THE IMPACT OF INVESTMENT TREATY LAW ON HOST STATES

Traditionally, international investment law was conceptualised as a set of norms aiming to ensure good governance for foreign investors, in exchange for their capital and know-how. However, the more recent narratives postulate that investment treaties and investor–state arbitration can improve governance not just for foreign investors but also for host communities. Investment treaty law can arguably foster good governance by holding host governments liable for a failure to ensure transparency, stability, predictability and consistency in their dealings with foreign investors. The recent proliferation of such narratives in investment treaty practice, arbitral awards and academic literature raises questions as to their juridical, conceptual and empirical underpinnings. What has propelled good governance from a set of normative ideals to enforceable treaty standards? Does international investment law possess the necessary characteristics to inspire changes at the national level? How do host states respond to investment treaty law? The overarching objective of this monograph is to unpack existing assumptions concerning the effects of international investment law on host states. By combining doctrinal, empirical, comparative analysis and unveiling the emerging 'nationally felt' responses to international investment norms, the book aims to facilitate a more informed understanding of the present contours and the nature of the interplay between international investment norms and national realities.

Volume 69 in the series Studies in International Law

Studies in International Law

Recent titles in this series

The Reception of Asylum Seekers under International Law:
Between Sovereignty and Equality
Lieneke Slingenberg

International Law and Child Soldiers
Gus Waschefort

The Contractual Nature of the Optional Clause
Gunnar Törber

Non-State Actors in International Law
Edited by Math Noortmann, August Reinisch and Cedric Ryngaert

The Rule of Law at the National and International Levels:
Contestations and Deference
Edited by Machiko Kanetake and André Nollkaemper

Human Rights Obligations of Non-State Armed Groups
Daragh Murray

Security and International Law
Edited by Mary E Footer, Julia Schmidt and Nigel D White

Complicity and its Limits in the Law of International Responsibility
Vladyslav Lanovoy

Complicity in International Criminal Law
Marina Aksenova

Arctic Law and Governance: The Role of China and Finland
Edited by Timo Koivurova, Qin Tianbao, Tapio Nykänen and Sébastien Duyck

States, the Law and Access to Refugee Protection: Fortresses and Fairness
Edited by Maria O'Sullivan and Dallal Stevens

Revisiting the Concept of Defence in the Jus ad Bellum:
The Dual Face of Defence
Johanna Friman

The International Legal Protection of Persons in Humanitarian Crises
Dug Cubie

The International Committee of the Red Cross and its Mandate to
Protect and Assist: Law and Practice
Christy Shucksmith

For a complete list of titles in this series, see www.bloomsburyprofessional.com/uk/series/studies-in-international-law

The Impact of Investment Treaty Law on Host States

Enabling Good Governance?

Mavluda Sattorova

• HART •

OXFORD • LONDON • NEW YORK • NEW DELHI • SYDNEY

HART PUBLISHING
Bloomsbury Publishing Plc
Kemp House, Chawley Park, Cumnor Hill, Oxford, OX2 9PH, UK

HART PUBLISHING, the Hart/Stag logo, BLOOMSBURY and the Diana logo are trademarks of Bloomsbury Publishing Plc
First published in Great Britain 2018

First published in hardback, 2018
Paperback edition, 2020

A catalogue record for this book is available from the British Library.

Library of Congress Cataloging-in-Publication Data

Names: Sattorova, Mavluda, author.

Title: The impact of investment treaty law on host states : enabling good governance? / Mavluda Sattorova.

Description: Portland, Oregon : Hart Publishing, 2018. | Series: Studies in international law | Includes bibliographical references and index.

Identifiers: LCCN 2017048788 (print) | LCCN 2017052191 (ebook) | ISBN 9781509901982 (Epub) | ISBN 9781849465854 (hardcover)

Subjects: LCSH: Investments, Foreign—Law and legislation | Investments, Foreign (International law) | Commercial treaties—Interpretation and construction.

Classification: LCC K3830 (ebook) | LCC K3830 .S29 2018 (print) | DDC 346/.092—dc23

LC record available at https://lccn.loc.gov/2017048788

ISBN: HB: 978-1-84946-585-4
PB: 978-1-50993-956-5
ePDF: 978-1-50990-197-5
ePub: 978-1-50990-198-2

Typeset by Compuscript Ltd, Shannon

To find out more about our authors and books visit www.hartpublishing.co.uk. Here you will find extracts, author information, details of forthcoming events and the option to sign up for our newsletters.

Acknowledgements

This monograph would not have been possible without help, inspiration and moral encouragement from many people. I am grateful to the University of Liverpool School of Law and Social Justice for the research and development funding that made my empirical work possible and for offering a generous period of research leave to produce the manuscript. I am grateful to Fiona Beveridge, Padraig McAuliffe, Sammie Currie, Christine Schwoebel-Patel, Sujitha Subramanian, and Gregory Messenger for reading various chapters of the draft and providing their valuable feedback. The book has also benefited from feedback received at various conferences, including the American Society of International Law Midyear Research Forum, the Stanford International Junior Research Forum, the European Society of International Law Conference in Vienna, the World Trade Institute Conference on the Role of States in Investor-State Arbitration (University of Bern) and the Society of Legal Scholars Annual Conference in Edinburgh. I also owe debt of gratitude to Lauge Poulsen, Andreas Kulick, and Jansen N Calamita for inviting me to present some of my earlier findings at workshops in Nuffield College (Oxford University), Tübingen University, and the Center for International Law (National University of Singapore) respectively. My thinking was also greatly helped by exchanges with Celine Tan, Lorenzo Cotula and Michael Waibel. It was my pleasure to work with Ohio Omiunu, Mustafa Erkan, Oleksandra Vytiaganets, and Iqboljon Qoraboyev in conducting interviews with government officials in Nigeria, Turkey, Ukraine and Kazakhstan. The case-study in Turkey has benefited from financial support granted by the British Institute at Ankara. The Lauterpacht Centre of International Law, Cambridge University provided a warm and intellectually stimulating home during the final months of writing up the monograph. Finally, I am enormously grateful to my friends and family, particularly my dear friend Gulara, my parents, my daughter Shirin, and Pete Lewis, for their unwavering support. The book is dedicated with love to Shirin.

Contents

1

Introduction

I. INTERNATIONAL INVESTMENT LAW: FROM GOOD GOVERNANCE FOR FOREIGN INVESTORS TO GOOD GOVERNANCE FOR ALL

CONTEMPORARY INTERNATIONAL INVESTMENT law has its historical roots in a system that was designed to protect interests of foreigners abroad—to ensure that foreign citizens in host states benefited from governance as good as that they enjoyed in their home states, even if a host state's legal systems fell below the acceptable standard. In his seminal speech in 1910 (which continues to be quoted with reference to the origins of the international minimum standard—one of the core provisions underpinning the modern investment treaty regime) Elihu Root famously articulated this notion of 'good governance for foreign citizens' in the following terms:

> There is a standard of justice, very simple, very fundamental, and of such general acceptance by all civilized countries as to form a part of the international law of the world. The condition upon which any country is entitled to measure the justice due from it to an alien by the justice which it accords to its own citizens is that its system of law and administration shall conform to this general standard. If any country's system of law and administration does not conform to that standard, although the people of the country may be content or compelled to live under it, no other country can be compelled to accept it as furnishing a satisfactory measure of treatment to its citizens.[1]
>
> ...
>
> The foreigner is entitled to have the protection and redress which the citizen is entitled to have, and the fact that the citizen may not have insisted upon his rights, and may be content with lax administration which fails to secure them to him, furnishes no reason why the foreigner should not insist upon them and no excuse for denying them to him.[2]

The core of the minimum standard of customary international law advocated by capital-exporting states was a set of norms encapsulating foreign

[1] Elihu Root, 'The Basis of Protection to Citizens Residing Abroad' (1910) 4 *AJIL* 517, 521–22.
[2] ibid 523.

subjects' entitlement to be treated in accordance with good governance precepts endorsed by 'civilised nations.'[3] The early references to the customary minimum standard show its function was primarily to protect aliens from the most egregious failures of governance such as in cases of denial of justice and uncompensated takings of property by host states.[4] As famously summarised by the US Secretary of State Cordell Hull in his historical note to the Mexican Government of 22 August 1938, 'under every rule of law and equity, no government is entitled to expropriate private property, for whatever purpose, without provision for prompt, adequate and effective payment thereof.'[5] Similar safeguards were being routinely incorporated in the early investment protection instruments. For instance, already the nineteenth century Friendship, Commerce and Navigation (FCN) treaties of the United States provided guarantees of '*full and perfect* protection' of property of US subjects abroad (emphasis added).[6]

Although the international minimum standard—an embodiment of the good governance benchmarks endorsed by civilised nations—was portrayed as a standard advantageous to a wider world community, it was designed to protect foreigners at the exclusion of nationals[7] and as such met with opposition from developing states. The most notable historic manifestation of refusal to endorse the international minimum standard was the national standard advocated by Latin American states. The national standard required that foreigners and their property be accorded treatment no more favourable than that accorded to the nationals of the host state.[8] The prominent embodiment of the standard is the Calvo doctrine, a principal tenet of which is the notion that when entering the territory of a host state a foreigner 'submits to local conditions with benefits and burdens' and that to grant a foreigner special treatment 'would be contrary to the principles of territorial jurisdiction and equality.'[9]

The idea of 'good governance for foreign investors' was also contested in the context of an historic opposition to the customary international

[3] See generally Andreas Hans Roth, *The Minimum Standard of International Law Applied to Aliens* (Leiden, A W Sijthoff's Uitgeversmaatschappij, 1949).

[4] ibid. See also Georg Schwarzenberger, *Foreign Investments and International Law* (London, Steven & Sons, 1969).

[5] See Burns H Weston and Frank G Dawson, '"Prompt, adequate, and effective"?: A Universal Standard of Compensation' (1961–1962) 30 *Fordham Law Review* 727, 735.

[6] Kenneth J Vandevelde, *U.S. International Investment Agreements* (Oxford, Oxford University Press, 2009) 20.

[7] Alireza Falsafi, 'The International Minimum Standard of Treatment of Foreign Investors' Property: A Contingent Standard' (2006–2007) 30 *Suffolk Transnational Law Review* 318, 321–22.

[8] Ian Brownlie, *Principles of Public International Law*, 6th edn (Oxford, Oxford University Press, 2003) 501–502.

[9] ibid.

law requirement of compensation for expropriation. In a number of landmark resolutions adopted under the aegis of the United Nations General Assembly, a coalition of newly-decolonised developing countries questioned the fairness and juridical basis of the customary international rules, and re-asserted the primacy of national treatment with regard to the foreigners' entitlement to compensation for expropriated and nationalised property.[10] This contestation reached its pinnacle with the promulgation of the 1974 UN Charter of Economic Rights and Duties of States, which provided that each state had the right to nationalise, expropriate or transfer ownership of foreign property, and that it was for the state to determine appropriate compensation, taking into account relevant national laws and regulations and all circumstances that it considered pertinent.[11]

Despite having encountered an overwhelming resistance from a wider international community, the ideas of special treatment—or 'better governance'—for foreigners have re-entered the corpus of international law through investment treaties. Although rejected by developing states in the UN General Assembly, various expressions of the international minimum standard found their way into bilateral and multilateral agreements on the promotion and protection of investment. As a wave of economic liberalisation processes swept across the globe in 1980s and 1990s, capital-exporting states embarked on negotiation of bilateral investment treaties with developing states. These treaty instruments were designed not just to protect investments from developed into developing countries but also, importantly, to address the prevailing uncertainty over the status of what had been previously postulated as the universally-accepted Hull rule of compensation for expropriation of property by host states.[12] This 'treatification'[13] process resulted in a hitherto unprecedented number of bilateral investment treaties whereby each contracting state committed to abide by a range of standards of treatment, including notably the guarantee against uncompensated expropriation, fair and equitable treatment, and non-discrimination. The salient and hitherto largely unprecedented feature of the investment treaty regime is that it grants foreign investors access to arbitration and the right to bring action directly against the host government.[14]

[10] See eg the UN GA Resolution No 1803 (14 December 1962) and No 3281 (12 December 1984).

[11] See Burns H Weston, 'The Charter of Economic Rights and Duties of States and the Deprivation of Foreign-Owned Wealth' (1981) 75 *AJIL* 437.

[12] Vandevelde, *U.S. International Investment Agreements*, 25–6.

[13] See generally Jeswald W Salacuse, 'The Treatification of International Investment Law' (2007) 13 *Law and Business Review of the Americas* 155.

[14] See Suria Subedi, *International Investment Law: Reconciling Policy and Principle* (Oxford, Hart Publishing, 2008) 149–50.

Supported by its own bespoke dispute settlement mechanism—the International Centre for Settlement of Investment Disputes founded under the Washington Convention in 1965—the newly-emerged investment treaty regime effectively reaffirmed the historically contested rules on special treatment of foreign investors. The regime was hailed as '[a] 21st century version of the 19th century club of "civilised nations" … though under different labels relating to contemporary notions of proper governance.'[15] Through their participation in bilateral arrangements on investment protection, developing countries were arguably 'sending a strong signal of their commitment to provide a predictable, stable and reliable legal environment for foreign direct investors, to stimulate investors' confidence and boost FDI flows.'[16] The advocates of the investment treaty regime reinforced the idea that one of the principal functions of investment treaty law was to ensure that foreign investors are treated in accordance with stronger, internationally recognised, good governance standards.

Subsequently, however, as the number of investment treaties has surged and investors turned to actively use the investor-state arbitration mechanism to challenge various host state actions, perceptions of the investment treaty regime and its functions have shifted somewhat. In contrast with the traditional customary international law rules on protection of foreign investment, the investment treaty regime possesses unique characteristics that have significantly changed the nature and scope of privileges conferred upon foreign investors. Investment treaties not only grant investors direct standing and right of action for damages against host states, but also allow investors in doing so to sidestep national remedies and to enforce awards against state assets located in other states.[17]

The scope of foreign investment protection and the extent of host state exposure to international adjudication and monetary liability have also dramatically expanded. Expropriation—or for that matter a denial of justice—are no longer primary causes of action to which foreign investors can resort in challenging host state conduct. The recent evolution of the investment treaty regime has been largely defined by the rise of non-expropriatory standards of treatment, such as the guarantee of fair and equitable treatment, the prohibition of arbitrary and discriminatory measures, and umbrella or sanctity of contract clauses. The availability of the whole arsenal of non-expropriatory standards has enhanced

[15] Todds Weiler and Thomas W Walde, 'Investment Arbitration under the Energy Charter Treaty in the Light of New NAFTA Precedents: Towards a Global Code of Conduct for Economic Regulation' (2004) 1 *Transnational Dispute Management* 1.

[16] UNCTAD 1999, UNCTAD Hosts Bilateral Investment Treaty Negotiations by Groups of Fifteen Countries. Press Release, 7 January 1999.

[17] See Gus Van Harten and Martin Loughlin, 'Investment Treaty Arbitration as a Species of Global Administrative Law' (2006) 17 *EJIL* 121, 332.

the protective reach and strength of investment treaties, transforming them into potent instruments that can be deployed by foreign investors against a diverse range of national measures in an infinite variety of socio-economic settings. Lack of transparency, stability, predictability as well as the lack of effective remedies and enforcement mechanisms at a national level can now lead to a host state's liability in damages. For instance, complying with the fair and equitable treatment standard 'may require states to create and maintain highly developed and particularised national institutions. Treating foreign investors equitably … demands a well-run administrative state highly protective of property rights and the expectations of those with capital.'[18] Investment treaty instruments have moved far beyond their original task of safeguarding foreign investors against outright takings of property and denial of justice, and now allow investors to claim redress even for governmental actions displaying 'a relatively lower degree of inappropriateness.'[19]

The shifts in the nature and scope of state responsibility before foreign investors—and the proliferation of the number of investment disputes against host states—has generated concerns on both a national and international scale. One such concern relates to the magnitude of financial consequences of investment arbitration for respondent states. Faced with the large sums that have been awarded to investors and the high cost of the arbitration process, developing countries in particular have found themselves vulnerable due to the detrimental financial impact of the awards on a country's budget.[20] As a study by UNCTAD points out, '[to] expedite payment of the awards, funds may be diverted from important development objectives, such as investment in infrastructure, education, health or other public goods.'[21] To exemplify the scale of financial consequences investment arbitration may entail for host states, in 2004 a claim by a Czech commercial bank against the Slovak Republic resulted in an award totalling approximately US$877 million in favour of the claimant investor.[22] Awards issued by ICSID tribunals against Argentina in 2007 alone exceeded US$600 million.[23] One of the highest awards in

[18] Jose E Alvarez, 'Contemporary Foreign Investment Law: An "Empire of Law" or the "Law of Empire"'? (2008–2009) 60 *Alabama Law Review* 943, 964 (commenting on a dictum from *Tecmed v Mexico*).

[19] *Saluka Investments BV v Czech Republic* (PCA—UNCITRAL, Partial Award, 17 March 2006) para 293.

[20] UNCTAD, *Best Practices in Investment for Development. How to prevent and manage investor-State disputes: Lessons from Peru*, Investment Advisory Series, Series B, number 10 (New York and Geneva, United Nations, 2011) 7.

[21] ibid 7.

[22] *Ceskoslovenska obchodni banka v Slovak Republic* (ICSID Case No ARB/97/4, Award, 29 December 2004) para 374.

[23] UNCTAD, *Best Practices in Investment*, 7.

the history of investment arbitration—US$1.77 billion plus pre-and post-award compound interest—was rendered in 2012 in the case of *Occidental v Ecuador*.[24]

Concerns have also been increasingly raised over the alarmingly asymmetric nature of international investment law. Investment treaties grant investors extensive substantive and procedural rights but not obligations, whilst subjecting states to an array of obligations unaccompanied by rights.[25] The creation of the investment treaty regime and the advent of investor-state dispute settlement was traditionally defended by reference to the need to depoliticise dispute settlement and to ensure equality of arms between foreign investors and host states.[26] It was designed to contribute to 'reducing the likelihood of unresolved conflicts between host countries and investors, and in particular by doing so in a manner which would eliminate the risk of a confrontation of the host country and the national State of the investor [sic]'.[27] Nevertheless, the first two decades of investor-state arbitration practice have prompted a growing perception that, 'despite the claims of neutrality and objectivity, both the system of international investment arbitration and the substantive rules of international investment law are deeply embedded in a political framework—but one that operates to the advantage of foreign investors.'[28]

These developments have inevitably prompted a perceived need for a re-conceptualisation of investment treaty law. First, the rapid evolution of investment arbitration practice and the emergence of novel (and at times far-reaching) interpretations of international treaty norms on investment protection have signalled the need to draw a stronger conceptual and methodological foundation to underpin the new regime. Second, numerous studies have questioned the role of investment treaties in advancing economic development of host states—something that has traditionally served as the principal justification for the internationalisation of rules on foreign investment protection.[29] It has been argued that the economic

[24] UNCTAD, Recent Developments In Investor-State Dispute Settlement (ISDS), No 1, April 2014, available at unctad.org/en/PublicationsLibrary/webdiaepcb2014d3_en.pdf.

[25] Jason Webb Yackee, 'Investment Treaties and Investor Corruption: An Emerging Defence for Host States?' (2012) 52 *Virginia Journal of International Law* 723.

[26] Aron Broches, 'Settlement of Investment Disputes' in Aron Broches (ed), *Selected Essays: World Bank, ICSID and Other Subjects of Public and Private International Law* (Dordrecht, Martinus Nijhoff Publishers, 1995) 161, 163.

[27] Aron Broches, 'The Convention on the Settlement of Investment Disputes between States and Nationals of Other States' (1972) (II) *Recueil Des Cours* 136, 337, 343.

[28] Kate Miles, *The Origins of International Investment Law: Empire, Environment and the Safeguarding of Capital* (Cambridge, Cambridge University Press, 2013) 86.

[29] Maria Carkovic and Ross Levine, 'Does foreign direct investment accelerate economic growth?' in Theodore Moran, Edward Graham and Magnus Blomstrom (eds), *Does Foreign Direct Investment Promote Development?* (Institute for International Economics, 2005) 219; Jason W Yackee, 'Do Bilateral Investment Treaties Promote Foreign Direct Investment? Some Hints from Alternative Evidence' (2011) 51 *Virginia Journal of International Law* 397, 399;

development rationale at the heart of investment treaty protection 'does not innately extend to a willingness to attract any kind of foreign capital, at all costs.'[30] As the number of investment claims continues to rise and the development function of the investment treaty regime is being increasingly contested, it was felt that investment arbitration 'must fulfil *some* useful societal function.'[31] Since the functional scope of investment treaties have been pushed beyond their original remit to redress sufficiently serious forms of host state interference with foreign investment, questions were raised about normative justifications for such expansion:

> … if investor-state arbitration is a component of global administrative law, which is in turn concerned with issues of transparency, public participation, and due process, for whom do these 'rule of law' principles operate? Are they solely for the benefit of the investor in their interaction with the host state?[32]

The idea of fostering the rule of law and good governance in developing states has thus been deployed to provide the much-needed normative content as well as additional justification for the evolving investment treaty norms. While traditionally the prevailing view was that international investment law aimed to ensure good governance for foreign investors (in exchange for their capital and know-how), the more recent narratives are premised on the idea of investment treaties altering outcomes not just for foreign investors but for host state communities also. Thus, even if investment treaties are unsuccessful in achieving their instrumental, economic objectives, their existence would still be justified by good governance norms enshrined in substantive standards of treatment that such treaties contain.[33] These good governance standards, although designed to benefit foreign investors, may eventually 'spill over into domestic law and

Eric Neumayer and Laura Spess, 'Do Bilateral Investment Treaties Increase Foreign Direct Investment to Developing Countries?' (2005) 33 *World Development* 1567, Karl Sauvant and Lisa Sachs (eds), *The Effect of Treaties on Foreign Direct Investment: Bilateral Investment Treaties, Double Taxation Treaties and Investment Flows* (Oxford, Oxford University Press, 2009). See further Jonathan Bonnitcha, 'Foreign Investment, Development and Governance: What international investment law can learn from the empirical literature on investment' (2016) 7 *Journal of International Dispute Settlement* 31, 36–44.

[30] Omar E García-Bolívar, 'Economic Development at the Core of the International Investment Regime' in Chester Brown and Kate Miles (eds), *Evolution in Investment Treaty Law and Arbitration* (Cambridge, Cambridge University Press, 2011) 587.

[31] Thomas Schultz and Cédric Dupont, 'Investment Arbitration: Promoting the Rule of Law or Over-empowering Investors? A Quantitative Empirical Study' (2014) 25 *EJIL* 1147, 1148.

[32] Miles, *The Origins of International Investment Law*, 332.

[33] Kenneth J Vandevelde, *Bilateral Investment Treaties: History, Policy, and Interpretation* (Oxford, Oxford University Press, 2010) 119; see also Jonathan Bonnitcha, *Substantive Protection under Investment Treaties: A Legal and Economic Analysis* (Oxford, Oxford University Press, 2014) 43.

may set new standards also for the domestic legal system.'[34] Especially in investor-state disputes relating to administrative law of host states, investment arbitration arguably 'may provide a powerful incentive to review and modernize their domestic legal systems.'[35] The mission of investment treaty law is therefore to 'reinforce and on occasion to institute, the rule of law internally' in host states.[36] It has been argued that '... investment treaties aim at binding states into a legal framework that gives them an incentive and a yardstick for transforming their legal systems into ones that are conducive to market-based investment activities and provide the institutions necessary for the functioning of such markets.'[37] This argument is also echoed in Vandevelde's normative claim that investment treaties 'embody norms that all countries committed to the rule of law should follow' and can therefore 'contribute greatly to institutional quality in host countries.'[38] A strong belief in the transformative function of international investment law underpins some of the recent writings of Echandi, who claims that international investment law can act as a deterrent mechanism against short-term policy reversals and assist developing countries in promoting greater effectiveness of the rule of law at the domestic level.[39] Investment treaties can arguably induce this result by subjecting host governments to strict standards, such as the prohibition of arbitrary conduct. Besides, the international investment regime can facilitate the strengthening of the rule of law in developing states through transparency-related commitments.[40] Owing to what has been variously described as the 'halo effect',[41] the 'desideratum effect',[42] or the 'signalling effect',[43] investment

[34] Peter Muchlinski, Federico Ortino and Christoph Schreuer, 'Preface' in Peter Muchlinski, Federico Ortino and Christoph Schreuer (eds), *The Oxford Handbook of International Investment Law* (Oxford, Oxford University Press, 2008) vi.

[35] Rudolf Dolzer, 'The Impact of International Investment Treaties on Domestic Administrative Law' (2005) 37 *New York University Journal of International Law and Policy* 972.

[36] Bonnitcha, *Substantive Protection*, 31, referring to James Crawford, 'International Law and the Rule of Law' (2003) 24 *Adelaide Law Review* 4.

[37] Stephan W Schill, *The Multilateralization of International Investment Law* (Cambridge, Cambridge University Press, 2009) 377.

[38] Kenneth J Vandevelde, 'Model Bilateral Investment Treaties: The Way Forward' (2012) 18 *Southwestern Journal International Law* 313.

[39] Roberto Echandi, 'What Do Developing Countries Expect from the International Investment Regime?' in Jose E Alvarez and Karl P Sauvant (eds), *The Evolving International Investment Regime: Expectations, Realities, Options* (Oxford, Oxford University Press, 2011) 13.

[40] ibid 13–14.

[41] World Bank, *World Development Report* (New York, Oxford University Press, 2005) 179 ('While ICSID is designed to encourage foreign investment, domestic firms can benefit from the halo effect provided by stronger constraints on arbitrary government action').

[42] Louis B Sohn and R Baxter, *Convention on the International Responsibility of States for Injuries to Aliens. Preliminary Draft with Explanatory Notes* (Cambridge, MA, Harvard Law School, 1959) 28 ('By the establishment of an international minimum standard, the law has not only protected aliens but has also suggested a desideratum for States in their relationships with their own nationals').

[43] Thomas W Walde, 'The "Umbrella Clause" in Investment Arbitration. A Comment on Original Intentions and Recent Cases' (2005) 6 *Journal of World Investment and Trade* 183, 188

treaties are said to act as *catalysts* of governance reforms in host states, providing the investment treaty regime with another raison d'etre and justifying its recent strides.

It was not until the first wave of investment arbitration disputes that the rhetoric of good governance was amplified and expressly embraced *de lege lata*. In a rising tide of investment claims challenging various host government actions and measures, the boundaries of the notion of internationally proscribed conduct have been pushed beyond the familiar. A string of arbitral awards, including the seminal *Metalclad*, *Tecmed*, and *Occidental* awards,[44] proclaimed that transparency, stability, predictability and consistency ought to be construed as elements of the fair and equitable treatment standard. A failure to create and maintain a transparent, stable and predictable regime was found to constitute a sufficient ground for claiming compensation against the host state. Some investment treaties now expressly require a host state to ensure 'effective means of asserting claims and enforcing rights' and to create and maintain 'a legal framework apt to guarantee to investors the continuity of legal treatment.'[45] The rapid uptake of the good governance narratives in the investment treaty practice and academic literature raises questions as to their juridical underpinnings. It necessitates an inquiry into the origins of the good governance rhetoric and the intentions of those who invoke it. What has propelled good governance from a set of normative ideals to enforceable treaty standards? How do host states respond to investment treaty norms? As investment treaty law has largely failed to deliver promised economic development,[46] is it capable of delivering improved governance?

('The example effect of treaty-based contract protection is likely to have an indirect effect also on the treatment of domestic investors, as it signals to the host-State institutions what a proper, international and universal standard of governance is. Such signalling effect provides a benchmark for domestic judicial procedures as well.')

[44] See *Metalclad Corpn v Mexico*, Award, 25 August 2000, ICSID Case No ARB(AF)/97/1, (2001) 40 ILM 36; *Técnicas Medioambientales Tecmed, SA v The United Mexican States*, Award 29 May 2003, 10 ICSID Rep 130, paras 154–64; *Occidental Exploration and Production Company v The Republic of Ecuador* (LCIA Case No UN 3467, Award, 1 July 2004) paras 184–91. Unless otherwise indicated, all cases cited in this chapter are available online at italaw.com. For a critique, see Santiago Montt, *State Liability in Investment Treaty Arbitration: Global Constitutional and Administrative Law in the BIT Generation* (Oxford, Hart Publishing, 2009) 309.

[45] See eg Art II(7) of the Treaty Between the United States of America and the Republic of Ecuador Concerning the Encouragement and Reciprocal Protection of Investment (1997); also Art 10(12) of the Energy Charter Treaty (signed 17 December 1994, entered into force 16 April 1998) 2080 UNTS 100.

[46] See Tienhaara noting that '[m]any African countries that have ratified numerous BITs have remained marginalized in terms of global investment flows': Kyla Tienhaara, *The Expropriation of Environmental Governance: Protecting Foreign Investors at the Expense of Public Policy* (Cambridge, Cambridge University Press, 2009) 59. See also Joseph E Stiglitz, 'Regulating Multinational Corporations: Towards Principles of Cross-Border Legal Frameworks in a Globalized World Balancing Rights with Responsibilities' (2008) 23 *American University International Law Review* 451, 455.

II. CONCEPTUAL FRAMEWORK

A. Why the Good Governance Lens?

Despite being increasingly popular (and contested), the good governance narratives represent only one distinct strand of legal discourse about the evolving functions and objectives of international investment law. One may therefore ponder why this book focuses on this seemingly narrow strand of legal thought. Why the good governance lens? Examining the recent evolution of investment treaty law through a critique of the good governance narratives provides the opportunity to engage with a broad array of issues underpinning the interaction between international investment law and host states, with particular focus on developing countries. It offers a useful conceptual framework to explore and critique international investment law from historical, doctrinal and normative angles, by taking a closer look at the evolution of the juridical foundations of the emerging interpretations, questioning their normative and practical implications, and identifying the shifting roles of various actors involved in the formation and functioning of the investment treaty regime.

Just like development, good governance 'has a very powerful and apparently universal appeal: all peoples and societies would surely seek a good governance—in much the same way that all peoples and societies were seen as desiring development.'[47] Just as is the case with economic development, which has long been regarded as one of the primary objectives of investment treaties, the question this book is preoccupied with is not whether fostering good governance is a desirable end. Rather, the question is what the language of good governance masks and whether change in domestic governance can at all be effectuated through international investment norms. Arguably, even the proponents of the good governance language in recent scholarship and doctrine are likely to agree (perhaps reluctantly) that such language supplies the moral and intellectual foundation for conceptualising and using investment treaty norms to 'manage … Third World states and Third World peoples.'[48] Yet there is very little analysis in academic literature on international investment law as to what 'good governance' means for those governed (or managed)—the developing states and host communities. Even less is known about the impact of the investment treaty regime and its good governance mission on host states.

Using the good governance lens provides the opportunity—or even renders it necessary—to evaluate the normative and causal assumptions

[47] Anthony Anghie, 'Civilization and Commerce: The Concept of Governance in Historical Perspective' (2000) 45 *Villanova Law Review* 887, 893.

[48] ibid 893–94.

about the effects of international investment law from an empirical angle and from the point of view of those whose behaviour international investment rules allegedly purport to influence (governments of developing states) and those who the regime promises to benefit through better, improved governance institutions and practices (host communities). This book seeks to make a novel contribution by offering empirical insights drawn from interviews with government officials and analysis of legislative data in developing states. While much has been written on why developing states sign investment treaties,[49] there is a dearth of studies on whether states comply with investment treaty norms and how the latter influence state decision-making. As Bonnitcha points out in his pioneering contribution to the literature on the subject, '[existing debate about investment treaties is relatively immature, in that both proponents and critics pay little attention to the normative and causal assumptions on which their arguments are based.'[50] To quote Broude, while in international law individual actions may be attributed to the state and give rise to state responsibility, ultimately many cases of compliance or non-compliance with international law are made by individuals.[51] Methodological statism ought to be avoided in favour of 'a recognition that states do not make decisions relating to international law; people do, or most often, groups of people.'[52] A critique of international investment law through the good governance lens invites us to go beyond purely legal formalistic analyses, to engage in conversation with government officials, and to take a step towards bridging the gap between the literature on investment treaty law and existing scholarship on law and development, political science and international relations studies on state compliance with international law.

The overarching objective of this book is to unpack existing assumptions concerning the effects of international investment law on host states. It aims to offer novel insights into real rather than abstractly imagined patterns of governmental behaviour in developing countries. By combining doctrinal, empirical, comparative and interdisciplinary approaches and thus unveiling the emerging 'nationally felt'[53] responses to international investment norms, the book aims to facilitate a more informed

[49] See eg Montt, *State Liability*; Andrew T Guzman, 'Why LDCs Sign Treaties that Hurt Them: Explaining the Popularity of Bilateral Investment Treaties' (1997–1998) 38 *Virginia Journal of International Law* 639, and more recently, Lauge N Skovgaard Poulsen, *Bounded Rationality and Economic Diplomacy: The Politics of Investment Treaties in Developing Countries* (Cambridge, Cambridge University Press, 2015).

[50] Bonnitcha, *Substantive Protection under Investment Treaties*, 11.

[51] Tomer Brouder, 'Behavioral International Law' (2015) 163 *University of Pennsylvania Law Review* 1099, 1130.

[52] ibid 1126.

[53] The term is borrowed from Harold Koh, 'How Is International Human Rights Law Enforced?' (1998) 74 *Indiana Law Journal* 1397, 1407.

understanding of present contours and the nature of the interplay between international norms and national realities. This, in turn, will provide a basis for analysing the ways in which such relationship can be optimised, including through reforming the existing norms and the creation of requisite legal and institutional mechanisms.

B. The Impact of Investment Treaty Law on Domestic Governance: Using a Compliance Lens

The principal question of this book is whether investment treaty law can exert a positive influence on host states by fostering greater state compliance with good governance standards. While compliance with international law has generated a considerable body of literature straddling international law and political science scholarship, state compliance with investment treaty law has so far received little attention. As observed by Simmons in her review of scholarship on treaty compliance, despite the evidence suggesting that international treaties have effects on state behaviour, 'large uncertainties remain and the conditions under which they can be effective are poorly understood.'[54] This book seeks to contribute to the existing knowledge by bringing to the fore and evaluating various factors determining the capacity of international investment law to alter the way governments operate. One of the key objectives of this study is to uncover how host states respond to investment treaty rules, ie how they *comply* with good governance prescriptions contained in international investment agreements. An inalienable part of this analysis is to identify which characteristics international investment norms ought to possess to be able to 'weigh the decision processes of states in the direction of compliance'.[55] For our purposes, compliance is understood as a process that goes beyond the formal ratification of international treaty instruments and comprises ex ante internalisation of the norms contained therein as well as ex post adjustment of national legal framework in line with decisions of international arbitral tribunals.

Whilst compliance with international investment norms has not to date been a subject of a comprehensive analysis, in undertaking a fresh inquiry into this subject matter one is aided by a considerable body of literature on compliance produced by scholars of international law and

[54] Leonardo Baccini and Johannes Urpelainen, 'Before Ratification: Understanding the Timing of International Treaty Effects on Domestic Policies' (2014) 58 *International Studies Quarterly* 29, 30.

[55] Abram Chayes and Antonia Handler Chayes, *The New Sovereignty: Compliance with International Regulatory Agreements* (Cambridge MA, Harvard University Press, 1995) 112.

political science.[56] In evaluating how host states respond to investment treaty prescriptions of good governance, a distinction must be made between compliance and effectiveness: host states may formally ratify investment treaties and comply with its dispute settlement awards whilst failing to honour the treaty obligation requiring them to refrain from mistreating investors in their daily practices. Investment treaties may be effective in forcing states to comply with provisions on the enforcement of awards rendered by dispute settlement bodies, but ineffective as far as the broader impact on domestic governance institutions and practices is concerned. For instance, host states may over-value foreign investors and refrain from harming them but fail to extend the same treatment to domestic investors,[57] and thus fall short of maintaining good governance across the board.

Compliance should also be disaggregated from implementation. Implementation is only a step on the way to compliance, and may comprise

> the enactment of legislation or the promulgation of regulations or a change in official policy, any of which may be combined with the activities of international institutions in monitoring and assisting national governments in putting their international commitments into practice.[58]

This book seeks to go beyond the formal expressions of implementation of investment treaty rules such as treaty ratification and enforcement of investment arbitration awards rendered in disputes brought under such treaties. As observed by Hathaway in her analysis of state compliance with human rights treaties, the ratification of a treaty, whilst constituting an implementation measure, may serve as a substitute for actual improvements in domestic practices.[59] Similar behaviour can be observed in connection with ratification of international investment treaties: with some minor exceptions, contracting state parties tend to signal their commitment to implementing such treaties through ratification whilst undertaking no or few measures to transpose investment treaty rules into domestic legal practice.

[56] See ibid, also Beth A Simmons, 'International Law and State Behavior: Commitment and Compliance in International Monetary Affairs' (2000) 94(4) *American Political Science Review* 819; Oona Hathaway, 'Between Power and Principle: An Integrated Theory of International Law' (2005) 72 *University of Chicago Law Review* 469; Thomas M Franck, 'Legitimacy in the International System' (1988) 82 *AJIL* 705; Harold Hongju Koh, 'Why Do Nations Obey International Law' (1977)106 *Yale Law Journal* 2599.

[57] Jonathan Bonnitcha, 'Outline of a Normative Framework for Evaluating Interpretations of Investment Treaty Protections' in Chester Brown and Kate Miles (eds), *Evolution in Investment Treaty Law and Arbitration* (Cambridge, Cambridge University Press, 2011) 128.

[58] Mary E Footer, 'Some Theoretical and Legal Perspectives on WTO Compliance' (2007) 38 *Netherlands Yearbook of International Law* 61, 66.

[59] Oona A Hathaway, 'Do Human Rights Treaties Make a Difference?' (2002) 111 *Yale Law Journal* 1935, 2005.

One aspect of implementation that falls squarely within the scope of our analysis concerns the ex post adjustment of national legal rules by host states following their exposure to investment treaty sanctions. Contracting state parties may formally enact domestic laws and regulations as a means of implementing investment treaty rules, yet such implementation measures may not lead to compliance with the letter and spirit of investment treaties in the practice of domestic institutions. Unlike the promulgation of national laws and regulations immediately following the signing of a treaty, the adjustment of national legal rules subsequent to the state's involvement in investor-state dispute settlement under the said treaty is more likely to reflect a change in host state behaviour which: (1) is precipitated by real as opposed to formal participation in the treaty regime; and (2) involves a more conscious decision-making in the sense of the host state government being more aware of the scale and consequences of treaty obligations and sanctions, and elaborating on the meaning of these norms and what they require in particular circumstances. By elucidating some of the actions and processes observed in developing states in the aftermath of their encounter with investment treaty law, this book seeks to uncover the hitherto less visible factors that may ultimately lead to compliance as 'a state of conformity or identity between an actor's behaviour and a specified rule'.[60] The crucial question is whether host state compliance with good governance standards for foreign investors can result in good governance for all.

III. OUTLINE OF CHAPTERS

Chapter 2 proceeds with tracing the emergence of good governance narratives in investment treaty practice and arbitral jurisprudence. It critically evaluates the doctrinal foundations and internal coherence of the argument which postulates that host states should be held liable for a failure to ensure compliance with good governance standards in domestic practices. The overarching aim is not to offer a comprehensive analysis of treaty practice and arbitral jurisprudence, but rather to expose cracks in the good governance narratives of international investment law by identifying and highlighting insufficiency in their legal foundations. It is argued that notwithstanding the proliferation of arbitral awards construing the fair and equitable treatment standard as an obligation to create and maintain a transparent, stable, predictable and consistent legal framework, such interpretation is not adequately supported by historical and doctrinal evidence pertaining to the evolution of the fair and

[60] Kal Raustiala, 'Compliance and Effectiveness in International Regulatory Cooperation' (2000) 32 *Case Western Reserve Journal of International Law* 387, 388.

equitable treatment standard. The interpretations of other 'good governance' standards, such as an investment treaty obligation to provide an effective means of asserting claims and enforcing rights are similarly questionable both for their insufficient legal underpinnings and their normative implications. Extending the scope of state responsibility in international law to such forms of governmental conduct as a failure to provide effective laws and to ensure time-efficient administration of justice drastically changes the function and scope of investment treaty law. Harnessing the language of good governance to justify the expansive interpretation of investment treaty rules is unlikely divert attention from the shortcomings of legal and normative reasoning underpinning the relevant arbitral awards. Rather, it may further heighten concerns over the regime's legitimacy and credibility.

Despite having recurred in various arbitral decisions and scholarly writings, the claim that investment treaties promote the rule of law and improve governance at a national level has not (yet) been supported either theoretically or through empirical appraisal. Chapter 3 intends to fill this gap by tapping into empirical data in examining the interplay between investment treaty disciplines and governmental conduct. The good governance narratives of international investment law are grounded in a set of assumptions about how host states *should* respond to investment treaty norms. It is presumed that the imposition of monetary liability on host states for a breach of good governance standards will not only deter host states from mistreating foreign investors but also encourage them to proactively reform legal and bureaucratic practices. For such deterrent and transformative effects to exist, however, government officials in host states need to be aware of the existence and meaning of investment treaty prescriptions. Furthermore, national legal and regulatory measures should be in place to discourage individual government officials from acting in breach of those prescriptions. To what extent are government officials actually aware of and influenced by investment treaty disciplines in making their decisions vis-à-vis foreign investors? Does the imposition of monetary sanctions on the host states prompt them to address the governance failures lying at the roots of investor-state disputes and to enhance accountability of relevant government agencies and officials? How do host states respond or react to their experience of defending themselves in investor-state disputes?

Chapter 3 engages with these questions by situating the good governance narratives within the emerging empirical data, including the findings obtained by this author through interviews with government officials and the analysis of national legislation in five developing states (Kazakhstan, Nigeria, Turkey, Ukraine and Uzbekistan). Notwithstanding their relatively limited scale, the case studies offer potentially illuminating insights. For instance, it transpires that even after the host states encountered investment arbitration in a respondent capacity, many government officials tended to remain unaware of investment treaty law and its implications. Even where government officials learnt about investment treaty law from their involvement in investor-state arbitration, such learning has not been translated into legal reforms. The interviews also reveal that, despite having gained a certain awareness and knowledge of investment treaty law, some host states continue to neglect the possible repercussions of their actions under that law. In some cases, rather than encouraging states to embark on governance reforms, dissatisfaction with investment arbitration may propel host states to seek retroactive changes in national laws on investment protection, and to withdraw from the investment treaty regime altogether.

Chapter 3 also examines the emerging trend towards the creation of national investment promotion and dispute settlement agencies, as illustrated in Brazil, Colombia, Kazakhstan, Peru, and Ukraine. Could the newly-established investment ombudsmen and similar dispute prevention bodies be a manifestation of a reformist impulse triggered by the host states learning from their encounter with investment treaty law, as predicted by the proponents of the good governance narratives? Both the analysis of national legislation, comparative studies and interviews are instructive insofar as they confirm no direct links between the creation of national investment ombudsmen and investment promotion agencies and investment treaty law. Rather, these policy developments appear to owe their origins to the investment facilitation agenda actively pursued by international institutions and Western donor organisations. Chapter 3 questions whether the involvement of international organisations in shaping national responses carries an enabling effect on governance in host states or whether it effectively prevents host states from formulating and implementing their own choices with respect to investment protection, promotion and dispute settlement.

The choice of questions addressed in the rest of the book has been inspired by the findings from our empirical case studies. Interviews with government officials have exposed a host of issues underpinning the interplay between international norms and national experiences. When sharing their views about international investment law and its good governance promise, our respondents expressed various degrees of hopefulness, scepticism, indifference, suspicion and resentment over international rules and actors and the latter's efforts to bring about change in the national realm. The key themes that emerged from the interviews form the basis of discussion in the remainder of the book.

Take, for instance, the assumption that the imposition of monetary liability will deter host states from breaching investment treaty prescriptions. The interviews with government officials (and evidence from investment arbitration jurisprudence) reveal that the pain of complying with damages awards does not necessarily produce either a deterrent effect or act as an incentive to proactively comply with investment treaty standards of good governance. Notwithstanding the threat of adverse financial consequences, host governments may choose to breach investment treaty norms in cases where they find it economically and politically more expedient. Chapter 4 examines whether investment treaty rules on liability are *by design* capable of inducing host states into compliance with treaty prescriptions on good governance. Can good governance at all be fostered through the externally imposed and crippling financial sanctions on host states? Law and development scholarship demonstrates that the use of financial incentives and sanctions in pushing for legal and institutional reforms has often resulted in expedited legislative changes but left no room for the internalisation of such reforms. Indeed, as one interviewee in our empirical case study put it, developing countries 'have perfect laws and perfect constitution, they simply don't work.'[61]

Existing studies show that financial sanctions may produce the desired effect on state behaviour but only if carefully designed and accompanied by effective communication and monitoring mechanisms. Are investment treaty remedies designed so as to deter future treaty breaches by host states? Investment treaties do not specifically require contracting states to adopt measures to foster and maintain good governance. Rather, they require that host states provide a set level of compensation for a failure to abide by good governance standards vis-à-vis foreign investors. When analysed from an historical and doctrinal perspective, and compared with other international regimes such as WTO law, the long-standing preference for monetary redress and the fact that the latter has rarely been accompanied by other remedies suggests that the primary goal investment treaty law has always been to indemnify the foreign investor, not to induce host states into compliance with investment treaty standards of good governance. Where the costs of breaching investment treaty provisions are less than the host state's gain from the same breach, the availability of monetary remedies may in fact render it considerably more attractive for the host state to choose breach over compliance. As long as the injured investor is compensated for its losses, investment treaty law implicitly allows host states to effectively opt out from the obligation to treat foreign investors in accordance with good governance standards. Chapter 4 explores the prospects and challenges of resorting to other forms of redress, such as the remedy of specific performance and injunction, in facilitating greater compliance with investment treaty norms.

Another question that has been prompted by our conversation with government officials in developing states is whether international investment law possesses the necessary characteristics to inspire domestic changes at

[61] Interview DFI.

the national level, to weigh the decision-making processes of host states in the direction of compliance. Drawing on investment treaty practice, investment arbitration jurisprudence as well as insights from the empirical case studies, Chapter 5 argues that investment treaty law, in its current form, lacks some of the vital characteristics necessary for its purported mission to act as a mechanism signalling what the universally acceptable standards of good governance are.[62] The much-criticised lack of clarity, consistency and predictability of investment treaty law is antithetical to the rule of law requirements.[63]

Chapter 5 also explores whether by effectively insulating foreign investors from the shortcomings of domestic regimes and by substituting the latter with an arguably stronger and more effective international alternative, the investment treaty regime reduces the incentive for host states to improve domestic governance institutions and practices. Since investor-state arbitration allows investors to escape the jurisdiction of domestic courts,[64] national judiciaries are not merely deprived of incentives to compete with international tribunals and enhance the quality of their governance outputs, but they are also effectively barred from otherwise embedding international standards of good governance in the legal and bureaucratic practices of host states. The empirical evidence also suggests that, due to its emphasis on the idea of foreign investors deserving special protection, the investment treaty regime contributes to a fragmentation of the national judicial and regulatory landscape and the emergence of special decision-making bodies and units specifically tasked with shielding foreign investors from the vicissitudes of dealing with national law and institutions. Rather than encouraging a comprehensive reform of national governance institutions and practices, host governments appear to favour 'good governance foreign investors' solutions. The externalisation and internationalisation of foreign investment protection tends to have an emasculating effect on national actors and institutions, hampering the emergence of local, home-grown expertise and of 'internally-felt' governance reforms.

Contrary to assumptions that foreign investors can foster good governance by lobbying host governments or otherwise pushing for reform, the emerging evidence from investment arbitration practice and the interviews reveal genuine grounds for concern over the negative impact of foreign investment on governance in host states. Through their contribution to

[62] Using the phrase from Walde, 'The "Umbrella Clause" in Investment Arbitration', 188.

[63] Benjamin K Guthrie, 'Beyond Investment Protection: An Examination of the Potential Influence of Investment Treaties on Domestic Rule of Law' (2012–2013) 45 *New York University Journal of International Law and Politics* 1151, 1196.

[64] Christoph Schreuer, 'Calvo's Grandchildren: The Return of Local Remedies in Investment Arbitration' (2005) 4 *Law and Practice International Courts and Tribunals* 1.

normalising corruption, bribery and regulatory capture, foreign investors may at times entrench poor governance in host states. Chapter 5 argues that the actual impact of the investment treaty regime on governance in host states would depend on the stance the regime takes on investor misconduct. If investment treaty instruments and arbitral tribunals turn a blind eye to illegal acts perpetrated by foreign investors in host states, including the instances of bribery and other forms of corruption, the investment treaty regime could be complicit in encouraging and perpetuating inadequate and undesirable patterns of behaviour by governments and foreign investors. Regrettably, the bulk of existing investment treaty instruments do not contain provisions to expressly address investor misconduct. Investment treaty law has long been criticised for is its asymmetric nature—for providing investor with rights, but not imposing any obligations. A failure to address lack of investor accountability in international investment agreements is starkly at odds with the investment treaty regime's proclaimed commitment to the ideals of rule of law and good governance.

When analysing the interaction between international investment law and those whose existence it purportedly aims to benefit through its promise of improved governance, one is reminded of the words of Cotterrell:

> Can international law be even more 'soulless' insofar as its links to networks of community are more indirect and potentially contradictory even than those of national law? With its vast, but abstract, potentially worldwide jurisdictional reach and its—so to speak—'high altitude' trajectory in 'thin legal air' far above most social life, could international law appear twice removed from the conditions of existence of the regulated insofar as it regulates mainly the relations of states and their agencies *rather than* social relations among their populations?[65]

Not only does investment treaty law remain far removed from the conditions of those it regulates, but it is also intrinsically inimical to the ideals of promoting democracy, participation, and political and socio-cultural rights of citizens. The regime's resistance to accommodate these ideals can be discerned both in the process of making investment treaty rules and their application in investor-state arbitration.

Chapter 6 will focus on the investment treaty regime's failure to embrace and maintain more inclusive and participatory approaches. Notwithstanding an emerging consensus that global norms of good governance should encompass such principles as accountability and an individual right of participation, investment treaty law remains largely indifferent to socio-political enablement in host states and instead stresses the need to insulate foreign investors from the national political process. Those who are

[65] Roger Cotterrell, 'Transnational networks of community and international economic law' in Amanda Perry-Kessaris (ed), *Socio-legal Approaches to International Economic Law: Text, Context, Subtext* (Abingdon, Routledge, 2013) 142.

expected to benefit from improved governance, which investment treaty law promises to deliver, remain largely excluded from the processes of formation, interpretation and application of investment protection rules. Developing states are particularly disadvantaged due to long-standing barriers hindering their meaningful input in the formation and change of investment treaty rules, including the so-called universally acceptable standards of good governance. Due to long-standing power asymmetries and the investment treaty regime's failure to offer legal and institutional means to address such asymmetries, developing countries traditionally end up as rule-takers, signing investment treaties that follow the developed state partner's model agreement. Likewise, developing countries are startlingly under-represented in the ranks of those who are vested with the task of interpreting and applying investment treaty rules. As recent empirical studies demonstrate, the rules on arbitrator appointment perpetuate a highly unequal system that hampers an input by developing countries into shaping investment arbitration jurisprudence.[66]

Can investment treaty law foster good governance if it forecloses any input from the general public and other stakeholders? With a few notable exceptions, even in developed states investment treaties continue to be drafted and negotiated in the absence of a meaningful political debate, with limited or at times non-existent public participation. Do recent moves towards greater transparency and stakeholder participation in the process of drafting and negotiating international investment agreements of the EU herald the dawn of a new era? Chapter 6 draws attention to the manner in which the Commission conducted the public consultation, its decision on the citizens' initiative concerning the Transatlantic Trade and Investment Partnership, and the European Parliament's ambivalence over (and its failure to mount effective opposition to) investor-state dispute settlement. Notwithstanding the significant strides made by the EU institutions towards a more participatory and democratic investment treaty-making, it is questioned whether the latest reforms carry an enabling effect or merely represent institutional efforts to create an illusion of participation to deflect the growing opposition to, and domestic contestation of, the investment treaty regime. To foster good governance in host states, investment treaty law must embrace the ideas of socio-political enablement and provide legal means to nurture, rather than impede, the emergence of robust domestic constituencies and their participation in the making and implementation of investment treaty norms.

[66] See eg Sergio Puig, 'Social Capital in the Arbitration Market' (2014) 25 *EJIL* 387; Michael Waibel, 'Abitrator Selection: Towards Greater State Control' in Andreas Kulick (ed), *Reassertion of Control over the Investment Treaty Regime* (Cambridge, Cambridge University Press, 2016) 333.

2

Genesis of 'Good Governance' Narratives in International Investment Law and Scholarship: An Historical and Doctrinal Analysis

I. CONCEPTUAL INSPIRATIONS BEHIND THE GOOD GOVERNANCE NARRATIVES OF INVESTMENT TREATY LAW

WHAT IS THE meaning of good governance in international investment law? An overview of the literature, which postulates virtuous effects of investment treaty rules on governance in host states, points to an overlapping or even interchangeable use of the terms 'good governance' and 'the rule of law'. Both narratives have a common core—the claim that one of the objectives of investment treaty law or one of its unintended but nonetheless significant benefits is to prompt host states to embrace transparency, stability, predictability, consistency and to ensure effective administrative and judicial remedies. The conceptual foundation for this claim is often derived from an extensive body of scholarship on the subject, including Raz's work on the rule of law and its virtues and the prolific body of research inspired by the World Bank's governance reforms in developing states.[1]

Most of the arguments positing the transformative impact of investment treaty law on the rule of law and governance in host states are premised on the so-called thin—or minimalist—conception of the rule of law as advanced in Raz's seminal essay on the subject. According to him, "[t]he rule of law' means literally what it says: the rule of the law. Taken in its broadest sense this means that people should obey the law and be ruled by it.'[2]

[1] See in particular a series of research papers on Worldwide Governance Indicators published under the aegis of the World Bank, available at info.worldbank.org/governance/wgi/#home.

[2] Joseph Raz, 'The Rule of Law and Its Virtue' in Joseph Raz, *The Authority of Law: Essays on Law and Morality* (Clarendon, Oxford, 1979) 212.

Stripped of any positive moral content,[3] this minimalist conception comprises the following requirements:

(1) all laws should be prospective, open, and clear;
(2) laws should be relatively stable;
(3) the making of particular laws (particular legal orders) should be guided by open, stable, clear and general rules;
(4) the independence of the judiciary must be guaranteed;
(5) the principles of natural justice must be observed;
(6) the courts should have review powers over the implementation of other principles;
(7) the courts should be easily accessible;
(8) the discretion of the crime-preventing agencies should not be allowed to pervert the law.[4]

Although the majority of scholars invoking the rule of law appear to espouse the thin conception in justifying the existence and workings of the investment treaty regime,[5] some have gone beyond the latter's primarily procedural content to argue that the rule of law also requires host states' compliance with requirements of reasonableness, security of property and contract, transparency and due process. Vandevelde, for instance, argues that investment treaty norms and investment arbitration practice embody and promote the elements of what is known as a thick conception of the rule of law.[6] In his view, investment treaties 'may serve to commit host countries to principles that have intrinsic worth and that will strengthen liberal democracy within those countries.'[7] Originating in the teachings of Rousseau and Dicey, the thick conception of the rule of law does not limit itself to the formal characteristics of legal systems and comprises egalitarian and antiauthoritarian ideals, such as freedom, deliberative

[3] Michael J Trebilcock and Ronald J Daniels, *Rule of Law Reform and Development: Charting the Fragile Path of Progress* (Cheltenham, Edward Elgar, 2008) 21–22 acknowledging that even the minimalist conceptions are imbued with quasi-moral principles. See further Michael Neumann, *The Rule of Law* (Burlingon VT, Ashgate, 2002) 11.

[4] Raz, 'The Rule of Law', 214–18.

[5] See, eg Rudolf Dolzer, 'The Impact of International Investment Treaties on Domestic Administrative Law' (2005) 37 *New York University Journal of International Law and Politics* 972, and Stephan W Schill, 'Fair and Equitable Treatment, the Rule of Law, and Comparative Public Law' in Stephan W Schill, *International Investment Law and Comparative Public Law* (Oxford, Oxford University Press, 2010) 154–61. See further Jonathan Bonnitcha, *Substantive Protection under Investment Treaties: A Legal and Economic Analysis* (Oxford, Oxford University Press, 2014) 43.

[6] See Kenneth J Vandevelde, *Bilateral Investment Treaties: History, Policy, and Interpretation* (Oxford, Oxford University Press, 2010) 113–14, 119.

[7] ibid 119. See also Bonnitcha, *Substantive Protection*, 43 (criticising Vandevelde's espousal of the thick conception of the rule of law).

democracy and constitutional protection of a wide range of individual rights, including the right to vote, the right of free expression, and the right to political property.[8] These elements of the thick conception of the rule of law can be discerned in some of the good governance narratives. For example, some have argued that

> ... investment treaties aim at binding States into a legal framework that gives them an incentive and a yardstick for transforming their legal systems into ones that are conducive to market-based investment activities and provide the institutions necessary for the functioning of such markets.[9]

The thick conception of the rule of law also underpins some of the arbitral interpretations of investment treaty standards, such as in cases where tribunals held that host states were under an obligation to guarantee total stability, predictability, consistency and effectiveness of a legal environment for investment.[10]

The thick conception of the rule of law has been criticised both in the broader literature on jurisprudence and in the investment treaty law context. In the words of Raz,

> the rule of law is just one of the virtues which a legal system may possess and by which it is to be judged. It is not to be confused with democracy, justice, equality (before the law or otherwise), human rights of any kind or respect for persons or for dignity of man.[11]

Some investment treaty scholars too have argued that as substantive conceptions involve normative judgments about the content of laws and legal systems,[12] using them in evaluating the influence of investment treaties on host states 'would run the risk of exporting Western institutions and ideals that are themselves imperfect or biased.'[13] Critics have pointed out that the ideals at the core of the thick conception of the rule of law are also far removed from what is regarded as the classical core of administrative law in developed legal systems.[14] There is growing consensus that the system

[8] See eg Cass Sunstein, *Democracy's Constitution* (New York, Oxford University Press, 2001) 7; see also Friedrich Hayek, *The Road to Serfdom* (London, Routledge, 1944) 63.

[9] Stephan W Schill, *The Multilateralization of International Investment Law* (Cambridge, Cambridge University Press, 2009) 377.

[10] See Section II below.

[11] Raz, 'The Rule of Law', 211.

[12] Benjamin K Guthrie, 'Beyond Investment Protection: An Examination of the Potential Influence of Investment Treaties on Domestic Rule of Law' (2012–2013) 45 *New York University Journal of International Law and Politics* 1151, 1163–64 (citations omitted).

[13] ibid 1164.

[14] Carol Harlow, 'Global Administrative Law: The Quest for Principles and Values' (2006) 17 *EJIL* 187, 193.

of governance based on such all-embracing precepts is 'simply not obtainable, particularly in resource-poor developing countries.'[15]

The elements of the thick or substantive conception of the rule of law largely mirror the notion of good governance. As Bonnitcha has suggested in his criticism of Vandevelde's conceptualisation of the investment treaty regime as the embodiment of the rule of law, the investment treaty prescriptions of reasonableness, security (of property and contract), non-discrimination, transparency and due process are better labelled as 'good governance' norms.[16] The narratives depicting investment treaty law as a mechanism for transforming domestic governance in host states appear to be largely inspired by the arguments advanced by law and development scholars in a series of studies that link failures of governance to low levels of development. One such study undertaken by the World Bank has found strong correlations between institutional quality, including the rule of law, as well as the overall quality of governance in a society on the one hand and development on the other.[17] To measure institutional quality and the overall quality of governance, the authors of the study went beyond rule of law indicators and looked into voice and accountability, political stability, government effectiveness, regulatory quality, and control of corruption.[18]

The rule of law is an essentially contested concept in that the disagreement about its precepts goes to its core.[19] An overview of its usage in the investment treaty law context evokes Waldron's observation that there is a tendency to use the term 'as a general stand-in for everything nice one could ever want to say about a political system, or everything good one could want from it.'[20] It falls outside the remit of this book to engage fully with extensive scholarship on the rule of law and good governance and their impact on development. Suffice it to say that law and development scholars have been sceptical about both the thin and thick conceptions of the rule of law. For instance, Trebilcock and Daniels have proposed their own alternative, the so-called thinner conception, which is linked to the goals of development and can therefore be of relevance in the investment treaty context. The normative benchmarks forming the core of this

[15] ibid 210.

[16] Bonnitcha, *Substantive Protection*, 43.

[17] Daniel Kaufmann, 'Governance Redux: The Empirical Challenge' (Washington DC, World Bank, 2004) 14, available at siteresources.worldbank.org/INTWBIGOVANTCOR/Resources/govredux.pdf. For the earlier iterations of this argument see Daniel Kaufmann, Aart Kraay, and Pablo Zoido-Lobaton, ' Governance Matters' (1999) World Bank Policy Research Working Papers No 2196.

[18] See Kaufmann, Kraay and Zoido-Lobaton, 'Governance Matters.'

[19] See Jeremy Waldron, 'Is the Rule of Law an Essentially Contested Concept (In Florida)?' (2002) 21 *Law and Philosophy* 137, 140.

[20] ibid.

conception of the rule of law are those characteristics of the legal system that contribute most to human development:[21]

(a) transparency in law-making and administration of justice;
(b) predictability (once adopted, laws should be enforced in a predictable and consistent way, relatively free from corruption, cronyism, patronage, or discrimination);
(c) stability (laws should not be subject to frequent, convulsive and sudden changes); and
(d) enforceability (laws should be effectively enforced by government or be effectively enforceable by private actors through the courts or other agencies).[22]

For Trebilcock and Daniels, these normative characteristics of a formal legal system—underpinned by the due process values as Western legal scholars might characterise them—are likely to be endorsed in most societies, because '[w]ithout them it is difficult to think of social purposes that a formal legal system could usefully serve as distinct from private purposes that the absence of one or more of these features might advance.'[23]

An overview of investment treaty law doctrine and scholarship suggests that it is something akin to this 'thinner' conception of the rule of law that serves as a baseline underlying most of the existing good governance narratives. To name one notable example, in conceptualising investment treaty law as an embodiment of, and a mechanism for, promoting the rule of law, Schill defines the latter in a manner largely mirroring the thinner conception with its emphasis on procedural fairness and due process.[24] The benchmarks of the 'thinner' conception of the rule of law can also be discerned in some of the arbitral interpretations of investment treaty rules as good governance standards.[25] In view of this largely overlapping use of rule of law and good governance paradigms in international investment law and scholarship, the remainder of this book will primarily use the term 'good governance' in engaging with legal and scholarly authorities which claim that investment treaty law can have a transformative impact on governmental conduct and domestic legal and bureaucratic culture. The aim of this work, once again, is not to support one or another vision of the rule of law or good governance but rather to trace and critically evaluate the legal meaning and jurisprudential bases of the recently proliferating narratives of international investment law as a mechanism for fostering changes in legal and bureaucratic practices of host states.

21 Trebilcock and Daniels, *Rule of Law Reform*, 25.
22 ibid 29–30.
23 ibid 30.
24 See generally Schill, 'Fair and Equitable Treatment', 154.
25 See below Section IIIB.

II. EMBODIMENTS OF GOOD GOVERNANCE PRECEPTS IN INVESTMENT TREATY LAW

A. Fair and Equitable Treatment as a Good Governance Standard: Transparency, Stability and Predictability

i. Transparency

Although the references to good governance and the rule of law can be traced back to the early days of 'treatification' of international investment law, it was not until the first wave of investment arbitrations in the 1990s that the rhetoric of good governance intensified and found its way into arbitral jurisprudence. *Metalclad v Mexico*[26] was among the first investment disputes in which the notion of transparency was invoked in determining a breach of the fair and equitable treatment standard and expropriation. The dispute concerned an investor's project for the construction and operation of a hazardous waste station and a landfill. Despite assurances by federal authorities that Metalclad had all necessary permits, the municipality ordered the cessation of construction works due to the absence of a municipal permit. The tribunal held Mexico responsible for a failure to 'ensure a transparent and predictable framework for Metalclad's business planning and investment.'[27] Relying on the NAFTA preamble which referred to the parties' agreement to 'ensure a predictable commercial framework for business planning and investment', the tribunal construed transparency as

> … the idea that all legal requirements for the purpose of initiating, completing and successfully operating investments made, or intended to be made, under the Agreement should be capable of being readily known to all affected investors of another party. There should be no room for doubt or uncertainty in such matters.[28]

In the tribunal's view, the absence of a clear rule as to the need to obtain a municipal construction permit as well as the absence of any established practice or procedure as to the manner of handling applications for such permits, constituted a failure on the part of Mexico to ensure the transparency required by NAFTA.[29] This finding was sufficient to establish a breach of the fair and equitable treatment standard under Article 1105.[30]

Tecmed v Mexico[31] is another seminal case whereby the fair and equitable treatment standard was construed to encompass a duty to ensure transparency. The dispute arose from a denial to renew the investor's

[26] *Metalclad Corpn v Mexico*, Award, 25 August 2000, ICSID Case No ARB(AF)/97/1, (2001) 40 ILM 36.

[27] ibid para 99.

[28] ibid para 76.

[29] ibid para 88.

[30] ibid para 101.

[31] *Técnicas Medioambientales Tecmed SA v Mexico*, Award, 29 May 2003, ARB(AF)/00/2, 10 ICSID Rep 130.

authorisation to operate the landfill. The decision to deny a renewal was explained by environmental violations which had allegedly been committed in the operation of the site. In the tribunal's view, the fair and equitable treatment standard entitled foreign investors to expect the host state to act

> … in a consistent manner, free from ambiguity and totally transparently in its relations with the foreign investors, so that it may know beforehand any rules and regulations that will govern its investments, as well as the goals of the relevant policies and administrative practices or directives, to be able to plan its investment and comply with such regulation.[32]

A lack of transparency was also at the heart of the tribunal's finding of unfair and inequitable treatment in *Saluka v Czech Republic*. An investor, one of the owners of a privatised bank, attempted to negotiate with the government a cooperative solution to the liquidity crisis. In the course of negotiations, some of the investor's correspondence addressed to the government agencies remained without any response.[33] At the final meeting between the investor, the Ministry of Finance and the Central Bank, the government representatives remained concerned about risks posed by the investor's proposal, which envisaged the transfer of assets but left open the possibility that certain toxic assets would remain in the possession of the bank.[34] While the investor was left with an impression that the negotiations would continue, the next day it was informed of the government's decision to put the bank into forced administration with the subsequent sales of its assets.[35] The tribunal found that by acting in such manner, the Czech government breached the fair and equitable treatment standard. It held that the government failed to deal with the investor's proposals in 'an unbiased, even-handed, transparent and consistent way.'[36] In particular, the exchange of views between the government and the investor were found to be not transparent enough to allow the investor to understand what the government's preconditions for an acceptable solution were.[37]

More recent iterations of transparency in investment arbitration practice show that, due to overwhelming endorsement by arbitral tribunals of the early jurisprudence and despite criticisms levelled against it being construed as an enforceable component of the fair and equitable treatment standard, a duty to maintain transparency has become entrenched in international investment law.[38] The tribunal in *Merrill & Ring Forestry*

[32] ibid para 154.
[33] ibid paras 392–96.
[34] ibid para 404.
[35] ibid para 405.
[36] ibid para 407.
[37] ibid para 420.
[38] See eg the definition of the fair and equitable treatment standard endorsed by the tribunal in *Mesa Power Group LLC v Government of Canada*, Award, 24 March 2016, PCA Case No 2012–17, para 502 and the Concurring and Dissenting Opinion of Charles Brower, paras 4, 17; *Crystallex International Corpn v Bolivarian Republic of Venezuela*, Award, 4 April 2016, ICSID Case No ARB(AF)/11/2, para 543.

v Canada went as far as to opine that transparency (and security of the legal environment) has now entered the corpus of general principles of law.[39]

ii. Stability and Predictability

The good governance precepts of stability and predictability have also entered the investment treaty law scene as elements of the fair and equitable treatment standard. In *Metalclad v Mexico*, the host state was found responsible for the failure to ensure transparency and predictability of the investment framework. While the tribunal did not elaborate on the notion of predictability, it made two brief references: once when referring to the NAFTA preamble where state parties agreed to 'ensure a predictable commercial framework'[40] and subsequently in its finding that Mexico failed to do so.[41] Later, the *Tecmed v Mexico* tribunal famously construed the fair and equitable treatment standard to include a state obligation to act in a totally transparent and consistent manner.[42] The *Tecmed* award, however, made no reference to stability and predictability. Despite having offered a very limited, if any at all, discussion of stability and predictability as elements of the fair and equitable treatment standard, both *Metalclad* and *Tecmed* awards have been heavily relied upon in subsequent arbitral interpretations of fair and equitable treatment. These awards construed the standard to include not only the host government's duty to ensure transparency and consistency, but also to maintain a stable and predictable legal environment for foreign investors.

For instance, it was by reference to *Tecmed* and *Metalclad* that the tribunal in *Occidental v Ecuador* elevated stability into an element of the fair and equitable treatment standard.[43] The dispute concerned a denial of VAT refunds to a foreign investor. The Ecuadorian tax agency annulled the previously-issued resolutions granting refunds on the ground that they had been based on a mistaken interpretation of the tax law. The arbitral tribunal found that the framework under which the investment had been made and operated was changed in an important manner by the tax agency's actions.[44] The tribunal stressed the significance of stability and predictability under international law,[45] and concluded that there was an international law obligation not to alter the legal and business environment in which the investment had been made.[46]

[39] *Merril & Ring Forestry LP v Canada*, Award, 31 March 2010, UNCITRAL-ICSID, para 187.
[40] *Metalclad v Mexico*, para 71.
[41] ibid para 99.
[42] *Tecmed v Mexico*, Award, para 154.
[43] *Occidental Exploration and Production Company v Ecuador*, Award, 1 July 2004, LCIA Case No UN 3467.
[44] ibid para 184.
[45] ibid para 191.
[46] ibid.

PSEG v Turkey provides another example where a lack of stability played a decisive role in the finding of the state in breach of the fair and equitable treatment standard. One of the claims brought before the tribunal concerned a series of legislative amendments that allegedly impeded the renegotiation of the investor's contract for the construction of an electric power plant. The tribunal criticised the government for what it characterised as 'a roller-coaster effect of the continuing changes in the legislation', including amendments relating to the legal status of the project company and the concession contract.[47] The tribunal held that

> [w]hile in complex negotiations, such as those involved in this case, many changes will occur beyond the control of the government, as was particularly the case with the increased costs, the issue is that the longer term outlook must not be altered in such a way that will end up being no outlook at all. In this case, it was not only the law that kept changing but notably the attitudes and policies of the administration.[48]

B. The Emerging Interpretations and their (Lacking) Juridical Foundations

Transparency, stability and predictability are not the only good governance requirements which tribunals have construed to be part of the fair and equitable treatment standard. Host states have also been found to be under a duty to ensure consistency of governmental action[49] and to be proactive as opposed to merely avoiding conduct prejudicial to the investors.[50] Unsurprisingly, the elevation of these normative benchmarks into the rank of enforceable components of the fair and equitable treatment standard have met with considerable criticism. In the words of Franck, 'the source of every rule—its *pedigree,* in the terminology of this essay—is *one* determinant of how strong its pull to compliance is likely to be.'[51] It is through its pedigree—various cues *pointing to* the 'historical origins, cultural or anthropological deep-rootedness'—that international norms exert a compliance pull.[52] Such pedigree of the good governance standards

[47] *PSEG Global Inc and Konya Ilgin Elektrik Üretim ve Ticaret Ltd Şirketi v Turkey,* Award and Annex, 19 January 2007, Case No ARB/02/5, para 250.

[48] ibid para 254.

[49] The tribunal in *Lauder v Czech Republic* (UNCITRAL, Final Award, 3 September 2001) paras 290–300, held that the fair and equitable treatment could be breached if domestic agencies acted inconsistently in applying domestic legislation.

[50] *MTD Equity Sdn Bhd and MTD Chile SA v Chile,* Award, 25 May 2004, ICSID Case No ARB/01/7, (2005) 44 ILM 91, para 113.

[51] Thomas M Franck, 'Legitimacy in the International System' (1988) 82 *American Journal of International Law* 705.

[52] ibid 725.

under investment treaties is troublingly insufficient. As one critic noted, transparency 'is actually not a standard at all; it is rather a description of a perfect public regulation in a perfect public world, to which all States should aspire, but very few (if any) will ever attain.'[53] A similar criticism has been made in regard to the *Tecmed* tribunal's unqualified language in defining the requirements of transparency and consistency: the tribunal pronounced that 'a state must act *totally* transparently; "*any and all* state actions" should be lawful and consistent with the goals underlying the laws in question' (emphasis added).[54] Such interpretations advance '[a] programme of good governance that no State in the world is capable of guaranteeing at all times.'[55] Even those who advocate the vision of the fair and equitable treatment as the embodiment of the rule of law have acknowledged that '[t]he stability and predictability of domestic law … should not be understood as an absolute requirement that would allow foreign investors to be effectively excluded from regulatory changes in the host state.'[56] Likewise, scholars supporting the good governance narrative have sounded a note of caution with regard to construing consistency as an element of the fair and equitable treatment standard: 'one should be aware that domestic regulatory frameworks are never completely free of inconsistencies.'[57]

Yet in spite of a welter of criticism from various quarters, a significant number of arbitral tribunals have endorsed the interpretation of fair and equitable treatment as a standard encapsulating an open-ended range of good governance precepts;[58] indeed, a few scholarly texts now cite those arbitral awards as expressions of positive law.[59]

It is unsurprising that, owing to its open-ended nature and lack of fixed content,[60] it was the fair and equitable treatment standard that has become the primary site for construing investment treaties as instruments of good governance and the rule of law. When arbitral tribunals first started to apply fair and equitable treatment in investment disputes, they faced lack

[53] Z Douglas, 'Nothing if Not Critical for Investment Treaty Arbitration: *Occidental, Eureko,* and *Methanex*' (2006) 22 *Arbitration International* 27, 28.

[54] Bonnitcha, *Substantive Protection*, 207.

[55] *El Paso Energy International Company v Argentina* (ICSID Case no ARB/03/15, Award, 31 October 2011) para 342.

[56] Schill, 'Fair and Equitable Treatment', 161 (footnotes omitted).

[57] Susan D Franck, 'International Decision: *Occidental Exploration & Production Co v. Republic of Ecuador*' (2005) 99 *AJIL* 676, 678.

[58] See above nn 38–39.

[59] See eg Marc Bundenberg, Jorn Griebel, Stephan Hobe, and August Reinsich (eds), *International Investment Law: A Handbook* (Oxford, Hart Publishing, 2015) 719; Rudolf Dolzer and Christoph Schreuer, *Principles of International Investment Law* (Oxford, Oxford University Press, 2008) 133–40; Jeswald W Salacuse, *The Law of Investment Treaties* (Oxford, Oxford University Press, 2010) 237–38.

[60] Iona Tudor, *The Fair and Equitable Treatment in the International Law of Foreign Investment* (Oxford, Oxford University Press, 2008) 131.

of textual guidance by reference to which the standard could be given a concrete meaning. Some tribunals have chosen to interpret the rule as a standard autonomous from the customary international minimum and therefore providing investors with protection that surpasses the minimum requirements of international law. An example of such reasoning can be found in *Vivendi v Argentina*, where the tribunal had to construe the fair and equitable treatment standard contained in the France-Argentina BIT.[61] As Article 3 of the treaty referred to fair and equitable treatment in *conformity* with the principles of international law and did not refer to the minimum standard of treatment, the tribunal refused to equate the provision with the minimum standard of treatment:

> [T]he reference to principles of international law supports a broader reading that invites consideration of a wider range of international law principles than the minimum standard alone … The wording of Article 3 requires that the fair and equitable treatment conform to the principles of international law, but the requirement for conformity can just as readily set a floor as a ceiling on the Treaty's fair and equitable treatment standard.[62]

Under such interpretation, 'anything that adversely affects investments and is economically unfavourable to their owners can constitute the breach of the relevant provisions of the bilateral investment treaties.'[63] A broadly similar approach was adopted in *Saluka v Czech Republic*, where the fair and equitable treatment was construed to provide protection surpassing that offered by the international minimum and could thus be used as a basis for holding states responsible for actions that would not have amounted to an international delict. The tribunal reasoned that fair and equitable treatment ought to be construed as a guarantee protecting investors against state conduct that displays *'a relatively lower degree of inappropriateness'* in comparison with the higher threshold required in establishing a violation of customary international law.[64] It concluded that precisely due to its autonomous nature, the fair and equitable treatment standard encompasses the host state's duty to ensure transparency, stability and predictability, and a duty to negotiate in good faith.[65]

The historical roots of the fair and equitable treatment standard, however, provide little support for construing the standard as an expression

[61] *Compañía de Aguas del Aconquija SA and Vivendi Universal SA v Argentina*, Award, 20 August 2007, ICSID Case No ARB/97/3, para 7.4.7.

[62] ibid. A similar stance was adopted in *Azurix Corp v Argentina*, Award, 23 June 2006, ICSID Case No ARB/01/12, para 361; and *Duke Energy Electroquil Partners and Electroquil SA v Ecuador*, Award, 12 August 2008, ICSID Case No ARB/04/19, para 336.

[63] Alexander Orakhelashvili, 'The Normative Basis of "Fair and Equitable Treatment": General International Law on Foreign Investment' (2008) 46 *Archiv des Völkerrechts* 74, 103.

[64] *Saluka Investments BV v Czech Republic*, Partial Award, 17 March 2006, PCA—UNCITRAL, para 293.

[65] See ibid paras 307, 329.

of the commitment by the state to maintain at all times compliance with good governance standards. Despite the autonomous interpretation of the fair and equitable treatment standard having garnered support among many tribunals and scholars, analysis of the early investment treaty models points to its origins in the international minimum standard. Fair and equitable treatment has its roots in the historical resistance to the international minimum standard by developing states that prompted the need for a more acceptable alternative.[66] The prototype of the modern fair and equitable treatment standard can be found in Article 1 of the 1967 OECD Draft Convention on the Protection of Foreign Property. As explained in the commentary to the Draft, the relevant clause was nothing but an expression of the minimum standard:

> The phrase 'fair and equitable treatment', customary in relevant bilateral agreements, indicates the standard set by international law for the treatment due by each State with regard to the property of foreign nationals … The standard required conforms in effect to the 'minimum standard' which forms part of customary international law.[67]

Subsequently, following the conclusion of a number of international investment agreements containing the fair and equitable treatment standard between the US and other countries, the OECD Committee on International Investment and Multinational Enterprises reaffirmed that the goal behind adopting a new terminology was to introduce '[a] substantive legal standard referring to general principles of international law even if this is not explicitly stated.'[68] That the fair and equitable treatment standard merely embodied customary international law was also confirmed in a 1979 statement issued by the Swiss Foreign Office.[69] A number of investment treaty scholars too have convincingly shown that 'fair and equitable treatment' was simply introduced into investment treaty language as a 'convenient, neutral and acceptable reference' to the much-discredited international minimum standard of treatment.[70]

The question is then whether the international minimum standard, as a customary international law predecessor of fair and equitable treatment,

[66] JC Thomas, 'Reflections on Article 1105 of NAFTA: History, State Practice and the Influence of Commentators' (2001) 17 *ICSID Review* 21.

[67] OECD Draft Convention on the Protection of Foreign Property (1968) 7 ILM 117, 120.

[68] OECD, Committee on International Investment and Multinational Enterprises, Intergovernmental Agreements Relating to Investment in Developing Countries (May 27, 1984) Doc. No 81/14, para 36.

[69] OECD, *Fair and Equitable Treatment Standard in International Investment Law*, Working Papers on International Investment (No 2004/3) 10.

[70] See Andrew Newcombe and Lluis Paradell, *Law and Practice of Investment Treaties: Standards of Treatment* (Alphen aan den Rijn, Kluwer Law International, 2009) 269; see also Martins Paparinskis, *The International Minimum Standard and Fair and Equitable Treatment* (Oxford, Oxford University Press, 2013) 163.

requires the sanctioning of states for a failure to ensure a transparent, stable, predictable and consistent legal framework. Historical analysis of the customary international minimum is useful inasmuch as it confirms the lack of legal basis for elevating lack of transparency, stability and predictability into enforceable breaches of international law. While the language of 'fair and equitable treatment' was embraced in investment treaties as a more politically neutral alternative to the contentious international minimum standard, the latter itself was long known as an ambiguous standard, providing for treatment that was 'incapable of exact definition.'[71] Although Elihu Root's speech described it as a standard generally endorsed 'by all civilized countries as to form a part of the international law of the world',[72] the notion of the international minimum did not draw on concrete evidence of state practice.[73] Existing scholarly expositions convincingly show that neither the nineteenth-century state practice, with its focus on the non-discriminatory aspects of the treatment of aliens and denial of justice, nor the subsequent elaboration of the standard in the landmark 1926 award in the US-Mexico General Claims Commission in the *LFH Neer and Pauline Neer* case and its emphasis on the element of 'procedural outrage'[74] provide any legal basis for construing the international minimum as a requirement of good governance and a ground of state responsibility for conduct exhibiting 'a relatively low degree of inappropriateness.'

The development of the content of the international minimum standard in the period following the Second World War was characterised by a shift from the protection of foreign private actors to the protection of foreign corporate actors and from denial of justice to compensation for expropriation.[75] While the international minimum evolved into a broader rubric, encompassing delicts that ranged from denial of justice and abuse of rights to protection of property,[76] relevant state practice during that period does not provide evidence to justify its expansion into a standard requiring transparency, stability and predictability in governmental conduct.

Lack of evidence of state practice and *opinio juris* to support the elevation of transparency, stability and predictability into a customary international standard may explain the fact that many investment tribunals have preferred to resort to alternative methods of establishing the emergence of a new international rule. Although some tribunals made general references to customary international law, most of the existing treaty-based

[71] Paparinskis, *The International Minimum*, 44 (referring to E Borchard, *Diplomatic Protection of Citizens Abroad* (New York, The Banks Law Publishing Co, 1915).

[72] Elihu Root, 'The Basis of Protection to Citizens Residing Abroad' (1910) 4 *AJIL* 517, 521.

[73] Paparinskis, *The International Minimum*, 39.

[74] ibid 64.

[75] Paparinskis, *The International Minimum*, 64–71.

[76] ibid 69.

interpretations of fair and equitable treatment as a good governance standard in investment arbitration practice have not drawn on evidence of a new international custom. An overview of arbitral jurisprudence shows that the language of transparency, stability, predictability and consistency has been imported into investment treaty law merely through: (1) references to treaty preambles; and (2) citing previous investment arbitration awards. For instance, the *Metalclad* tribunal's interpretation of transparency as an element of the fair and equitable treatment standard was based on the NAFTA preamble, which referred to the parties' agreement to 'ensure a predictable commercial framework for business planning and investment'.[77] The *Metalclad* award was subsequently partially set aside in judicial review by the Supreme Court of British Columbia precisely because: (1) transparency was not part of the Chapter 11 obligations and fell outside the scope of investor-state arbitration;[78] (2) no authority was cited or evidence introduced to establish that transparency has become part of customary international law.[79] Despite the fact that its finding of a breach of transparency was ruled out by the reviewing national court, the *Metalclad* award has exerted a considerable influence on the subsequent tribunal decisions, which reaffirmed transparency and predictability requirements as elements of the fair and equitable treatment standard.[80]

A similar lack of jurisprudential basis can be observed in arbitral awards that construed the fair and equitable treatment standard as requiring host states to ensure stability and predictability of an investment framework. Prior to the *Occidental* award, there had been no customary international rule which would require a host state to be held to monetary responsibility if its investment framework was not stable and predictable. To interpret stability and predictability as requirements under the fair and equitable treatment standard it was necessary to show the existence of a relevant international custom. The *Occidental* tribunal failed to do so. As a matter of treaty interpretation, in order to conclude that the fair and equitable treatment standard encompasses an obligation to maintain a stable and predictable environment a tribunal would need to base its interpretative reasoning on the wording of the applicable investment treaty

[77] The North American Free Trade Agreement, Preamble (1993) 32 ILM 289, 605.

[78] *United Mexican States v Metalclad Corp* [2001] 89 BCLR 3d 359, para 58.

[79] ibid para 68.

[80] See further John Hanna Jr, 'Is Transparency of Governmental Administration Customary International Law in Investor-Sovereign Arbitrations? Courts and Arbitrators May Differ' (2005) 21 *Arbitration International* 187; Akira Kotera, 'Regulatory Transparency' in Peter Muchlinski, Federico Ortino and Christoph Schreuer (eds), *The Oxford Handbook of International Investment Law* (Oxford, Oxford University Press, 2008) 617; Lluis Paradell, 'The BIT Experience of the Fair and Equitable Treatment Standard' in Federico Ortino, Lahra Liberti, Audley Sheppard and Hugo Warner (eds), *Investment Treaty Law: Current Issues II* (London, British Institute of International and Comparative Law, 2007) 131–34.

instrument, which the *Occidental* tribunal likewise failed to do.[81] Instead, drawing exclusively on the arbitral pronouncements in *Metalclad* and *Tecmed*, the tribunal merely vested a duty to ensure a stable and predictable environment with a status of customary international norm.[82] Despite the clearly insufficient legal basis on which the *Occidental* tribunal predicated the existence of an international obligation to ensure the stability and predictability of an investment framework, a number of tribunals have subsequently followed a similar stance.[83] Just like the *Occidental* tribunal, however, the respective tribunals failed to substantiate their findings by reference to customary international law or substantive treaty provisions.

It could be argued, of course, that customary international law has evolved and 'no longer requires showing outrageousness and other extreme forms of illegality in state behaviour as a precondition for establishing a breach of [the fair and equitable treatment standard],'[84] and that the good governance prescriptions have now become part of the modern customary international law enshrined in the relevant investment treaty provisions. Yet, the tribunal in *Glamis Gold* convincingly rejected the argument that customary international law has evolved to the point where the investor becomes entitled to additional, higher guarantees than those provided by the customary minimum. The tribunal noted common agreement that, as a minimum, 'the treatment of an alien, in order to constitute an international delinquency, should amount to an outrage, to bad faith, to wilful neglect of duty, or to an insufficiency of governmental action so far short of international standards that every reasonable and impartial man would readily recognize its insufficiency.'[85] While acknowledging that what the international community regards as 'outrageous' may have changed over time, the tribunal nevertheless pointed to lack of state practice and *opinio juris* to support the proposition that customary international law has moved beyond the minimum standard as articulated in *Neer*.[86]

It should be acknowledged that, outside customary international law, support for interpreting the good governance prescriptions as substantive

[81] See *Glamis Gold Ltd v United States*, Ad Hoc—UNCITRAL Award, 14 May 2009, paras 614–16 (the tribunal rejecting the argument that customary international law has evolved to the point where the investor becomes entitled to additional, higher guarantees. The tribunal pointed to the lack of state practice and *opinio juris* to support such an interpretation).

[82] *Occidental v Ecuador*, para 190.

[83] For instance, in *CMS Gas Transmission Co v Argentina* (2005) 44 ILM 120, para 274, the treaty preamble stating that fair and equitable treatment is desirable 'to maintain a stable framework for investments and maximum effective use of economic resources' was relied upon by the tribunal to conclude that a stable legal and business environment should be regarded an essential element of fair and equitable treatment.

[84] *Mondev International Ltd v United States*, Award, 11 October 2002, ICSID Case No ARB(AF)/99/2, para 116.

[85] *Glamis Gold v United States*, para 612.

[86] ibid para 614.

and enforceable treaty obligations could be drawn from certain investment treaty texts. For instance, Article 11 of the 2007 US-Uruguay BIT requires, in a sufficiently concrete language, that contracting host states ensure transparency through: (1) the designation of a contact point to facilitate communication; (2) the publication and provision of information pertaining to measures that might affect the operation of the treaty; (3) the conduct of administrative proceedings, including reasonable notice and an opportunity for affected persons to present facts and arguments in support of their position. The NAFTA Chapter 18 contains similar provisions. It is clear that, unlike arbitral statements that construed transparency as an element of fair and equitable treatment requiring the host state 'to act in a totally transparent manner', the provisions on transparency as found in NAFTA Chapter 18 and the US-Uruguay BIT are more concrete, fleshed out and agreed upon by the contracting state parties. Where an investment treaty instrument expressly requires transparency, the finding of a host state liable for lack of transparency would necessitate examining whether the disputed conduct violates any of the specifically outlined duties on notification and publication of information, and the conduct of proceedings. Even then, it has been suggested that 'the interpretation of fair and equitable treatment should not overstretch the position and function of administrative agencies by developing them into consultative units and insurers for the implementation of foreign investment.'[87]

Crucially, where investment treaties expressly stipulate transparency obligations, such instruments do not allow investors to claim damages for the host state's failure to maintain transparency. For instance, the transparency obligations in Article 11 of the US Model BIT and NAFTA Chapter 18 fall outside the scope of matters which can be brought by a foreign investor before an investment tribunal in proceeding initiated directly against a host state.[88] Similarly, Canada's most recent model investment treaty exempts transparency provisions from the scope of its investor-state dispute resolution mechanism.[89] Under these treaties, a foreign investor cannot claim a breach of the transparency provisions as a ground of state responsibility as it remains a prerogative of the state parties to determine the matter by resorting to the state-to-state dispute settlement mechanism. One is therefore safe to conclude that, to

[87] Stephan W Schill, 'Revisiting a Landmark: Indirect Expropriation and Fair and Equitable Treatment in the ICSID case Tecmed' (2006) 3(2) *Transnational Dispute Management*.

[88] NAFTA State parties have stated that no general transparency requirement exists in Art 1105. See *Glamis Gold v United States*, para 580 (referring to *Methanex*, Rejoinder Memorial of the United States on Jurisdiction, Admissibility and the Proposed Amendment, 33 (27 June 2001); *Metalclad*, Amended Petition of Mexico to the Supreme Court of British Columbia (Sup Ct BC) para 72 (27 October 2000); *Metalclad*, Outline of Argument of Intervenor Attorney General of Canada (Sup Ct BC) paras 31–33 (16 February 2001)).

[89] See, for instance, Arts 12 and 20 of the Kuwait-Canada bilateral investment treaty (signed 2011, entered into force 2014).

date, neither customary international law nor international investment treaties provide sufficient support for interpreting transparency, stability, predictability and consistency as enforceable components of the fair and equitable treatment standard, non-compliance with which could trigger a host state's obligation to compensate the disaffected foreign investor.

C. Other Good Governance Standards

i. Obligation to Provide Effective Means of Asserting Claims and Enforcing Rights

Beyond the fair and equitable treatment standard, good governance prescriptions could arguably be found in other investment treaty provisions. Some treaties, among them the Energy Charter Treaty and a number of US investment treaties, explicitly require that host states ensure 'effective means of asserting claims and enforcing rights.'[90] One may argue that the obligation to provide effective means of asserting claims and enforcing rights is nothing but a positive statement of the obligation not to deny justice. However, it is also possible to construe the effective means standard as a provision that requires states to do more than just refrain from a denial of justice: a negative duty to refrain from a denial of justice could be narrower in its scope than a positive duty to provide effective means of justice. Such was the case in *AMTO v Ukraine*, where the investor argued for a considerably broader interpretation of the standard and contended that the host state should be held to monetary responsibility for failing to create and maintain effective bankruptcy legislation.[91] While acknowledging that the claimant's experience of Ukrainian bankruptcy proceedings might have been frustrating, the *AMTO* tribunal concluded that the investor failed to prove 'any legal error, abuse, undue delay or interference in the process by the Ukrainian courts'.[92] The tribunal found that the investor's claims demonstrated 'unrealistic expectations of a simple and rapid result, in a judicial structure where there were many other interests and competing rights to be considered.'[93] Nevertheless, it construed the effective means obligation in Article 10(12) as a qualitative standard of good governance: legislation ought to be not only constitutional and accessible but also effective.[94] Having acknowledged the difficulty of identifying criteria by reference to which the effectiveness of the legislation could be assessed, the tribunal drew guidance from the object and purpose of the Energy Charter

[90] See eg Art II(7) of the investment treaty between the United States of America and the Republic of Ecuador signed 1993; also Art 10(12) of the Energy Charter Treaty, 17 December 1994, 2080 UNTS 100.

[91] *AMTO v Ukraine*, Final Award, 26 March 2008, SCC Case No 080/2005, paras 75, 85.

[92] ibid para 84.

[93] ibid.

[94] ibid para 87.

Treaty and concluded that 'effectiveness' under Article 10(12) implied a systematic, comparative, progressive and practical standard.[95]

The tribunal's reasoning, while remaining largely within the boundaries of ordinary and effective interpretation of the treaty terms, nevertheless suggests that the effective means standard is not limited to the obligation to provide a fair and efficient system of justice, but also to ensure effectiveness of legislation as may be necessary for the assertion of claims and the enforcement of rights by foreign investors. It has been observed that

> where tribunals interpret the standard to focus on the quality of the legal system in general—either instead of or in addition to the treatment of investors in any individual case—effective means provisions essentially require states to provide not only foreign investors, but also domestic parties, with a legal system that corresponds to the basic demands of the rule of law.[96]

However, the interpretation of the standard in *AMTO v Ukraine* seems to transcend even the basic demands of the rule of law. Although the tribunal found that, on the facts of the case, the investor's expectations of judicial governance in Ukraine were unrealistic, its emphasis on viewing the effective means provision as a qualitative standard renders the latter open to interpretation which would impose on host states obligations going far beyond what a procedural or thin conception of the rule law encapsulates. In particular, the requirement that a legal framework be not only accessible but also effective may entail normative judgments about the content of host state laws,[97] potentially resulting in a situation where Western institutions and normative ideals are used as benchmarks of effectiveness and legality and host states held to monetary responsibility when espousing qualitatively different approaches.

Even where the effective means standard is construed in a narrower manner—as a host state duty to establish a proper system of laws, with the emphasis on procedural as opposed to substantive effectiveness—its implications for developing countries are still troubling. For instance, the tribunal in *Chevron v Ecuador* held that congestion and backlogs in national courts could be relevant factors in establishing whether the effective means standard has been breached.[98] In the tribunal's view, '[t]o the extent that generalized court congestion could alone produce the persistent and long delays of the kind observed here, it would evidence a systemic problem with the design and operation of the Ecuadorian judicial system and would breach Article II(7).'[99] The tribunal also held that, if

[95] ibid para 88.
[96] Guthrie, 'Beyond Investment Protection', 1192.
[97] See Guthrie 1163–64, citations omitted.
[98] *Chevron Corpn and Texaco Petroleum Corpn v Ecuador*, UNCITRAL, Partial Award on Merits, 30 March 2010, para 250.
[99] ibid para 263.

used in evaluating claims concerning the administration of justice by the host state courts, the effective means standard would entail a potentially less demanding test than that involved in establishing a denial of justice in customary international law, in the sense that state responsibility could be established even in cases where the disputed conduct does not rise to the level of denial of justice.[100] This interpretation has been endorsed in other subsequent awards,[101] and is troubling for a number of reasons. For one, the very creation of investor-state arbitration was historically justified by the fact that national courts in capital-importing developing countries were deemed too biased, corrupt, lacking expertise and controlled by the executive to provide a fair and efficient forum for the resolution of disputes between investors and host governments.[102] Thus, an historical lack of institutional and legal capacity in developing states has already resulted in an important part of judicial powers being removed from national courts to international investment tribunals. By subjecting host states to monetary responsibility for a failure to ensure effective administration of justice in individual cases, international investment law effectively punishes developing states twice: once by restricting national adjudicative control over investment disputes due to an historical inability of developing states to meet the high institutional and legal benchmarks, and subsequently by sanctioning host governments in each individual case where such benchmarks were not met.

Another troubling aspect of holding developing states responsible for regular and systemic judicial delays and backlogs is a tendency to examine deficiencies of national judicial systems through different lenses depending on the status of a respondent state. This disparity in treatment is instantly discernible if one compares two leading investment arbitration cases on denial of justice: *Loewen v United States* and *Saipem v Bangladesh*. In the former, despite having acknowledged the critical failure of the US trial courts to render justice and ensure impartial and non-discriminatory treatment of a foreign litigant, the tribunal famously (or rather infamously) refrained from finding the US responsible for a denial of justice. The tribunal was able to reach this outcome by insisting on the prior exhaustion of local remedies as a precondition for claiming a denial of justice. This approach to cases involving judicial misconduct was endorsed in a number of subsequent cases, only to be later dispensed with in *Saipem v Bangladesh*, where an Italian investor succeeded in its claim against Bangladesh even despite the fact that the disputed conduct was a

[100] ibid para 244.

[101] See eg *White Industries Australia Ltd v India*, UNCITRAL, Award, 30 November 2011, para 11.3.

[102] See eg Salacuse, *The Law of Investment Treaties*, 358; Dolzer and Schreuer, *Principles of International Investment Law*, 214–15.

denial of justice and the investor did not exhaust local remedies.[103] While both cases involved a denial of justice by national courts, the respective arbitral tribunals appeared to be less inclined to find a breach in the claim brought against the United States but were prepared to do so in the case against Bangladesh.

An overview of arbitral practice and commentary tends to suggest that a protracted judicial procedure in, for instance, Ecuador and India is likely to be characterised as an international wrong while a similar feature of the Italian judicial system is unlikely to be internationally condemned and sanctioned, despite its notoriety and the degree of criticism it attracted.[104] As incisively observed by Anghie, the legal and political shortcomings that afflict developed states 'are rarely if ever discussed in terms of internationally articulated norms of good governance.'[105] One is also reminded of the words of Harlow that there is '[a] measure of hypocrisy in seeking to impose external standards on the poor and under-privileged, which the self-styled "good countries" are unwilling and sometimes unable to meet.'[106] The imposition—and enforcement—of the obligation to create and maintain effective means of asserting claims betrays this hypocrisy. It also raises an important question as to whether the use of monetary sanctions, such as the remedy of damages, is suitable and desirable in rectifying deficiencies in domestic governance, particularly when such deficiencies are caused by an historical lack of institutional, legal and human capacity and, importantly, are known to investors at the time of making a decision to invest.

ii. An Obligation to Create Favourable Conditions for Foreign Investment

Good governance prescriptions can also be discerned in investment treaty provisions declaring contracting state parties' commitment to 'create and maintain in its territory a legal framework apt to guarantee to investors the continuity of legal treatment.'[107] Another variation of this provision is a treaty clause whereby contracting states undertake to encourage the creation of favourable conditions.[108] For example, Article II(1) of

[103] *Saipem v Bangladesh*, Award 20 June 2009, ICSID Case ARB/05/7, para 181.

[104] See also recent political science analyses showing that developed states with higher rule of law rankings are significantly less likely to lose in investment arbitration cases: Daniel Behn, Tarald Laudal Berge and Malcolm Langford, 'Poor States or Poor Governance? Explaining Outcomes in Investment Treaty Arbitration' (2017) *Northwestern Journal of International Law & Business* (forthcoming).

[105] Anthony Anghie, 'Civilization and Commerce: The Concept of Governance in Historical Perspective' (2000) 45 *Villanova Law Review* 887, 893.

[106] Harlow, 'Global Administrative Law', 211.

[107] See Art 2(4) of the Italy-Jordan BIT, discussed in *Salini v Jordan*, Decision on Jurisdiction, 15 November 2004, (2005) 44 ILM 563, para 126.

[108] See Art II of the United States-Panama BIT.

the Canada-Ecuador BIT stipulates that each contracting party shall encourage the creation of favourable conditions for investors of the other contracting party to make investments in its territory. It has been argued that the obligations on the creation of favourable conditions can operate as substantive and enforceable treaty provisions. According to Reisman and Sloane, a commitment to create favourable conditions should be construed as an enforceable standard of good governance:

> The 'favourable conditions' established by BITs consist, not merely of natural phenomena such as climate resources, and access to the sea, nor even an educated population in the host state receptive to and eager to participate in the benefits of foreign investment; they also contemplate, more significantly and innovatively, an effective normative framework: impartial courts, an efficient and legally restrained bureaucracy, and the measure of transparency …
>
> … In a BIT regime, the host state must do far more than open its doors to foreign investment and refrain from overt expropriation. It must establish and maintain an appropriate legal, administrative, and regulatory framework, the legal environment that modern investment theory has come to recognize as a *conditio sine qua non* of the success of private enterprise.[109]

Newcombe and Paradell have also espoused the view, albeit with some reservations, that an obligation to create favourable conditions should be viewed as a substantive and enforceable standard.[110] While noting that an obligation to create and maintain favourable conditions should not be viewed as imposing specific types of market-based regulatory policies such as privatisation and deregulation, Newcombe and Paradell suggest that the term 'favourable conditions' might be interpreted as 'the minimal legal administrative and regulatory framework that fosters and sustains investment in industrialised capital-exporting states.'[111]

It is abundantly clear that the arguments interpreting a commitment to the creation of favourable conditions as an enforceable treaty standard reflect a vision of international investment law as a mechanism whose function is to enhance domestic governance in host states. However, for 'favourable conditions' to be construed as a standard encompassing the efficient legislation, impartial judiciary and restrained bureaucracy, such an interpretation must be firmly grounded within the established sources of international law. The inherent vagueness of the term 'favourable conditions' and the sheer scale of a promise contained therein would make it too easy for investors to allege a breach, thus dramatically expanding the scope of host state responsibility under investment treaties.

[109] W Michael Reisman and Robert D Sloane, 'Indirect Expropriation and Its Valuation in the BIT Generation' (2004) 74 *British Yearbook of International Law* 115, 117.

[110] Newcombe and Paradell, *Law and Practice*, 131.

[111] ibid 132.

In contrast with other good governance obligations, the idea of treating the commitment to create favourable conditions as a substantive standard met with little support in arbitral practice. For instance, in *Toto v Lebanon*, the tribunal dismissed as unfounded the claimant's assertion that an increase in customs and duties and taxes constituted a failure to maintain 'favourable economic and legal conditions' of the investment. It held that for the tribunal to have jurisdiction over the dispute, the investor would need to demonstrate that these changes in legislation were discriminatory, unreasonable, or otherwise in violation of the treaty.[112]

White Industries v India provides another example of a case where an investor argued that a commitment to encourage and promote favourable conditions for investors under the Australia-India bilateral investment treaty ought to be construed as an enforceable good governance obligation. The investor contended that, at the very least, the relevant provision comprised three distinct obligations on the part of the host state: to create a suitable governance framework for supervising the conduct of state-owned enterprises in their dealings with foreign investors; to ensure that arbitration laws were in line with the New York Convention; and to 'take step to reduce the backlogs of cases in its courts, given the prospect that such backlog must necessarily have significant effect on domestic and international businesses …'.[113] The tribunal noted a general consensus in the academic commentary that commitments to create favourable conditions should not be treated as a basis of substantive investor rights, and concluded that, owing to a lack of sufficient content, the relevant provision was 'far too general' to give rise to the specific obligations asserted by the investor.[114]

Although the prevailing view in investment arbitration doctrine seems to be that declaratory commitments to the creation of favourable conditions are just that—hortatory devices, it is nevertheless troubling that a number of scholars and claimant-investors have argued for the provision to be construed as a substantive and enforceable standard. Trends in investment arbitration practice so far also suggest that despite their declaratory tone, such commitments are capable of being harnessed as textual guidance in establishing the object and purpose of a relevant investment treaty instrument and thus may have a certain bearing on the interpretation of substantive treaty obligations as good governance standards.

[112] *Toto Costruzioni Generali SpA v Lebanon* (ICSID Case No ARB/07/12, Decision on Jurisdiction, 8 September 2009) paras 129–30.

[113] *White Industries*, para 9.2.1.

[114] ibid para 9.2.12.

III. COMPETING VISIONS OF INVESTMENT TREATY LAW AND ITS GOOD GOVERNANCE PROMISE

A. What Does the Good Governance Rhetoric Mask?

Why the expansive interpretation of investment treaty norms as good governance standards? The doctrinal analysis of investment arbitration and treaty practice suggests that the prolific invocation of the good governance language has been driven by a range of factors that can be brought under a common rubric of mission creep. Driven as it seems by an inherent interest in the continuation of investment treaty practice and investor-state dispute settlement,[115] arbitrators created new causes of action and new grounds of state responsibility in international law by reading various good governance benchmarks into the vague and open-ended investment treaty provisions, prominently the fair and equitable treatment standard and the obligation to create and maintain effective means of redress. The elevation of good governance benchmarks into enforceable treaty standards significantly expands the scope of state responsibility under investment treaties and correspondingly enables foreign investors to claim damages in a broader range of circumstances.[116] References to good governance requirements were imported into arbitral practice to supply the otherwise lacking justifications for the new, very broad and dubiously-founded interpretations of investment treaty standards. Good governance has also been invoked as a new raison d'etre of investment treaty law to justify the growing exposure of states to adverse financial implications of arbitral awards and to compensate for the increasingly questionable contribution of investment treaties to economic development. As argued by Vandevelde, good governance norms enshrined in substantive standards of treatment have 'intrinsic worth' that would offer justification for the existence of investment treaties even if the latter fail to deliver on their economic objectives.[117]

The 'divinely ordained and morally justified civilisation mission'[118] of the international investment treaty regime has already been questioned

[115] Anthea Roberts, 'Power and Persuasion in Investment Treaty Interpretation: The Dual Role of States' (2010) 104 *AJIL* 179, 198; see also Yves Dezalay and Bryant G Garth, *Dealing in Virtue: International Commercial Arbitration and the Construction of a Transnational Legal Order* (Chicago University Press, 1996) 8, 70; similarly Kate Miles, *The Origins of International Investment Law: Empire, Environment and the Safeguarding of Capital* (Cambridge, Cambridge University Press, 2013) 343.

[116] See S Subedi, *International Investment Law: Reconciling Policy and Principle* (Oxford, Hart Publishing, 2008) 140–41 criticising the emerging jurisprudence for transforming the minimum protection into the maximum protection.

[117] Vandevelde, *Bilateral Investment Treaties*, 119. For a critique, see Bonnitcha, *Substantive Protection*, 43.

[118] Jose E Alvarez, 'Contemporary Foreign Investment Law: An "Empire of Law" or the "Law of Empire"?' (2008–2009) 60 *Alabama Law Review* 943, 944.

from historical and normative and doctrinal angles. To some, the increasingly expansive reach of investment treaty law and its evolving objectives is yet another manifestation of 'repetitive assertions of power and responses to power.'[119] Others point out that historically the notion of governance was never preoccupied with well-being of peoples in developing states; rather, it was understood that the whole purpose of governance was to facilitate the 'inexhaustible expansion of European commerce' in the global South.[120] Critics also highlight the shortcomings of legal and interpretive approaches through which the language of good governance was introduced in investment treaty law. In the words of Montt, 'the relatively free invention of new rules without proper methodological foundation' undermines the rule of law legitimacy of the system.[121] It has also been argued that

> … the current framing of investor-state arbitration as the embodiment of good governance and the rule of law is representative solely of the perspectives of political and private elites. And it will remain so without the incorporation of substantive principles from other areas of international law …[122]

Crucially, competing visions of international investment law have long been crystallising in investment treaty law and arbitral jurisprudence. There is an ample body of case law and literature which convincingly seek to contest the far-reaching interpretation of investment treaty protections and expose critical insufficiencies of legal reasoning in arbitral interpretations of the fair and equitable treatment and other good governance standards. Some arbitral tribunals and scholars have been vocal in alerting to the dangers of construing investment treaty norms autonomously from treaty texts and customary rules. Given the inherent vagueness of the terms 'fair and equitable', an arbitral tribunal's failure to situate the interpretation of the fair and equitable treatment standard within a broader corpus of public international law leaves the outcomes precariously open to individual preferences. Unrestrained by customary international law or a treaty text, tribunals might add new elements to the already growing notion of a fair and equitable treatment standard, broadening the scope of state responsibility to foreign investors. The following sections will focus on investment treaty practice and arbitral awards which support the vision of investment treaty law as a mechanism for redressing serious procedural irregularities adversely affecting investors, and not as a mechanism for

[119] Miles, *The Origins of International Investment Law*, 7, citing Lauren A Benton, *Law and Colonial Cultures: Legal Regime in World History, 1400–1900* (New York, Cambridge University Press, 2002) 11.

[120] Anghie, 'Civilization and Commerce', 902.

[121] Santiago Montt, *State Liability in Investment Treaty Arbitration: Global Constitutional and Administrative Law in the BIT Generation* (Oxford, Hart Publishing, 2009) 153.

[122] Miles, *The Origins of International Investment Law*, 335.

holding states liable for a failure to treat investors in accordance with best international standards of good governance. Particular attention will also be drawn to the notion of investor responsibilities and the role the latter should play in conceptualising foreign investors' entitlement to enjoy good governance when investing in developing states.

B. Fair and Equitable Treatment as Due Process

In contrast with transparency, stability, predictability and the creation of favourable conditions for foreign investment, a duty to ensure due process—another good governance standard by which host states are arguably bound under international investment law—appears to be less contentious both in terms of its content and its legal foundations. Historically, references to due process have entered investment treaty law through early friendship, commerce and navigation treaties and bilateral investment treaties, which frequently required that foreign investments ought not to be expropriated except where such expropriation is non-discriminatory, carried out under due process of law and accompanied by compensation.[123] Due process has thus come to be regarded as one of the 'conduct requirements' that must be satisfied for an expropriation to be lawful.[124] There is support for the view that a host state's duty to ensure due process in carrying out expropriation implies the availability of judicial review so that an independent host state tribunal can assess the amount of compensation due to a foreign investor for the expropriated investment.[125]

From 2004, US model treaties have also been featuring a reference to due process as the key element of an obligation to treat investors fairly and equitably. The fair and equitable treatment standard now incorporates the obligation 'not to deny justice in criminal, civil, or administrative adjudicatory proceedings in accordance with the principle of *due process* embodied in the principal legal systems of the world.'[126] Just as is the case with other good governance obligations, the meaning of a duty to ensure due process has crystallised primarily through interpretations of the fair and equitable treatment standard in arbitral and judicial practice. What is noteworthy here is that the existing treaty practice and case law overwhelmingly support the procedural aspects of due process, such as

[123] See UNCTAD, *Taking of Property* (United Nations, New York and Geneva 2000) 15–16.

[124] See eg August Reinisch, 'Legality of Expropriations' in August Reinisch (ed), *Standards of Investment Protection* (Oxford, Oxford University Press, 2008) 171.

[125] For instance, the 2005 Afghanistan-Germany BIT requires that the legality of expropriation, nationalisation or comparable measure and the amount of compensation 'shall be subject to review by due process of law'.

[126] Art 5(2)(a) of the 2004 US Model BIT.

lawful procedure, reasonable advance notice, access to a court, and a fair hearing.[127] For instance, in *Waste Management v Mexico* the tribunal held that a breach of fair and equitable treatment could result from '*a lack of due process* leading to an outcome which offends judicial propriety—as might be the case with a manifest failure of natural justice in judicial proceedings or a complete lack of transparency and candour in an administrative process.'[128] In *Tecmed*, the tribunal construed the standard to require a reasonable notice and access to fair hearing. In the dispute before it, an investor challenged a refusal to renew its permit to operate a waste landfill. The tribunal pointed to the fact that the environmental authority did not enter into any form of dialogue through which the investor would become aware of the possibility of non-renewal of its permit and also could rectify deficiencies that would later be the grounds for the environmental authority's decision to discontinue the operation of the landfill site. The investor had thus been deprived of an opportunity, prior to the resolution, to inform the environmental authority of its position or to provide an explanation with respect to such deficiencies.[129] In a similar vein, notification and an opportunity to respond were at the heart of the investor's claim in *Rumeli Telekom v Kazakhstan*.[130] The dispute involved the termination of an investment contract, which had subsequently led to divestment of the investor's shareholding in a telecommunications enterprise. The tribunal found several breaches of due process. In terminating the contract on the grounds of an alleged failure to file reports, the investment committee failed to notify the investor of the reasons for such termination.[131] Following the termination of the contract, the government appointed a working group which had to examine the fulfilment by the investor of its investment obligations. The tribunal found that the working group confirmed the validity of the decision terminating the investor's contract without giving the investor a real possibility to present its position.[132]

One significant implication of interpreting the due process obligation as a procedural standard is that such interpretation is based on understanding the fair and equitable treatment standard in the same manner as the customary international minimum—as a rule designed to address formal and procedural aspects rather than to engage with substantive elements of governmental conduct.[133] The obligation of due process appears to have

127 Paparinskis, *The International Minimum*, 72–73.

128 *Waste Management Inc v Mexico*, Award, 30 April 2004 (2004) 43 ILM 967, para 98 (emphasis added).

129 *Tecmed v Mexico*, para 173.

130 *Rumeli Telekom v Republic of Kazakhstan*, Award, 29 July 2008, ICSID Case No ARB/05/16.

131 ibid para 614.

132 ibid paras 616–18.

133 Paparinskis, *The International Minimum Standard*, 73.

a stronger legal basis in state practice and contemporary international investment law, and thus—at least in doctrinal terms—does not raise the same concerns as other good governance obligations. Yet even the more temperate interpretations of the fair and equitable treatment standard as an obligation of due process might be problematic for their broader normative implications. As Harlow reminds us,

> … there is a degree of wilful blindness involved … in the belief that increased doses of Western style bureaucracy or due process procedures necessarily benefit citizens; to the contrary, the adjudicative methods dear to economic liberals are designedly biased to benefit those who can afford to use them, normally states and multinational enterprises, with skilful in-house lawyers.[134]

Even the competing interpretations of the fair and equitable treatment standard—interpretations that show greater judicial restraint and care in complying with the established canons of treaty interpretation—raise the question whether certain 'baseline' good governance benchmarks might deserve a status of an international norm (providing that there is enough support for it in treaty text or a custom) or whether any of the so-called 'universally accepted' standards of due process and procedural fairness are beneficial for host communities.

C. Good Governance and the Doctrine of Legitimate Expectations

Is it fair, desirable, and appropriate to hold a host state to monetary liability for a failure to ensure good governance, where such failure is the result of the host state's lack of financial, institutional, political and social capacity? Should investors be entitled to claim redress for harm caused by poor governance where the investor had been aware, at the time of making its decision to invest, of the host state's inability to meet high legal and institutional standards? From a normative standpoint, the expansive interpretation of the fair and equitable treatment has been criticised for disproportionately affecting developing countries.

Ironically, although arbitral tribunals are responsible for transplanting good governance obligations into the investment treaty law context, arbitral jurisprudence on the fair and equitable treatment standard also offers what can arguably be seen as a very potent means of exposing the shortcomings of the good governance narratives and countering them in investor-state arbitration. Of particular relevance here is the doctrine of legitimate expectations, which a string of arbitral tribunals relied upon in their construction of the fair and equitable treatment standard as encompassing the duty to provide transparency, stability, predictability

[134] Harlow, 'Global Administrative Law', 211 (citations omitted).

and consistency.[135] Whilst enabling tribunals to interpret the fair and equitable treatment standard in broad and far-reaching terms, the doctrine of legitimate expectations can also offer the much-needed legal and conceptual framework for scaling back the scope of state responsibility in international investment law by focusing on the conduct of investor and implied duties investors are bound by in making their claims against host states. Most instances where legitimate expectations have been invoked, either by a claimant investor or an arbitral tribunal, tend to highlight that good governance is a two-way street, and investors' entitlement to good governance must be measured against investors' responsibilities.

Since international investment treaties barely contain any reference to the concept of legitimate expectations,[136] the early iterations of legitimate expectations in the investment arbitration practice invoked the public international law principle of good faith and the related doctrine of estoppel, as well as general principles of law, as a basis of the proposition that a failure of the state to inform others of the proposed changes in policy or to retreat from previously made assurances may lead to an obligation to indemnify the party which placed reliance upon the pre-existing state of affairs to its own detriment.[137] Thus, where a host state's conduct creates reasonable and justifiable expectations on the part of an investor to act in reliance on the said conduct, a failure by the host state to honour those expectations may cause the investor or investment to suffer damages which the state is then responsible to indemnify.[138]

The protection of investors' legitimate expectations has become part of the fair and equitable treatment standard much in the same way as transparency, stability and predictability—with tribunals predominantly relying on relatively few authorities outside investment treaty texts and customary rules on investment protection.[139] Despite the questionable manner in which the doctrine of legitimate expectations has been

[135] See Francisco Orrego Vicuna, 'Regulatory Authority and Legitimate Expectations: Balancing the Rights of the State and the Individual under International Law in a Global Society' (2003) *Intl L Forum* 188, 193–94; Elizabeth Snodgrass, 'Protecting Investors' Legitimate Expectations: Recognizing and Delimiting a General Principle' (2007) 21 *ICSID Review* 1.

[136] Explanatory notes to expropriation clauses in the BITs and FTAs, especially those concluded by the US, contain reference to investment-backed expectations, the latter concept originating in the US jurisprudence on regulatory takings. See *Penn Central Transport Co v New York City* 438 US 104 (1978); *Lucas v South Carolina Coastal Council* 505 US 1029 (1992).

[137] Bin Cheng, *General Principles of Law as applied by International Courts and Tribunals* (Cambridge, Cambridge University Press, 1994) 137–43. See also W Michael Reisman and Mahnoush H Arsanjani, 'The Question of Unilateral Governmental Statements as Applicable Law in Investment Disputes' (2005) *ICSID Review* 328.

[138] *International Thunderbird Gaming Corpn v Mexico*, UNCITRAL, Award, 26 January 2006, para 147.

[139] See generally, Martins Paparinskis, 'Good Faith and Fair and Equitable Treatment in International Investment Law' in Andrew D Mitchell, M Sornarajah, and Tania Voon, *Good Faith and International Economic Law* (Oxford, Oxford University Press, 2015) 168.

imported into international investment law, it has played a crucial part in supplying the (insufficient) legal basis for raising transparency, stability, predictability and other good governance standards into the rank of host state obligations. Both the *Metalclad* and *Tecmed* awards—and their progeny in subsequent arbitral practice—referred to foreign investors' *expectations* that host states would act in a transparent, consistent and predictable manner, and concluded that a frustration of such expectations ought to give rise to the host states' obligation to redress investors for the resulting economic harm.[140]

The pertinent question is: to what extent can the investor's expectations of transparency, stability and predictability be regarded as legitimate and deserving of protection under investment treaties? For an investor's expectation to be entitled to protection under the fair and equitable treatment standard, it must be based on a commitment, assurance, or representation by a state party. The significance of specific commitments as a central element of the legitimate expectations analysis has been widely endorsed in arbitral practice. For instance, in examining the disputed conduct against the doctrine of legitimate expectations, the *LG&E* tribunal reasoned that for an investor's expectations to be 'fair' such expectations should be 'based on the conditions offered by the host state at the time of the investment; they may not be established unilaterally by one of the parties; they must exist and be enforceable by law.'[141] The *EDF v Romania* tribunal reached a similar conclusion in its examination of the investor's claims under the fair and equitable treatment clause:

> [e]xcept where specific promises or representations are made by the State to the investor, the latter may not rely on a bilateral investment treaty as a kind of insurance policy against the risk of any changes in the host State's legal and economic framework. Such expectation would be neither legitimate nor reasonable.[142]

Another criterion of the legitimacy of an investor's expectations is the reasonableness of reliance. To what extent is it reasonable for an investor to expect a host government's adherence to good governance standards? Arbitral practice has so far overwhelmingly endorsed the view that an expectation of *total* stability and predictability is unreasonable. As summarised by the tribunal in *EDF v Romania*,

> the idea that legitimate expectations, and therefore [the fair and equitable treatment standard], imply the stability of the legal and business framework, may not be correct if stated in an overly-broad and unqualified formulation.

[140] See *Tecmed v Mexico*, para 154; *Metalclad v Mexico*, paras 89, 99.

[141] *LG & E Energy Corpn v Argentina*, Decision on Liability, 3 October 2006, ICSID Case No ARB 02/1, (2007) 46 ILM 36, para 130.

[142] *EDF (Services) Ltd v Romania*, Award, 2 October 2009, ICSID Case No RB/05/13, para 217.

> The FET might then mean the virtual freezing of the regulation of economic activities, in contrast with the State's normal regulatory power and the evolutionary character of economic life.[143]

In examining the reasonableness of expectations arbitral tribunals have also considered the investor's conduct. There is a growing support for the view that a foreign investor must act as a prudent and responsible actor, refrain from unconscionable dealings, undertake reasonable assessment of investment risks in the host country and operate an investment in a reasonable manner.[144] As far as stability and predictability are concerned, an investor's expectation should hinge on whether it has understood the risk of foreseeable future regulatory change prior to entering the host state. Before a decision to invest is made, foreign investors ought to assess the shortcomings of the existing legal and regulatory framework.[145]

To mention one example where the reasonableness of investor expectations was evaluated by reference to the investor's conduct, in *Saluka v Czech Republic* the investor alleged a breach of fair and equitable treatment, including a failure by the host state to ensure a predictable and transparent regulatory framework to enable financial institutions to enforce loan security. The tribunal noted that while it was undisputed between the parties that Czech law failed to provide effective mechanisms to enforce a loan security, such legal shortcomings ought to have been known to the claimant when its investment had been made and an expectation that such shortcomings would quickly be fixed by the Czech legislature was unfounded.[146]

The tribunal in *Parkerings v Lithuania* similarly stressed the investor's duty to assess the legal and political environment in the host state.[147] As part of its examination of the investor's claims relating to an alleged lack of stability and predictability in the legislative framework of the investment, the tribunal drew attention to the fact that at the time the concession agreement had been concluded between the investor and the government, Lithuania was in the process of transition from its past status of having been part of the Soviet Republic to being a member of the European Union. Legislative changes were therefore to be reasonably expected. The tribunal concluded that

> [a]s any businessman would, the Claimant was aware of the risk that changes of laws would probably occur after the conclusion of the Agreement.

143 *EDF v Romania*, para 217.

144 See Peter Muchlinski, '"Caveat Investor?" The Relevance of the Conduct of the Investor under The Fair and Fair Equitable Treatment Standard' (2006) 55 *ICLQ* 527; more recently, Jorge E Vinuales, 'Investor Diligence in Investment Arbitration: Sources and Arguments' (2017) 32 *ICSID Review* 346.

145 Muchlinski, 'Caveat Investor', 544–51.

146 *Saluka v Czech Republic*, paras 359–60.

147 *Parkerings-Compagniet AS v Lithuania*, Award, 11 September 2007, ICSID Case No ARB/05/8.

> The circumstances surrounding the decision to invest in Lithuania were certainly not an indication of stability of the legal environment. Therefore, in such a situation, no expectation that the laws would remain unchanged was legitimate.[148]

The tribunal held that by deciding to invest notwithstanding the possible instability, the investor assumed the business risk of legislative changes likely to be detrimental to its investment.[149]

In *Duke Energy v Ecuador*, the tribunal endorsed a wider interpretation of fair and equitable treatment as being inclusive of stability and predictability requirements.[150] Nevertheless, it indicated that in order to be entitled to protection the investor's expectations ought to be legitimate and reasonable at the time when the investor had made the investment.[151] The tribunal emphasised the importance of establishing the legitimacy of investor expectations against a wider context, including 'not only the facts surrounding the investment, but also the political, socioeconomic, cultural and historical conditions prevailing in the host State.'[152] In assessing the reasonableness of the investor's expectations, the tribunal pointed to the fact that the investment had been made in the political and economic context of Ecuador's energy crisis.[153]

The importance of taking into account the country risk in evaluating the reasonableness of investor expectations has not, however, been commonly endorsed in arbitral practice and scholarship.[154] For instance, some argue that setting the international minimum standard according to the level of development of the host state would result in 'relativism' contrary to an objectively-determined minimum level of protection.[155] Others have proposed to construe fair and equitable treatment as an objective and non-relative standard but suggested that other investment protection standards—such as an obligation to provide full protection and security (the standard of due diligence)—would allow for adjustments to be made depending on a state's particular circumstances.[156] It has been

[148] ibid para 335.

[149] ibid para 336.

[150] *Duke Energy v Ecuador*, see n 62 above, para 339.

[151] ibid para 340.

[152] ibid para 340.

[153] ibid para 347.

[154] See generally Nick Gallus, 'The Influence of the Host State's Level of Development on International Investment Treaty Standards of Protection' (2005) 6 *Journal of World Investment Trade* 711. For an earlier work, see Ian Brownlie, 'Treatment of Aliens: Assumption of Risk and the International Standard' in W Flume and others (eds), *International Law and Economic Order: Essays in honour of F.A. Mann* (München, Verlag CH Beck, 1977) 309.

[155] See eg Kaj Hober, *Investment Arbitration in Eastern Europe: In Search of a Definition of Expropriation* (New York, JurisNet, 2007) 125, 225–26.

[156] Newcombe and Paradell, *Law and Practice*, 310.

acknowledged that, for instance, 'an investor investing in an area with endemic civil strife and poor governance cannot have the same expectation of physical security as one investing in London, New York or Tokyo.'[157]

Debates about the relevance of a country risk as a factor in the assessment of the legitimacy of investor expectations point to the importance of distinguishing between the customary international minimum standard and the expectations of a perfect public regulation in a perfect state.[158] The key problem here is that the expectation of legal security of an investment—of a perfect governance framework in the host state—is sometimes regarded as an investor's entitlement, despite the fact that such an entitlement lacks legal support in treaty texts or customary international law. As observed by the arbitrator in *Pantechniki*, 'foreigners who enter a poor country are not entitled to assume that they will be given things like verbatim transcripts of all judicial proceedings—but they are entitled to decision-making which is neither xenophobic nor arbitrary.'[159]

Those who argue that a host state's level of development ought not to be taken into account in determining claims under the fair and equitable treatment standard effectively conflate two distinct issues: the relevance of the host state's socio-economic and political conditions in establishing the level of investment protection on the one hand, and the investor's duty to act in a prudent manner and to undertake reasonable assessment of investment risks in the host country on the other. It should be conceded that the meaning of what is fair and equitable should not vary depending on which country is in a respondent seat. However, construing the fair and equitable treatment/international minimum standard as an objective standard does not obviate the need to examine the investor's conduct in evaluating reasonableness of investor expectations. Put differently, the level of development is not per se determinative of the outcome but is crucial insofar as it presupposes the investor's duty to take into account the level of the host state's development when making its decision to invest.

Precisely because the notions of fairness and equity constitute the core of the fair and equitable treatment standard, the investor must not be entitled to a remedy where its high expectations have been frustrated because of a host state's inability to meet certain the standards of good governance, such as total transparency, stability, predictability and efficiency. It

157 ibid. See also *American Manufacturing & Trading, Inc v Zaire*, Award and Separate Opinion, 11 February 1997, (1997) 36 ILM 1531, paras 7.14–7.15.

158 Douglas, 'Nothing if Not Critical', 28.

159 *Pantechniki SA Contractors and Engineers v Albania*, Award, 28 July 2009, ICSID Case No ARB/07/21, para 76. It is, however, difficult to agree with the arbitrator's view that the standard should be objective because if the standard were set according to the level of the host state development it would provide no incentive to improve (ibid). This argument is based on an unsubstantiated premise that holding host states liable leads to improved governance and political stability.

would be unfair and inequitable to grant an investor compensation for the state's administrative failures and weak governance in the case where such shortcomings were known to the investor, and even formed the basis of the investor's decision to enter the market. It has been observed that foreign investors frequently '[t]ake advantage of the lack of administrative capacities and technical expertise in developing countries to get away with things they could not get away with in developed countries.'[160] In 2000, an empirical study revealed that foreign investors frequently did not conduct a full investigation of the legal system of the host state before investing.[161] Moreover, the study showed that despite perceiving most aspects of the domestic legal system 'to have characteristics which would cause it to be described as inefficient and unpredictable', many investors reported that they would still have invested if they had known then about its legal system. Thus, 'knowledge of the fact that the host state's legal system was 'ineffective' by the standard definition would not have prevented them from investing.'[162] If investors fail to investigate host states' legal systems or invest despite being aware of weak domestic governance and institutions, doubt arises as to their entitlement to claim losses for governance failures at the post-establishment stage.

Some arbitral tribunals have acknowledged the importance of calibrating investor expectations by reference to the conditions prevailing at the host state at the time a decision to invest was made. Moreover, they have been cognisant of the fact that when deciding to invest foreign investors may in fact be attracted by low levels of development and weak governance in a host state. For instance, in *Generation Ukraine v Ukraine* the tribunal addressed the investor's claim concerning an alleged interference by the Ukrainian authorities in the investor's real estate project. In examining whether the investor's expectations had been frustrated, the tribunal found it necessary to take into account the transitional state of the host economy. It observed that the investor had been attracted to the Ukraine '[b]ecause of the possibility of earning a rate of return on its capital in significant excess to the other investment opportunities in more developed economies.'[163]

[160] Joseph E Stiglitz, 'Regulating Multinational Corporations: Towards Principles of Cross-Border Legal Frameworks in a Globalized World Balancing Rights with Responsibilities' (2008) 23 *American University International Law Review* 451, 478. 'Worse still, some MNCs are exploiting the lack of administrative capacity as the basis of claims against developing countries under BIT provisions providing for "fair and equitable treatment"—even though they should have been fully aware of these limitations at the time they made the investments' (ibid 479).

[161] Amanda Perry, 'Effective Legal Systems and Foreign Direct Investment: In Search of the Evidence' (2000) 49 *ICLQ* 779, 786.

[162] Perry, 'Effective Legal Systems', 786.

[163] *Generation Ukraine, Inc v Ukraine*, Award, 15 September 2003, (2005) 44 ILM 404, para 20.37.

The tribunal concluded that the investor '[i]nvested in the Ukraine on notice of both the prospects and the potential pitfalls.'[164] The tribunal's decision aptly illustrates the reality of an investor's decision-making process whereby the absence or lack of democratic institutions and civil society may often be seen as an economic advantage. In such circumstances, allowing the investor to claim a breach of fair and equitable treatment—or a failure to abide by good governance standards—would be contrary to the notions of equity and fairness.

More recently, the tribunal in *Mamidoil v Albania*[165] also reaffirmed the centrality of the notions of fairness and equity as well as the relevance of due diligence by investors at the time of making an investment in a country with weak governance. The tribunal stressed the fact that at the time of the investment Albania 'was in a dilapidated situation, with its infrastructure run down and with its legal framework, regulation and independent justice absent and with no stability'.[166] While the tribunal held that '[a]n investor may have been entitled to rely on Albania's efforts to live up to its obligations under international treaties', the claimant-investor 'was not entitled to believe that these efforts would generate the same results of stability as in Great Britain, USA or Japan.'[167] The tribunal emphasised that it was the investor's duty to exercise due diligence with respect to the investment environment of the host State and to act accordingly. In the tribunal's view, the fair and equitable treatment standard is '[a]ddressed to both the State and the investor. Fairness and equitableness cannot be established adequately without an adequate and balanced appraisal of both parties' conduct.'[168]

Support for a greater emphasis on the investor conduct—and on the importance of risk assessment prior to making a decision to invest—in determining the scope and meaning of fair and equitable treatment (and other good governance standards) can be found in arbitral cases brought against developed states. In *Methanex v United States*, for instance, the investor contended that an environmental ban on the use of methanol-based fuel additive amounted to expropriation and breach of FET.[169] The tribunal emphasised the need to take into account the specificity of the overall framework in which the investment had been made and the fact of

[164] ibid para 20.37.

[165] *Mamidoil Jetoil Greek Petroleum Products v Albania*, Award, 30 March 2015, ICSID Case No ARB/11/24, para 623.

[166] ibid, para 625.

[167] ibid, para 626.

[168] ibid, para 634.

[169] *Methanex Corpn v United States*, UNCITRAL, Final Award on Jurisdiction and Merits, 3 August 2005, (2005) 44 ILM 1345.

voluntary assumption of risk by the investor. It stressed the fact that the investor voluntarily

> entered a political economy in which it was widely known, if not notorious, that governmental environmental and health protection institutions at the federal and state level, operating under the vigilant eyes of the media, interested corporations, non-governmental organizations and a politically active electorate, continuously monitored the use and impact of chemical compounds and commonly prohibited or restricted the use of some of those compounds for environmental and/or health reasons.[170]

As the foregoing discussion shows, the assumption by an investor of a risk (political, regulatory or economic) has already been regarded by some tribunals as a key element in the assessment of whether an investor's specific expectations are reasonable. Such interpretation does not undermine the baseline function of fair and equitable treatment, and does not detract from the protective value of investment treaties. It does, however, cast considerable doubt on the validity of narratives which justify the subjecting of host states—in particular developing countries—to monetary liability for failure to meet the high standards of good governance. From a doctrinal perspective, the application of the doctrine of legitimate expectations, and in particular the identification of specific commitments and reasonable reliance, should preclude holding host states responsible for failure to meet good governance standards in cases where the shortcomings of domestic institutions and legal culture had been known to investors at the time a decision to invest was made.

IV. CONCLUSION

The overarching aim of this chapter was to evaluate the genesis of good governance narratives in investment treaty practice, arbitral case law and legal scholarship. Rather than offering a comprehensive analysis of treaty practice and arbitral jurisprudence, it has sought to expose cracks in the good governance narratives of international investment law by identifying and highlighting their shaky legal foundations. Despite the proliferation of arbitral awards interpreting the fair and equitable standard as an obligation to create and maintain a transparent, stable,

[170] ibid Part IV Chapter D, para 9. See also *LG & E Energy Corpn v Argentina*, para 130: 'the investor's fair expectations cannot fail to consider parameters such as business risk or industry's regular patterns.' See further Jean Kalicki and Suzana Medeiros, 'Fair, Equitable and Ambiguous: What is Fair and Equitable Treatment in International Investment Law?' (2008) 22 *ICSID Review* 24, 46.

predictable and consistent legal framework, such interpretation are not sufficiently supported by historical and doctrinal evidence pertaining to the evolution of the fair and equitable treatment standard. There is overwhelming support for interpreting the treaty standard of fair and equitable treatment in the same manner as its customary counterpart: as an obligation whose principal function is to provide redress for serious formal and procedural shortcomings of host states' conduct, and not as a basis for holding host states liable for a failure to live up to exacting standards of good governance.

Similar charges of a lacking jurisprudential basis can be levelled against other 'good governance' standards, such as an investment treaty obligation to provide an effective means of asserting claims and enforcing rights. The existing interpretations of the effective means obligation as a qualitative standard are questionable not only for their insufficient legal underpinnings but also their overarching normative implications. The remit of state responsibility towards foreign investors was historically confined to certain categories of internationally proscribed conduct, such as unlawful takings of property and denial of justice. Expanding the notion of 'internationally proscribed conduct' to a failure to provide effective laws and to ensure time-efficient administration of justice radically transforms the function and scope of investment treaty law. Questions also arise whether these good governance standards can be enforced equally against developed and developing states. Evidence from investment arbitration practice suggests that governments of developing states are more likely to be found liable for failing to ensure the effective laws and enforcement mechanisms.[171] Although the arbitration practice offers examples of judicial and administrative failures in developed states, these are less likely to be presented as shortcomings of good governance, even less so sanctioned.

The doctrinal analysis of investment arbitration and treaty practice suggests that the enthusiasm with which the good governance language was embraced among those supporting the investment treaty regime has been driven by the opportunity such language offered to expand the scope of investment treaty protection whilst also buttressing the otherwise lacking justifications for the new, very expansive and often unfounded interpretations of investment treaty standards. Good governance has

[171] See Behn and others, 'Poor States', demonstrating that poorer states are significantly more likely to lose in investment arbitration than wealthier states. The comparison of cases concerning the administration of justice also support this finding: See Mavluda Sattorova, 'Denial of Justice Disguised: Investment Arbitration and the Protection of Foreign Investors from Judicial Misconduct' (2012) 61 *ICLQ* 223.

been deployed as both a new raison d'etre of investment treaty law and a powerful means to deflect concerns voiced by critics—or, in the words of Tan, as an instrument of crisis containment and rehabilitation of the normative and institutional credibility of the regime.[172] Yet the harnessing of the good governance narratives to justify a more expansive interpretation of investment protection rules is unlikely to redress the failures of legal and normative reasoning. Rather, the startlingly insufficient doctrinal foundations underpinning much of the existing arbitral jurisprudence on good governance standards are likely to amplify the growing concerns about the regime's legitimacy, credibility and desirability.

[172] Celine Tan, 'Navigating New Landscapes: Socio-legal mapping of plurality and power in international economic law' in Amanda Perry-Kessaris (ed), *Socio-legal Approaches to International Economic Law: Text, Context, Subtext* (Abingdon, Routledge, 2013) 148.

3

How Do Host States Respond to Investment Treaty Law?

I. THE IMPACT OF INVESTMENT TREATY LAW ON GOVERNANCE IN HOST STATES: KEY EMPIRICAL QUESTIONS

WHAT EFFECT DO international investment law and its dispute settlement mechanism have on host state behaviour? At the heart of the argument that posits a transformative impact of investment treaty law on governance in host states lies an assumption that investment treaty rules act as 'a deterrent mechanism against short-term policy reversals and assist developing countries in promoting greater effectiveness of the rule of law at the domestic level.'[1] The proponents of good governance narratives argue that

> [w]hile tribunals cannot quash domestic acts or compel States to bring their domestic legal order into line with investment treaty obligations, the monetary sanctions they can impose exert considerable pressure on states to bring their domestic legal orders into conformity with their investment treaty obligations.'[2]

Yet the claims of virtuous effects of international investment law on host states remain, by and large, empirically and theoretically untested.[3] The good governance narratives of international investment law are undergirded by a set of assumptions relating to how states *should* respond to investment treaty disciplines. It is presupposed that investment treaty law will have certain deterrent and transformative effects on future government behaviour: not only is the host state expected to refrain from mistreating foreign investors in the future, but it is also expected to take

[1] Roberto Echandi, 'What Do Developing Countries Expect from the International Investment Regime?' in Jose E Alvarez et al, *The Evolving International Investment Regime: Expectations, Realities, Options* (Oxford, Oxford University Press, 2011) 13.

[2] Stephan W Schill, 'System Building in Investment Treaty Arbitration and Lawmaking' (2001) 12 *German Law Journal* 1083, 1085.

[3] Jonathan Bonnitcha, *Substantive Protection under Investment Treaties: A Legal and Economic Analysis* (Oxford, Oxford University Press, 2014) 11, 138.

positive steps to change its legal and bureaucratic practices (which supposedly are lacking and therefore lead to investor-state disputes). Yet for such deterrent and transformative effects to exist, government actors in host states need to be aware of the existence of investment treaties and concerned about the monetary implications of damages awards in cases where foreign investors are successful in their claims against host governments.[4] If investment treaty law were to act as a mechanism encouraging host states to adjust their legal orders and to foster compliance with good governance standards prescribed by investment treaties (thus preventing future investor claims and their financial consequences), government officials ought to understand the scope and meaning of investment protection guarantees under existing bilateral and multilateral agreements. The question is: to what extent are government officials actually aware of investment treaty disciplines?

Another neglected aspect of the interplay between international investment law and governance in host states is the question of internalisation. For international investment law to bring about a change of a positive nature (eg improved governance), government officials in host states should not only be aware of investment treaty prescriptions and the implications of non-compliance but also be prepared to take measures to avoid future sanctions that such non-compliance may entail. In theory, holding a host state liable for an investment treaty breach should compel the state to create a governmental agency responsible for detecting, identifying, and controlling risk-increasing activities in which its government agencies and officials may engage.[5] In the words of Puig, '[i]f government officials or agencies know that they will be held to account, they will be less likely to commit violations in the first place.'[6] The capacity of the investment treaty regime to induce government officials to respond to investment treaty rules in a certain way would therefore depend on the government's 'monitoring ability'—its capacity to put in place an internal loss-allocation regime to ensure that monetary losses incurred as a result of damages awards are shifted to the governmental agency which has managerial, supervisory, and budgetary authority and political power over bureaucrats whose activities lead to state liability.[7] For such a mechanism to

[4] ibid 118; see also Susan Frank, 'The Legitimacy Crisis in Investment Treaty Arbitration: Privatising Public International Law Through Inconsistent Decisions' (2005) 73 *Fordham Law Review* 1521, 1592.

[5] See David Cohen, 'Regulating Regulators: The Legal Environment of the State' (1990) 40 *University of Toronto Law Journal* 245.

[6] Sergio Puig, 'No Right Without a Remedy: Foundations of Investor-state Arbitration' in Zachary Douglas, Joost Pauwelyn and Jorge E Viñuales (eds), *The Foundations of International Investment Law: Bringing Theory into Practice* (Oxford, Oxford University Press, 2014) 235.

[7] Cohen, *Regulating Regulators*, 213.

have not only a preventative but also a transformative effect, two major prerequisites are: (1) governance prescriptions of investment treaty law should be embedded into daily practices of relevant government agencies; and (2) national legal and regulatory measures should be in place to enable the 'learning process' and to discourage individual government officials from acting in breach of those prescriptions.

The good governance narratives of international investment law by and large assume the existence of such mechanisms and tend to ignore the crucial question of learning, internalisation, and accountability. Such narratives presuppose that host states would respond to investment treaties in a certain way, ie by undertaking a reform of domestic governance institutions and practices. Are there legal frameworks that would enable investment treaty prescriptions to be internalised and embedded in daily interactions between government officials and foreign investors? Does the holding of a host state liable for a breach of investment treaty standards prompt the host government to reform the domestic legal and bureaucratic environment and to address the governance failures lying at the roots of investor-state disputes? Might the application of investment treaty rules to host states entail negative effects on national agencies and decision-makers? How do host states respond or react to their experience of acting as a respondent in investor-state disputes?

This chapter seeks to engage with these questions and evaluate the hypotheses underpinning the good governance narratives with the aid of empirical and comparative insights obtained through interviews with government officials in developing states and the analysis of national legislation. Whilst acknowledging that a comprehensive analysis necessitates a large-scale, longitudinal empirical investigation across a large number of states that have been involved in investment treaty practice and investor-state arbitration, this chapter argues that insights from small-scale case studies can be still be illuminating and useful in testing the existing assumptions about the objectives and effects of investment treaty law. In critically evaluating the good governance narratives of investment treaty law with the aid of empirical data, this chapter goes beyond analysing the formal characteristics of the investment treaty regime to examine the practical experiences of host states and government officials, with particular focus on developing countries. Empirical case studies are incorporated into analysis to both complement and contextualise the existing conceptual and doctrinal accounts of the law by providing some tangible examples of how investment treaty law influences host state behaviour and what responses it has engendered so far. The overarching objective is to provide the currently missing empirical insights into how international investment law is perceived 'on the ground'. By doing so, the chapter aims to bridge what Cotterrell refers to as 'moral distance between the regulators and the regulated',[8] and to challenge the investment treaty regime's 'inability (or unwillingness) to learn adequately about the conditions, expectations and motivations of the regulated.'[9]

II. METHODOLOGY

The research on which this chapter is based was carried out between 2013 and 2017 and focused specifically on the views and perceptions about investment treaties and their effects in host states that have been parties to investment treaties and had acted as respondents in investment arbitration cases. The case studies comprise comparative analysis of national legal and policy documents and five sets of country-specific qualitative interviews conducted in Kazakhstan, Nigeria, Turkey, Ukraine and Uzbekistan (54 interviews in total).[10] Interviews were carried out with government officials who work or have worked in the ministries and agencies that have had involvement in investment treaty making and dispute settlement, as well as government officials who interact with foreign investors outside the context of investment treaty law and dispute settlement, ie in the process of making, implementing and otherwise applying national laws in domestic, not international, settings. The respondents were drawn from a variety of agencies and ministries responsible for economic development, energy and natural resources, financial regulation, justice, municipal administration, state prosecution and internal affairs, as well as legislature and the judiciary. The interviews were conducted using a snowball sampling method whereby some of the initially approached respondents referred us onto other participants. Despite its limitations, this methodology allowed access to government officials whose experiences would otherwise have been excluded from our study.

In addition to these country-specific case studies, the findings made in this chapter resonate with a number of encounter interviews undertaken with government officials from Armenia, Azerbaijan, Belarus, Georgia, Kenya, Kyrgyzstan, Lebanon, Mongolia, Russia, Sri Lanka, Tajikistan, and Jordan (15 respondents in total). As these interviews were limited to one or two government officials from each respective country, the resulting findings cannot be seen as manifesting experience of the relevant country

[8] Roger Cotterrell, 'Transnational networks of community and international economic law' in Amanda Perry-Kessaris (ed), *Socio-legal Approaches to International Economic Law: Text, Context, Subtext* (Abingdon, Routledge, 2013) 142.

[9] ibid.

[10] Some of the earlier findings from case studies in Nigeria, Turkey and Uzbekistan have been discussed in Mavluda Sattorova, Mustafa Erkan, Ohio Omiunu, 'How Do Host States Respond to Investment Treaty Law?: Some Empirical Observations' (2017) *The European Yearbook of International Economic Law* (Springer, forthcoming).

as a whole but remain useful inasmuch as they provide snapshots into how international investment law is currently known and perceived among government officials in developing states.

The interviews were semi-structured, open-ended and sought to engage the participants in a conversation. In designing this study, we have been conscious of the importance of disentangling two distinct but interrelated issues: (1) the extent of awareness of investment treaty law; and (2) the ways in which investment treaty law is perceived and internalised. The conversation revolved around the following key questions:

1 What law do you use/rely upon in your workings with foreign investors?
   1.1. Do you apply international law? Which treaties/conventions are most relevant to your area of work?
   1.2. To what extent are international investment treaties relevant or taken into account in your or your department's dealings with foreign investors?
2 If there is a disagreement or a problem between a foreign investor and your department, how would the situation usually be resolved?
3 [In cases where the respondent shows little or no knowledge of investment treaties and their relevance]: Investment treaties and the national law on foreign investment allow investors to take their disputes to international investment arbitration. [Your country] has been involved in a number of investor-state arbitration cases. In your line of work, have you heard of these cases or been involved in them? If you have been involved, directly or indirectly, could you tell us more what you think about investment arbitration?
4 [If the respondent had an involvement in investment arbitration] Has anything changed after those investment arbitration cases? Have there been any changes to prevent such cases in future?

Additionally, where appropriate and possible, interviewees were also encouraged to share their thoughts about the effectiveness of national and international legal regulation of foreign investment, challenges and prospects of improving the investment climate, the interplay between foreign investment and public policy regulation, and constraints faced by government officials in dealing with foreign investment-related issues.

Since the interviewees were given assurances of confidentiality and anonymity, in reporting our findings it has been necessary to avoid identifying any specific government ministry, position, or role of a respondent. In most instances, the considerations of anonymity and the need to prevent our interviewees from being identified also rendered it necessary to avoid mentioning which country they were from. In some instances, direct reporting of interviewee statements has been used to be provide the reader with a more nuanced picture and allow them to evaluate the findings in their context.

The primary goal of the case studies has been to produce qualitative insights into the effects of investment treaty law on national governance from the perspective of host states and their government officials. The overarching objective is to expose some of the on-the-ground perceptions and experiences that often remain unseen behind purely formal and conceptual analyses. Although investment treaty scholarship has recently witnessed a rise in empirical and in particular quantitative approaches,[11] there is a dearth of qualitative studies addressing how investment treaty disciplines are received by, and influence, government officials in host countries, in particular developing countries.[12] This chapter seeks to go beyond assumptions and statistics and elucidate the views, experiences, and decision-making patterns of those whom investment treaty law seeks to influence through its rules and remedies.

The findings from the empirical case studies are harnessed to highlight particular experiences of the host states in which the interviews were undertaken. The sample presented here does not contend to paint a representative picture of the overall experience of the broad array of state parties to investment treaties, but rather to offer new insights into the experiences of some of those that have been involved in investment treaty-making, investment arbitration and dealing with foreign investors on a day-to-day basis. The case studies do not set out to construct a new theory but rather to provide a fresh empirical context within which the existing theoretical assumptions regarding the impact of investment treaty law on government behaviour can be evaluated and contested.

By doing so, this chapter aims to make a novel contribution to promote better understanding of international investment law in its social

[11] Some of the notable studies adopting an empirical lens include Lauge N Skovgaard Poulsen, *Bounded Rationality and Economic Diplomacy: The Politics of Investment Treaties in Developing Countries* (Cambridge, Cambridge University Press, 2015); Christine Côté, *A chilling effect? The impact of international investment agreements on national regulatory autonomy in the areas of health, safety and the environment*, PhD thesis, London School of Economics and Political Science (LSE, 2014); Jason Webb Yackee, 'Do Bilateral Investment Treaties Promote Foreign Direct Investment? Some Hints from Alternative Evidence' (2010–2011) 51 *Virginia Journal of International Law* 397; Susan D Franck, 'Development and Outcomes of Investment Treaty Arbitration' (2009) 50 *Harvard Journal International Law* 435. See more recently, Thomas Schultz and Cédric Dupont, 'Investment Arbitration: Promoting the Rule of Law or Over-empowering Investors? A Quantitative Empirical Study' (2014) 25 *EJIL* 1147; Daniel Behn, Tarald Laudal Berge and Malcolm Langford, 'Poor States or Poor Governance? Explaining Outcomes in Investment Treaty Arbitration' (2017) *Northwestern Journal of International Law & Business*.

[12] Gregory Shaffer, 'A New Legal Realism: Method in International Economic Law Scholarship' in Colin B Picker, Isabella D Bunn, and Douglas Arner (eds), *International Economic Law: The State and Future of the Discipline* (Oxford, Hart Publishing, 2008) 42: 'Although more quantitative and qualitative empirical work is emerging, the total is small in light of the international economic law work being published, work that can have significant effects on how the legal community prioritises the creation of new international economic law and interprets existing international economic law …'.

context, both as a producer and product of social change.[13] The overarching objective is to offer a more contextualised framework for an inquiry into how investment treaty norms interact with domestic governance in host states. It seeks to not only challenge the existing theories through which international investment law is being narrated and advocated, but also, by grounding the enquiry in its social context and by bringing together the national and international dimensions, to promote de-specialisation and de-fragmentation of legal discourse on international investment law.[14] Scholarship on international investment law continues to be dominated by expert views, critical or otherwise, emanating from traditional capital-exporting states and primarily focusing on the international, not national, aspects of the interplay between investment treaty rules and host state behaviour. The experiences of government agencies and officials in developing states continue to be under-explored. The chapter aims to fill this gap and unveil the hitherto less visible intended and unintended effects of international norms on national realities.

Whilst highlighting the significance of empirically-grounded approaches to investigating the impact of international investment law on host states, it is crucial to acknowledge both the difficulties and the limitations of such studies. The most obvious methodological hurdle in greater use of empirical approaches is the fact that most researchers (including this author) have limited access to government decision-makers on a scale that would satisfy the demanding sampling requirements and in a way that would overcome the charges of cognitive bias. The availability factor certainly played a key role in determining the choice of countries in our case studies: the fact that our interviews were conducted in Kazakhstan, Nigeria, Turkey, Ukraine and Uzbekistan was due to our success in gaining access to government officials. Conveniently for our study, these countries share their 'developing country' status, the fact that they have been active in signing investment treaties and have had some experience with investment arbitration, and their established record of reforms and other initiatives to address governance shortcomings at a national level.

As investment treaty scholars acknowledge, '[j]ust as there are perils with quantitative research, qualitative methods involve their own pitfalls.'[15] Interviewees may slant their portrayal of realities to fit their

[13] David Nelken, 'Comparative Sociology of Law' in Reza Banakar and Max Travers (eds), *An Introduction to Law and Social Theory* (Oxford, Hart Publishing, 2002) 330.

[14] Amanda Perry-Kessaris, 'What does it mean to take a socio-legal approach to international economic law?' in Amanda Perry-Kessaris (ed), *Socio-legal Approaches to International Economic Law: Text, Context, Subtext* (Abingdon, Routledge, 2013) 11, referring to a period of disciplinarity, during which 'the surface structures' of academic institutions trended towards 'specialisation, professionalization, departmentalization, and fragmentation.'

[15] Poulsen, *Bounded Rationality*, 23.

own individual preferences or institutional mandate. To address this problem, we have endeavoured to corroborate individual responses with the data emerging from other developing states. Throughout the study, the analysis of national legislation and policy documents has been used to complement the interviews and provide a broader and more detailed picture. Furthermore, wherever possible, the study also draws on the analysis of legal and policy innovations in developing states that are not included in our empirical studies. Thus, experiences of Brazil, Colombia, and Peru are discussed so as to offer additional comparative insights and facilitate a more nuanced understanding of the interplay between international norms on investment protection and national decision-making.

III. ARE GOVERNMENT OFFICIALS AWARE OF INTERNATIONAL INVESTMENT LAW AND ITS GOOD GOVERNANCE PRESCRIPTIONS?

If investment treaty law indeed serves as a mechanism encouraging or otherwise prompting host states to adjust their legal orders and to ensure compliance with good governance standards prescribed by investment treaties, it is essential that 'all levels of government and agencies that interact with foreign investors understand the scope and consequences of the commitments under investment treaties and the practical implications for their day-to-day activities.'[16] Now that many host states have experienced the effect of investment treaty law and its arbitration mechanism in a respondent capacity, the question is: to what extent are government officials actually aware of and influenced by investment treaty disciplines in their dealings with foreign investors?

Even prior to the emergence of empirical scholarship on the interplay between international investment law and national decision-making, it was argued that government officials—particularly those in administrative agencies of developing states—who do not have direct or regular dealings with foreign investors are unlikely to be aware of international investment agreements and their prescriptions.[17] As a consequence, such decision-makers are unlikely 'to internalise the constraints of investment treaty protections'[18] not only when evaluating the adoption of new

[16] UNCTAD, *Best Practices in Investment for Development. How to prevent and manage investor-State disputes: Lessons from Peru*, Investment Advisory Series, Series B, number 10 (New York and Geneva, United Nations, 2011) 11.

[17] Jack Coe Jr and Noah Rubins, 'Regulatory Expropriation and the *Tecmed* Case: Context and Contributions' in Todd Weiler (ed), *International Investment Law and Arbitration: Leading Cases from the ICSID, NAFTA, Bilateral Treaties and Customary International Law* (London, Cameron May, 2005) 599.

[18] Bonnitcha, *Substantive Protection*, 122.

governmental measures but also in exercising their day-to-day decision-making powers vis-à-vis foreign investors. This argument resonates with findings from our case studies. The interviews show that the first exposure to investment arbitration claims entailed some rise in the levels of awareness of investment treaty law among government officials who were directly involved in regulating and implementing foreign investment projects and investor-state dispute settlement (ie ministries of energy and natural resources, justice and foreign affairs). However, lack of awareness has been observed among officials in other branches of the government (such the judiciary, the legislature, public health and environment protection ministries, municipal authorities, anti-corruption agencies, financial regulation authorities, and state prosecutor offices).

For instance, Uzbekistan was named a respondent in at least nine investor-state arbitration claims, of which one was decided in favour of a claimant investor, two decided in favour of the state, a further two were discontinued, and the other cases were still pending.[19] The first investor-state challenges against Uzbekistan were brought in 2006,[20] and in the following years the government continued to sign bilateral investment treaties. Uzbekistan has a total of 53 investment treaties, of which seven were concluded after the country's first encounter with investor-state arbitration.[21]

The relatively active involvement of Uzbekistan in the signing of international investment treaties and dealing with investment claims should have arguably led to increased levels of awareness and, as posited by the proponents of the good governance narratives, resulted in concerted governmental efforts to reform domestic governance structures and processes so as to prevent future investor-state disputes. Nonetheless, the data collected in Uzbekistan suggests that even after a number of high-profile investment disputes were brought against Uzbekistan, many governmental officials in various key ministries and agencies remained unaware of international investment treaties and their liability implications for the government. This is despite the fact that these respondents had dealings with foreign investors in an executive, legislative or judicial capacity. For example, four out of five respondents from the judiciary (regional and Supreme Court judges—all with extensive experience of adjudicating claims involving foreign investors, either in the form of a joint venture or a

[19] The statistics are drawn from UNCTAD's Investment Dispute Settlement Navigator (investmentpolicyhub.unctad.org/ISDS/CountryCases/226?partyRole=2) and the ICSID's case database (icsid.worldbank.org/apps/ICSIDWEB/cases/Pages/AdvancedSearch.aspx?rntly=ST152).

[20] *Newmont USA Ltd and Newmont (Uzbekistan) Ltd v Republic of Uzbekistan*, ICSID Case No ARB/06/20, registered 12 December 2006.

[21] See investmentpolicyhub.unctad.org/IIA/CountryBits/226#iiaInnerMenu.

foreign-owned enterprise) were surprised to learn that a foreign investor's dispute with a government body might lead to investor-state arbitration under investment treaties.[22] The respondents explained their lack of prior awareness about investment treaties and their implications by the fact that their daily activities would mainly involve invocation and application of national law and that international law, despite being constitutionally recognised as one of the primary sources of legal norms, is rarely—if at all—considered as relevant by national government agencies.[23] Furthermore, as one respondent opined, international treaties and international arbitration would usually be regarded by investors as a last resort; hence their limited relevance for (and limited awareness about their existence among) government officials who deal with foreign investors on a day-to-day basis.[24] Initiation of investor-state arbitration by a foreign investor would be seen by the government as an irreversible end of their relationship, thus making arbitration a viable option only to those investors who have exited Uzbekistan's market or are in the process of doing so.

Similar findings emerge from the case study of Turkey. By the time the interviews were completed, Turkey had faced a considerable number of investor-state disputes in a respondent capacity, including the high-profile *Libananco* case.[25] So far, the country has been a respondent in 11 investor-state cases, some of which are still pending, one resolved in favour of the investor, and others in favour of the state.[26] Since the first investor-state arbitration was brought against Turkey in 2002, the country has continued to actively sign international investment agreements (42 out of 109 investment treaties concluded with Turkey were signed in the period following the country's first encounter with investor-state arbitration).[27] The prolific signing of international investment treaties and a comparatively high rate of involvement in investor-state arbitration in a respondent capacity should, as the proponents of the good governance narrative argue, have entailed the correspondingly growing levels of awareness about international investment law, and prompted the government of Turkey to embark on a reform of domestic governance to address the root causes of investor-state disputes. However, our case study unveils a more nuanced picture. Five out of ten respondents linked their awareness of investment treaty law with the first large scale and well-publicised arbitration claim

[22] Interviews HSG, HSK, HSD, HSR.

[23] ibid.

[24] Interviews HSR, also AA.

[25] *Libananco Holdings Co Ltd v Republic of Turkey*, Award, 2 September 2011, ICSID Case No ARB/06/8.

[26] At investmentpolicyhub.unctad.org/ISDS/CountryCases/214?partyRole=2.

[27] At investmentpolicyhub.unctad.org/IIA/CountryBits/214#iiaInnerMenu.

made against the country.[28] However, the interviews showed that, even after several cases were brought against Turkey, government officials in a range of bodies and agencies dealing with foreign investors remained unaware of Turkey's investment treaties and of their relevance to their day-to-day behaviour vis-à-vis foreign investors. Neither were they aware of the fact that their acts or omissions affecting foreign investors could potentially lead to investment arbitration claims.[29] Three respondents expressly mentioned primacy of national law and regulations in governing any dealings between the state and foreign investors in Turkey.[30] One respondent referred to the prevalence of national law in explaining the fact that international investment treaty rules were rarely, if ever, considered in governmental decision-making in dealing with day-to-day aspects of foreign investment activities, such as taxation, environmental control and financial markets regulation.[31] Echoing responses from our case study in Uzbekistan, one Turkish respondent suggested that international treaties, and in particular international dispute settlement, would be considered by investors as a last resort and only in circumstances where the working relationship with the government was unlikely to be salvaged by other means.[32]

Nigeria is currently a party to at least 29 bilateral investment treaties, of which 15 are in force,[33] and 9 other investment agreements.[34] So far it has faced three major investment claims, all instigated under the ICSID Convention.[35] It was reported that in *Shell Nigeria Ultra Deep Ltd v Federal Republic of Nigeria*, the investor sought damages in excess of US$ 5.2 billion.[36] Despite its comparatively limited exposure to

[28] Interviews MFA1, MED, MEN1, MEN2, MIT.

[29] Interviews FRT, ICT, APP, CMB, MEN.

[30] Interviews FRT, MFA1, MEN2.

[31] Interview ICT.

[32] Interview APP.

[33] The statistics are provided by the ICSID at investmentpolicyhub.unctad.org/IIA/CountryBits/153, accessed 11 July 2017. For a comprehensive breakdown of the composition of investment protection clauses in Nigeria's investment treaties, see generally Global Arbitration Review (12 November 2014), available at: globalarbitrationreview.com/know-how/topics/66/jurisdictions/18/nigeria/.

[34] ibid.

[35] *Guadalupe Gas Products Corpn v Nigeria*, ICSID Case No ARB/78/1, was discontinued on 22 July 1980 with settlement agreed by parties; *Shell Nigeria Ultra Deep Ltd v Federal Republic of Nigeria*, ICSID Case No ARB/07/18, was discontinued on 1 August 2011; *Interocean Oil Development Co and Interocean Oil Exploration Co v Federal Republic of Nigeria*, ICSID Case No ARB/13/20, is currently ongoing.

[36] See Innocent Anaba and Ikechukwu Nnochiri, 'Court voids two arbitration awards worth N840bn against NNPC' *Vanguard* (33 April 2012) available at www.vanguardngr.com/2012/04/court-voids-two-arbitration-awards-worth-n840bn-against-nnpc/#sthash.84SqQflw.dpuf, and Paul Idornigie, 'Investment Treaty Arbitration and Emerging Markets: Issues, prospects and challenges' (Abuja, Nigerian Institute of Advanced Legal Studies, 2011) 15. See further Sattorova, Erkan and Ominunu, 'How Do Host States Respond'.

investor-state arbitration, the magnitude and high profile of claims Nigeria has faced so far should have arguably produced increased awareness of the investment treaty law and its liability rules. Yet only one out of the seven respondents interviewed was aware of investment treaties and investor-state arbitration. This awareness might be explained by the fact that *Shell v Federal Republic of Nigeria* led to a parallel dispute in the Nigerian courts, and involved the agency where the interviewee worked.[37]

Ukraine has been actively involved in both signing investment treaty instruments and engaging with investment arbitration. It is currently a signatory to 73 bilateral investment treaties[38] and has been named as a respondent in at least 21 investor-state arbitration disputes.[39] To exemplify the extent of financial exposure faced by the country, in *Lemire v Ukraine (II)* the investor succeeded in obtaining a damages award totalling US$8.70 million.[40] Even though Ukraine has successfully defended itself in the overwhelming majority of cases brought against it, it nevertheless incurred a considerable financial burden in the form of arbitration costs as well as its own legal costs and expenses. Notwithstanding a comparatively long and active record of engagement with investment treaty law and arbitration, our interviews with Ukrainian government officials point to a prevailing lack of awareness about international investment norms.[41] Of 18 respondents, only four were aware of international investment law and its investor-state arbitration mechanism; these respondents gained their awareness through being associated with the departments that were involved in defending Ukrainian interests in investment arbitration.[42] One further respondent admitted having heard of an arbitration case recently resorted to by a foreign corporation (the case was mentioned at a reception organised by the embassy of Spain in Ukraine). This interviewee was not certain if the case in point was investment treaty arbitration.[43] Other interviewees reported no knowledge of investment treaty law and its arbitration mechanism. When prompted to elaborate on the reasons why Ukraine's engagement with international investment law remained unknown to government officials, one interviewee pointed to a lack of communication and coordination between various government ministries

[37] Interview NRN.

[38] See investmentpolicyhub.unctad.org/IIA/CountryBits/219#iiaInnerMenu.

[39] See further investmentpolicyhub.unctad.org/ISDS/CountryCases/219?partyRole=2.

[40] *Joseph Charles Lemire v Ukraine*, Award, 28 March 201, ICSID Case No ARB/06/18.

[41] For a further analysis, see Mavluda Sattorova and Oleksandra Vytiaganets, 'Investment Treaty Law and Its Lessons for Developing States' (2017) available at papers.ssrn.com/sol3/papers.cfm?abstract_id=3002067.

[42] Interviews MUL, MUT.

[43] Interview MPU.

and agencies: 'Everyone works autonomously, everyone is by himself'.[44] Two interviewees pointed out that most learning about investment arbitration is concentrated in a special department in the Ministry of Justice, yet this department is not involved in consultation processes and drafting of legislative and treaty instruments on foreign investment.[45]

Kazakhstan has signed 48 investment treaties, and experienced the full bite of investment treaty law, with significant sums in damages awarded to investor-claimants in a number of cases (five out of 17 cases decided in favour of investor, one settled).[46] The extent of Kazakhstan's liabilities under investment arbitration awards[47] to date should arguably have prompted the government to revise the scope of its investment treaty commitments and undertake a comprehensive governance reform so as to internalise the lessons from investment arbitration. Two out of seven interviewed officials showed awareness of the investment treaty regime and its arbitration mechanism.[48] However, these officials were associated with one of the key government agencies tasked with the promotion and protection of foreign investment in Kazakhstan. Illuminatingly, one high-ranking official involved in designing Kazakhstan's FDI promotion strategy acknowledged that investor-state disputes often arise due to the lack of awareness and 'shared vision' between officials in central government agencies and regional/municipal authorities: 'It is as if we are on opposite sides of the barricade.'[49]

IV. HOW HOST STATES 'LEARN' FROM INVESTMENT ARBITRATION

A. 'Limited' Internalisation: Scaling Back the Scope of National Laws on Investment Protection

For international investment law to have a preventative effect and, moreover, to encourage governance reforms in host states, it is crucial that all levels of government that interact with investors are aware of the scope and consequences of the state's obligations under investment treaties and their practical implications for the day-to-day activities of the relevant agencies.[50] Furthermore, the host government should acknowledge the importance of, and commit to, governance reforms. Our case studies

[44] Interview DFI.

[45] Interviews MUH, MUD, MUL.

[46] See further at investmentpolicyhub.unctad.org/ISDS/CountryCases/107?partyRole=2.

[47] A brief look at the awards rendered against Kazakhstan indicate that its liabilities thereunder exceed US$ 640 million (cost of arbitration and legal expenses excluded).

[48] Interviews IDM1, IDM2.

[49] Interview IDM1.

[50] See UNCTAD, *Best Practices in Investment*, 11.

suggest that investment treaty law tends to be internalised by government officials in host states but not necessarily in the way predicted by the proponents of the good governance narratives.

An historical analysis of developments in the national policy on foreign investment in Uzbekistan shows that, just like in case of many other developing countries, the government may not have been fully aware of the meaning and scope of some investment protection commitments enshrined in national statutes and international investment treaties. It transpires that, even after the host state had the experience of investment arbitration and the relevant government officials gained some awareness of investment treaties and their liability implications, such knowledge did not necessarily motivate the government to treat foreign investment projects in line with investment treaty prescriptions of good governance or to launch a reform of governance practices. Instead, as some scholars have shown, after experiencing the first bite of investor-state arbitration[51] the host country may endeavour to scale back its investment protection commitments—as was illustrated in case of Uzbekistan and its attempt to retroactively limit access to investment arbitration through constitutional review of the relevant national legislation.[52]

Such an attempt was made in 2006 when, following a number of claims brought against Uzbekistan by foreign investors, the Cabinet of Ministers launched proceedings in the Constitutional Court of the Republic of Uzbekistan requesting interpretation of a dispute settlement provision in the Law on Guarantees and Measures for the Protection of Rights of Foreign Investors.[53] The clause in question, contained in Article 10, appears to have been modelled on a dispute settlement clause featuring in many traditional investment treaties. It provides that a dispute, directly or indirectly relating to foreign investment, shall be settled through consultation; and, should the parties fail to reach settlement, such a dispute should be resolved by an economic court of the Republic of Uzbekistan *or* through arbitration in accordance with rules and procedures of international agreements on settlement of investment disputes. In its decision the Constitutional Court held that certain investors 'mistakenly construed' provisions contained in Article 10, in particular the provision concerning the settlement of an investment dispute by means of international arbitration, as an expression of state consent to ICSID arbitration.[54] In support of this

[51] Lauge N Skovgaard Poulson and Emma Aisbett, 'When the Claims Hit: Bilateral Investment Treaties and Bounded Rational Learning' (2013) 65 *World Politics* 273, 282.

[52] See Mavluda Sattorova, 'International Investment Law in Central Asia: The Making, Implementation and Change of Investment Rules from a Regionalist Perspective' (2015) 16 *Journal of World Investment and Trade* 1089, 1105.

[53] Law No 611-I of 30 April 1998, available at www.lex.uz.

[54] Sattorova, 'International Investment Law in Central Asia', 105–106.

finding, the Constitutional Court invoked the principle of supremacy of the Constitution of Uzbekistan and referred to Article 111 of the Constitution according to which competence over the adjudication of disputes between business actors and state administration organs is vested in the Supreme Economic Court and the Economic Courts of Uzbekistan. It concluded that the relevant provision of Article 10 of the said law merely enumerated the various possible options of resolving investment disputes and could not as such be construed as containing Uzbekistan's express consent to either of the stipulated options.[55] Therefore, the Court concluded, Article 10 could not be invoked as an expression of consent to ICSID arbitration and that express and written consent to arbitration ought to be obtained by investor claimants in each individual case.[56]

While this attempt to retrospectively scale back the scope of its investment protection commitments can be seen as an expression of its dissatisfaction with and growing scepticism over international investment law, the government of Uzbekistan did not take further steps to tangibly amend the relevant provisions in either the national statutes or subsequent investment treaties.[57] In May 2013, Uzbekistan's Deputy Minister of Justice reportedly announced that amendments would be made to the Law on Guarantees and Measures for the Protection of Rights of Foreign Investors to clarify that Article 10 did not offer a free-standing consent to investment arbitration.[58] However, although a number of changes to the law were approved by parliament in 2014, Article 10 survived in its original wording and arguably can still be relied upon by investors as a unilateral expression of Uzbekistan's consent to investor-state arbitration.[59] Two respondents recounted informal guidance issued by a ministerial body instructing government officials to prevent the inclusion of arbitration clauses in agreements involving foreign investors (although it was not clear whether the guidance concerned investment contracts or investment treaties).[60]

Neither has the government announced any further plans to reform the existing legal framework for foreign investors with the aim of preventing future investor-state disputes or otherwise delimiting its exposure to such disputes. Our interviews reveal that, in some cases, despite their

[55] Ibid 106.

[56] Decision of the Constitutional Court of the Republic of Uzbekistan 'On interpretation of part 1 of Article 10 of the Law of the Republic of Uzbekistan on Guarantees and Measures of Protection of Foreign Investor Rights' (translated by the author; a version in Russian is available at www.lex.uz/pages/getpage.aspx?lact_id=1267669, accessed 11 July 2017).

[57] Sattorova, 'International Investment Law in Central Asia', 106.

[58] ibid.

[59] ibid.

[60] Interview MUI, HSR.

awareness of the state's previous exposure to investment treaty arbitration claims, government officials chose to ignore the risk of a new claim that their treatment of a certain foreign investment project could entail. One interviewee, for instance, referred to an incident where a high-ranking official disregarded legal advice about the potential risk of investment arbitration. The official reasoned that even if in breach of international investment law, the governmental action at issue was 'economically significant' and therefore ought to be maintained despite other considerations.[61]

It has also emerged from a number of interviews and from analysis of the national legislation of Uzbekistan that, although its initial encounters with investment treaty law in a respondent capacity have prompted the questioning of the scope of its international investment treaty commitments, no concrete institutional changes were made in the sense of establishing an internal mechanism of prevention and management of investment disputes. The Ministry of Justice remains responsible for representation of the government interests in investment arbitration, and no special unit or department has been created to prevent and manage investment disputes. Neither have there been any changes to the existing legal framework on the payment of awards and judgments rendered against government organs and/or their officials.[62] No formal measures have been taken to address the issue of accountability of government officials whose actions and omissions result in investor-state arbitration.

B. Optimising the Defence of Host State Interests in Investment Arbitration

In line with our findings in the case study of Uzbekistan, Turkey's encounter with international investment law does not appear to have entailed the expected rise in the level of awareness among government officials on the ground. Rather, the learning has been confined to a small number of agencies. Neither has the government taken any significant steps to prevent future investment disputes changing domestic governance norms and practices. Unlike Uzbekistan, Turkey has not attempted to scale back its investment treaty commitments. In fact, after the first well-publicised investment disputes against Turkey took place (the most notable of them, *Libananco v Turkey* was resolved in 2006), the country continued to actively

[61] Interview MUI.

[62] The Uzbek language version of the Decree governing the payment of judgments and awards of compensation for damages caused by government bodies and officials is available at www.lex.uz. (Ministry of Justice, No 1095, 12 January 2002).

sign investment treaties. Almost one third of Turkey's investment treaty stock was signed in the period between 2006–16, ie after the country experienced the bite of investor-state arbitration. Notably, even after Turkish officials in the key agencies became increasingly aware of investment treaties and their financial implications, on some occasions the government ignored its previous experience when evaluating future implications of investment treaties. For instance, two respondents recalled their frustration over an incident whereby the government pushed for a ratification of an investment treaty without a proper legal screening, despite having been earlier drawn into a number of high-profile investment arbitration disputes which ought to have prompted the government to reflect on and revise the scope of its investment treaty commitments.[63]

As far as changes in domestic legal and regulatory frameworks are concerned, an overview of national legislation and data from interviews suggests that no significant steps were undertaken by the Turkish government to address the root causes of investment disputes and to launch relevant governance reforms. Instead, in the aftermath of the first wave of investment claims the government enacted an executive decree No 659 regulating the provision of legal services for government agencies and ministries, which vests the Legal Department of Prime Minister's Office with the responsibility to defend Turkey's interests in international disputes, including investor-state arbitration claims.[64] The decree stipulates that the Legal Department may handle the claims by itself or coordinate actions of the government authorities involved in the dispute. The decree makes no express mention of the need to prevent investment disputes or to enhance accountability of government agencies for actions that may result in Turkey's international responsibility.

One high-ranking official referred to Turkey's imperial past in explaining why the government abstained from any significant change in its investment treaty policy. 'We are the former Ottoman Empire. This sets us apart from any other developing countries … we have been involved in making international treaties for centuries, and as a respectable country we continue to sign them.'[65] This response echoes Poulsen's observation that

> [j]ust as 'civilized' nations had to adhere to certain standards during the Imperial era, for instance, countries with widely different backgrounds also use a

[63] Interviews MID, MEN1. A similar experience has been reported by the interviewees from Ukraine: even though most learning about investment arbitration is concentrated in a special department in the Ministry of Justice, this department is not involved in consultation processes and drafting of legislative and treaty instruments on foreign investment (interviews MUH, MUD).

[64] Law No 659 of 29 September 2011 (the Turkish language version is available at mevzuat.basbakanlik.gov.tr/.

[65] Interview MIT.

number of policy programmes today to signal their commitment to the norms of political and economic liberalism without necessarily having the capacity, or even inclination, to implement them in practice.[66]

Interviews with Turkish and Ukrainian government officials also point to another important intersection between international investment law and national governance: the embedding of good governance prescriptions of investment treaties into national law. As mentioned earlier, the majority of respondents stressed that international investment law was primarily relevant for government agencies directly involved in investment disputes at an international level.[67] A number of respondents concurred in their view that, while investment treaty rules were not directly applied by many governmental bodies in their day-to-day dealings with foreign investors, incorporating investment treaty norms into national laws was not necessary because, as one interviewee from the Turkish government put it: 'national laws are good, we just have problems with enforcing them and generally with a legal culture.'[68] A similar view was expressed by an interviewee in Ukraine: 'We have a perfect Constitution, perfect laws; it's just they don't really work.'[69] This view was shared by a number of interviewees from other countries also. It raises the question that has long been discussed in law and development literature: to what extent can the mere incorporation of international good governance standards into national legal frameworks effectively transform national legal cultures?[70] The interviews also point to a shared scepticism about the potency of either international law or national law to effectuate any significant changes in legal and bureaucratic *culture* on the ground.

C. Establishing Dispute Prevention and Management Mechanisms

One common feature in the way Uzbekistan and Turkey responded to their encounter with investment treaty law and arbitration is the fact neither government has made efforts to introduce or strengthen existing legal frameworks on accountability of individual officials or government agencies for financial harm caused to the state as a result of investor-state disputes caused by their actions. A similar experience can be observed in Ukraine. The participants in the Ukrainian case study have pointed out

[66] Poulsen, *Bounded Rationality*, 13.
[67] Interviews MFA1, MED, MEN1, MEN2.
[68] Interview CMB.
[69] Interview DFI.
[70] See eg John Hewko, 'Foreign Direct Investment: Does the Rule of Law Matter?' Carnegie Endowment for International Peace Rule of Law Series, Democracy and Rule of Law Project, Working Paper No 26, April 2012, 2.

that formal legal mechanisms exist to impose disciplinary and criminal sanctions, however they have never been used.[71] Other countries in our case studies show different approaches.

While some host states appear to have reacted to their encounter with the investment treaty regime by scaling back the scope of investment protection commitments in national law and focused on the strengthening of the defence of governmental interests in investor-state arbitration cases, our case studies show that in a number of host states new agencies have been founded with the aim to improve the investment climate and prevent investor-state disputes. For instance, in Kazakhstan a new government department was created within the Ministry of Justice specifically tasked with defending state interests in investor-state disputes.[72] While the principal function of the agency is to represent and protect Kazakhstan's interests in investor-state arbitration and other international disputes, its other key objective is to prevent investment disputes. In furtherance of its dispute prevention function, the department is vested with responsibility for legal expert evaluation of investment contracts and international agreements as well as analysis of the matters relating to harmonisation and implementation of international norms into national legislation.[73] However, the law creating the agency does not elaborate on how learning from Kazakhstan's involvement in investment arbitration is to be translated into concrete changes in the legal environment so as to address governance shortcomings that lead to investment disputes.[74] Our interviews with those directly involved in the design and implementation of foreign investment policy of Kazakhstan reveal that, as part of its prerogative to issue post-dispute recommendations, the department has already taken steps to 'educate' other government agencies about the best ways in which the state interests could be safeguarded, primarily through taking greater care in drafting dispute settlement/international arbitration clauses in investor-state contracts.[75] Yet the department's expertise appears to be siloed. It does not feature prominently in any of the recent reform initiatives spearheaded by the Committee on Foreign Investment and aimed at the improvement of an investment climate in Kazakhstan.

[71] Interviews MUH, MUD.

[72] See www.adilet.gov.kz/ru/node/694.

[73] The outline of the department's mandate in Russian language is available on the website of the Ministry of Justice of the Republic of Kazakhstan at http://www.adilet.gov.kz/ru/node/694. See also https://kapital.kz/business/27535/ne-tolko-zacshicshatsya-no-i-vnimatelnee-chitat-kontrakty.html.

[74] See, for instance, the United States Department of State, Bureau of Economic and Business Affairs, 2013 Investment Climate Statement—Kazakhstan, February 2013, available at www.state.gov/e/eb/rls/othr/ics/2013/204668.htm.

[75] Interviews IDM1, IDM2.

An overview of developments in the legislative and regulatory landscape of Kazakhstan points to a growing recognition by the government of the importance of investor-state dispute prevention. The most pertinent example is the recent amendment to the Law on Investments establishing the investment ombudsman agency.[76] Among other functions, the ombudsman is designed to provide a rapid response system for difficulties which foreign investors may experience in their dealings with various government bodies and agencies in Kazakhstan. The ombudsman is vested with responsibility for: (1) solving issues related to rights and interests of foreign investments during implementation of investment projects; (2) mediating settlement of disputes between investors and state authorities; (3) offering support in legal proceedings; (4) where problems cannot be solved under the existing legislation, designing and submitting proposals on the improvement of the legislation to the competent legislative organs of the Republic of Kazakhstan.[77]

Since the official statements accompanying the creation of the ombudsman did not expressly link it with concerns relating to Kazakhstan's exposure to investor-state claims, it remains unclear whether this development has been prompted by the government's reflection on the scale of financial losses it incurred as a respondent in investment arbitration. It would be useful to know whether the creation of the ombudsman was driven specifically by the government's desire to reduce its exposure to investor-state claims and their financial consequences, or whether it was an unrelated development prompted by the government's desire to attract greater flows of inward foreign investment. The media briefs suggest that the ombudsman was modelled on the South Korean experience, where the eponymous institution played a key role in Korea's investment promotion strategy (as opposed to being designed to prevent investment disputes).[78] The question is: is South Korean model itself based on a certain blueprint?

The interviews, together with comparative analysis of similar developments in other countries of the region, offer further insights. While the respondents did not expressly link the creation of the ombudsman with Kazakhstan's experience in investment arbitration, the initiative was reportedly sponsored by the World Bank and other international organisations.[79] The ombudsman role is currently played by the Minister

[76] Estabished by Government Decree of the Republic of Kazakhstan No 1153 dated 30 October 2014.

[77] See Art 12-1 of the Law No 373-II on Investments, 8 January 2003, as amended 12 June 2014.

[78] See Sattorova et al, 'How Do Host States Respond to Investment Treaty Law'.

[79] Interview IDM1.

for Investment and Development, who works in conjunction with a group of other stakeholders from key ministries and agencies. As one interviewee suggested, there is a sense that the Ombudsman 'does not have competence to do much, mostly to issue recommendations. It needs prerogatives to impose obligations and other executive powers.'[80] Nevertheless, despite this institutional disadvantage, the Ombudsman is already seen as capable of making effective intervention in an effort to prevent investor-state controversies from escalating into investment arbitration disputes. This type of intervention, however, is ad hoc, very informal and, as one interviewee put it, 'may have no basis in law'—in cases where existing laws provide only limited or cumbersome and protracted solutions.[81]

Other pertinent policy developments include the setting up of a national investment promotion agency, Kazakh Invest. Conceived as an independent, non-governmental investment advisory board, Kazakh Invest is expected to assume a major part in attracting FDI. In doing so, the agency will work closely with the Ministry of Investment and Development, in particular the Committee for Investments and the Investment Ombudsman. While it has no formal powers with respect to dispute settlement, Kazakh Invest is expected to act as an informal facilitator and thus complement the role currently played by Ombudsman. The interviews suggest that the creation of the agency was supported by international organisations, including the World Bank.[82]

Similar developments have taken place in Ukraine. Invest Ukraine was established as an independent advisory agency on 19 October 2016. The initiative was sponsored by external donors.[83] Invest Ukraine is expected to work closely with the office for reform delivery by the Prime Minister. The latter is part of the European Bank for Reconstruction and Development (EBRD) and EU-sponsored initiative establishing the dedicated Reform Support Teams (RSTs) comprising experts from outside the Ukrainian civil service who are envisaged to work in ministries on a temporary basis to implement reforms and transform the ministries. Although the principal role of Invest Ukraine is to provide independent expertise and support the government in attracting investment into Ukraine, it is also expected to work closely with the Investment Commissioner (a representative from the Ministry of Finance) and the Business Ombudsman in facilitating effective and amicable resolution of any disputes between investors and local government agencies.[84] Invest Ukraine is not, however, formally involved

[80] ibid.
[81] Interviews IDM1, AFM1.
[82] Interview IK1.
[83] Interview IU1.
[84] Interview IU1.

in resolving investment disputes; rather it is expected to refer investor grievances to the Ombudsman. Neither does it have the power of legislative initiative to initiate reforms to address governance issues affecting foreign investors in Ukraine.[85]

Just like its equivalent in Kazakhstan, the Business Ombudsman Council of Ukraine owes its origins to international donor organisations and a number of Western governments.[86] Its key objective, however, is formulated in slightly different terms and focuses primarily on combating corruption as part of a major step forward towards the improvement of the investment climate in Ukraine.[87] The Business Ombudsman Council is conceived to serve as the first and focal point of contact for companies seeking redress against unfair treatment and to facilitate greater transparency for business practices in Ukraine. The Business Ombudsman Council is composed of the Business Ombudsman, two Deputies, and other staff represented by 'distinguished experts with mostly western education and practical experience in law, strategic management, economics, auditing, and risk management.'[88] Although our requests for an interview meeting did not receive any response, interviews with government officials from other agencies and ministries show that the Ombudsman is already well-known as a new and key agency to which all foreign investor grievances should be addressed for resolution.[89]

D. Dispute Prevention Versus Systemic Governance Reforms

Before turning to the analysis of the variety of ways in which the host states in our case studies appear to have responded to international rules on investment protection, it is important to briefly discuss responses the regime has so far elicited among other developing states, such as Peru, Colombia and Brazil. While it has not been possible to obtain empirical data to complement and contextualise our analysis of legal and policy developments in these countries, nevertheless, even in the absence of such empirical data, a comparative snapshot provides valuable insights into how international investment law influences national governance. Why Peru, Colombia and Brazil? These countries offer a very interesting case

[85] ibid.

[86] The BOC is funded through the Multi-donor Account for Ukraine set up at the EBRD in 2014. The donors of the Multi-donor Account for Ukraine include Denmark, Finland, France, Germany, Japan, the Netherlands, Poland, Sweden, Switzerland, the United Kingdom, the United States and the European Union.

[87] For an overview of the Ombudsman's mission, see boi.org.ua/en/about.

[88] ibid.

[89] Interviews DFI, AC1, IU1, MUL.

study insofar as their approach to addressing the risk of future investment claims highlights a fundamental difference between domestic prevention of investor-state disputes and systemic governance reforms.

i. Peru

The first investment arbitration claim against Peru was brought by a French investor Compagnie Minière in 1998.[90] The case was settled in 2003, but in the following years the country continued to experience a steady drip of investor-state claims. Consequently, as an UNCTAD study reports, the government of Peru 'realized that the institutional framework required to optimally defend the State in ISDS cases was not in place.'[91] The government was particularly concerned about:

— lack of understanding by government officials of the scope and implications of international arbitration clauses included in investors-state contracts;
— problems with coordinating actions after disputes emerged at different levels of government, or coordinating actions with the agency that adopted the measure triggering the dispute;
— the absence of a legal mechanism to make government agencies and officials accountable for the consequences of their actions where such actions were found to be in breach of investment treaty standards.[92]

To address these issues, in 2006 Peru adopted Law No 28933 (followed by a number of implementing regulatory decrees in 2008 and 2009) that founded the International Investment Disputes State Coordination and Response System (hereinafter the Response System).[93] The aim of the Response System was to bring together the different state agencies playing key roles in the international investment legal framework, such as the Ministry of Economy and Finance, the Ministry of Foreign Affairs, ProInversion (a treaty negotiation team), the Ministry of Justice, and the Ministry of Trade and Tourism.[94] The three crucial pillars of the system are: (1) a direct link enabling investors to register their concerns or investment problems so that they can be addressed before escalating into an investment arbitration dispute;[95] (2) an obligation imposed on government agencies to promptly report to the Response System Coordinator

[90] *Compagnie Minière v Peru*, ICSID Case No ARB/98/6, settled 23 February 2001.
[91] UNCTAD, *Best Practices in Investment for Development*, 19.
[92] ibid 20.
[93] ibid.
[94] ibid 22.
[95] ibid 25.

any investment disagreement or dispute that may result in an investment arbitration case;[96] (3) making the agency that took measures which triggered an investment dispute eventually responsible for the financial costs of Peru's involvement in the dispute.[97]

Two salient features of Peru's Response System are: (1) the creation of a direct gateway through which investors can register their concerns has been designed to 'allow more time to resolve a problem, prepare a case … or facilitate an amicable settlement, or at least … provide the State with more time to prepare a strong and complete case for arbitration';[98] and (2) the imposition of ultimate responsibility on the agency involved in the dispute aims to render government bodies accountable for taking measures in violation of Peru's investment treaty commitments.[99] Peru's Response System empowers the Coordinator to require the agency whose action resulted in the dispute to bear the costs of the process and of any award against the government. Although the funds to cover the state's involvement in investment arbitration are factored in the budget of the Ministry of Economy and Finance and released in accordance with the decisions made by the System Coordinator, it is the responsible agency itself that is ultimately liable for the payment of any settlement, mediation, conciliation or award.[100] An overarching aim of the policy is to 'serve as a deterrent of measures not compatible with investment treaties, and encourage agencies to reach out to the central investment contact point to consult on measures before they are taken or when problems do arise, thereby promoting early detection.'[101] By far, Peru offers an example of a very sophisticated approach to prevention of investment disputes at a national level—the approach that combines raising awareness about investment treaty law, internalisation of investment treaty prescriptions, and accountability of agencies and officials for a failure to comply with those prescriptions in treatment of foreign investors. The latter is missing in the institutional reforms undertaken in countries such as Kazakhstan and Ukraine.

ii. Colombia

In contrast with other developing countries, Colombia has established a legal framework for preventing and managing investor-state disputes before it faced any investor-state claims. In 2010, the National Council of

96 ibid 30.
97 ibid 32–33.
98 ibid 30.
99 ibid 31.
100 ibid 32–33.
101 ibid 46.

Social and Economic Policy adopted a policy document formulating the government's strategy for preventing and managing investor-state disputes including through the creation of an efficient and reliable system if and when the government does face a dispute.[102] The strategy was premised on the necessity to guarantee the state's compliance with the international commitments enshrined in investment agreements, and to prevent and manage appropriately disputes that may arise between foreign investors and Colombia.[103] The government acknowledged that lack of awareness of and experience with investment treaty commitments among government officials could increase the likelihood of investment treaty rules being violated when such officials interact with foreign investors.[104] It also stressed the importance of designating a lead agency to facilitate efficient and effective defence of the state in arbitration proceedings.[105] The implementation of the strategy resulted in the founding of a high-level government body with responsibility to advise and make recommendations to prevent investment disputes and manage them when they arise. Its members are drawn from representatives of the Minister of Justice and Law, the Minister of Finance, the Minister of Foreign Affairs, the Minister of Trade, Industry, and Tourism, the Legal Secretary of the Office of the President, and external advisors. The principal functions of the high-level government body include: (1) coordinating, directing and developing recommendations for preventing and managing disputes and defending national interests in investor-state arbitrations; (2) designing measures to prevent and resolve international investment disputes; and (3) facilitating a timely and continuous defence of the state in any international investment disputes.[106]

Although the original text of the policy document outlining Colombia's strategy for prevention and management of investor-state disputes emphasised the importance of 'defining procedures so that the agency that has triggered the dispute (involved agency) bears the costs of the process and any amounts awarded to the claimant',[107] there is little evidence as to whether the subsequent implementation of the strategy successfully incorporated these measures to ensure accountability of relevant government agencies and officials.

[102] The strategy is set out in CONPES 36842 of 2010 (a national policy document adopted by the National Council of Social and Economic Policy) and Decree 1859 of 2012.

[103] See USAID/APEC, Investor-State Dispute Prevention Strategies: Selected Case Studies, 2013, available at www.apec.org/Groups/Committee-on-Trade-and-Investment/~/media/Files/Groups/IEG/20130625_IEG-DisputePrevention.pdf, 13.

[104] ibid 14.

[105] ibid 15.

[106] ibid 15.

[107] ibid.

iii. Brazil

While Brazil's experience closely resembles the path followed by Peru and Colombia, it is remarkable in the sense that a commitment to the prevention of investment disputes has been internationalised, ie enshrined in the new Brazil model bilateral investment protection agreement. Unlike model investment treaties of other states, the Brazilian Investment Cooperation and Facilitation Agreement (CFIA) does not offer the possibility of investor-state arbitration but instead prioritises investment promotion and dispute prevention.[108] It makes an express reference to institutional governance as a vehicle to achieve the treaty's primary objective of investment cooperation and facilitation. The institutional governance is to be effectuated through: (1) the establishment of an agenda on investment cooperation and facilitation; and (2) the development of mechanisms for risk mitigation and prevention of disputes, among other instruments mutually agreed on by the parties. The overarching treaty objective is to improve 'the investment climate and to provide a transparent legal regime for foreign investors during the whole life of their investments.'[109]

In concrete terms, the Brazilian model envisages the creation of the national focal points or 'Ombudsmen'[110] and the Joint Committee in order to resolve any disputes between the parties.[111] The principal role of the focal points is to serve as communication channels between foreign investors and the host state, in order to propose inter alia improvements to the business environment, to prevent disputes and facilitate their amicable resolution.[112] In contrast with the traditional bilateral investment treaties, the Brazilian model provides for an institutional mechanism for the implementation of 'the mutually agreed cooperation and facilitation agendas.'[113] The task of coordinating such implementation lies with the Joint Committee, composed of government representatives of both contracting state parties.[114]

[108] The texts of recently signed investment facilitation and cooperation agreement (ICFA) with Malawi can be found at investmentpolicyhub.unctad.org/Download/TreatyFile/4715. For commentary, see Katia Fach Gómez and Catharine Titi, 'International Investment Law and ISDS: Mapping Contemporary Latin America' (2016) 17 *Journal of World Investment and Trade* 515, 523.

[109] Nitish Monebhurrun, 'Novelty in International Investment Law: The Brazilian Agreement on Cooperation and Facilitation of Investments as a Different International Investment Agreement Model' (2017) 8 *Journal of International Dispute Settlement* 79.

[110] Brazil-Malawi ICFA (2015), Art 4.

[111] ibid Art 3.

[112] ibid Art 4.

[113] ibid Art 7.

[114] ibid Art 3.

The Brazilian model investment treaty is notable both for its shift away from investor-state arbitration as a primary means of settling investment disputes and for its internationalisation of state commitments to dispute prevention, investment promotion and improvement of a national investment governance framework. In the latter sense, Brazil's approach departs from the prevailing tendency to assign investment protection to investment treaties and dispute prevention to national legislation. The Brazilian model treaty is uniquely innovative not only because it expressly envisages the creation of implementation mechanisms but also because it brings together the international and national domains.

V. NEGATIVE INTERNALISATION: OVER-PROTECTION AND WITHDRAWAL

Host state efforts to delimit exposure to future investor-state disputes through dispute prevention measures could arguably be seen as an illustration of the positive effect of international investment protection norms and practices on national governance. Yet the recent developments in investment treaty practice across the globe demonstrate that international norms do not always generate a positive 'compliance pull.'[115] Instead of entailing legal reforms and fostering more rule-oriented governance practices, the encounter with international investment law and its arbitration mechanism might provoke adverse reactions on the part of host states. As discussed earlier, in an attempt to avoid the painful financial implications of investment arbitration, host states may start questioning the scope of investment protection commitments in national laws. Others may be pushed to reconsider their participation in the international investment treaty regime. International norms on investment protection may also lead to over-protection of foreign investors. These effects confound the good governance narratives of investment treaty law whilst also raising important questions about the design of mechanisms through which host states are pressured or encouraged to reform national institutions and practices.

A. Investment Treaties and Over-protection of Foreign Investors

Long before the emergence of empirical studies on the impact of investment treaty law on government behaviour, some scholars have persuasively

[115] The phrase is borrowed from a seminal article by Thomas M Franck, 'Legitimacy in the International System' (1988) 82 *American Journal of International Law* 705.

argued that '[r]equiring governments to compensate foreign investors for their losses, while not extending equivalent protection to other private actors, is likely to lead decision-makers to over-value the interests of foreign investors.'[116] Holding the state liable for failing to maintain good governance standards vis-à-vis foreign investors may translate into a pressure to treat foreign investors better than other businesses, as opposed to changing the generally prevailing governance culture and practices that had led to liability in the first place. This argument resonates with findings from our empirical case studies. Rather than embarking on comprehensive and systemic reforms of governance institutions and practices, some host governments—in particular in developing countries—appear to opt for short-term and localised solutions aimed solely at safeguarding the special treatment of foreign investors and optimising the defence of state interests in investment arbitration disputes. Furthermore, our empirical studies indicate that by enabling foreign investors to benefit from stronger protections, international investment law not only leads to reverse discrimination against domestic investors (to whom such rights and remedies are not available) but also appears to hamper the formation of a domestic business constituency that would see its interests and values as aligned with the promotion of good governance. This, in turn, only contributes to the pervasive scepticism about international norms as a force for change. International investment norms and institutions entrench the role of developing states as rule-takers rather than rule-makers and impede the emergence of 'nationally felt' norms of good governance.

An overwhelming number of respondents in our case studies revealed that the improvement of investment climate is often seen as synonymous with creating legal enclaves for foreign investors. As one respondent (a former judge) recalled, the government would frequently issue formal and informal executive orders demanding that foreign investors be accorded special protection in judicial proceedings.[117] Interviews in Kazakhstan and Ukraine also point to the growing popularity of national foreign investment promotion agencies as well as investment ombudsmen specifically tasked with providing 'a tailor-made, door-to-door' protection to foreign investors. When interviewed, one representative of a newly-established investment promotion agency told us that the privilege of a 'door-to-door' protection will be extended only to foreign investments of a certain size and in strategic sectors of economy.[118] An interviewee from

[116] Jonathan Bonnitcha, 'Outline of a Normative Framework for Evaluating Interpretations of Investment Treaty Protections' in Chester Brown and Kate Miles (eds), *Evolution in Investment Treaty Law and Arbitration* (Cambridge, Cambridge University Press, 2011) 128.

[117] Interview THS. This claim was corroborated by interviews HSG and HSK1.

[118] Interview IK1. Similar testimony is found in interview IU1.

one national ministry recounted the government's intention to introduce an overarching framework which would, among other things, enable an expedited visa and entry clearance procedures for foreign investors and their personnel.[119] To this end, agencies responsible for border control and internal affairs would work closely with the ministries and departments responsible for the promotion of foreign investment. Another respondent mentioned the government's intention to introduce a ranking system whereby heads of municipal authorities would be rated for their success in attracting and retaining foreign investments within their respective jurisdictions.[120] None of these initiatives have been explicitly linked to investment treaties and to the respective government's encounter with investment arbitration but rather appear to have been advocated and sponsored by international organisations, such as EBRD, OECD and the World Bank.

Interviews in Kazakhstan also pointed out the government's ambition to transform the investment landscape through the establishment of the Astana International Financial Centre (AIFC), a special economic zone to promote capital markets development, facilitate the privatisation of state-owned enterprises by foreign investors, and generally foster the improvement of local financial system, human and technological capital, cementing Kazakhstan's role as the financial and logistics hub of the Eurasian region.[121] A particularly noteworthy feature of this initiative is the fact that the newly-created AIFC will operate as a special jurisdiction with an independent legal framework based on common law. According to Article 13(2) of the Constitutional Law of the Republic of Kazakhstan 'On Astana International Financial Centre', the AIFC Court shall be independent in its activity and shall not be a part of the judicial system of the Republic of Kazakhstan.[122] Even more notable is the fact that Kazakh law will not be applicable law; rather the Court will be governed by rules 'based on the procedural principles and norms of England and Wales and (or) standards of the world leading financial centres.'[123] The interviews with Kazakh government officials reveal that judges of the AIFC court judges will be selected from foreign experts with professional reputations and an established track record of previous experience in common law jurisdiction countries.[124] The underlying idea is to afford foreign investors with special privileges by insulating them from national law and the national judicial system.

[119] Interview IDM1.

[120] ibid.

[121] The Constitutional Law of the Republic of Kazakhstan 'On Astana International Financial Centre' (entered into force 1 January 2017).

[122] ibid, the full text is available at www.kazembassy.org.uk/en/pages/page/88.

[123] ibid Art 13(5).

[124] Interview MFA1.

The emerging picture suggests that, in an effort to improve national regulatory environment, some host governments have been favouring not a systemic reform that would result in 'good governance for all', but rather solutions that over-protect foreign investors by creating special legal enclaves and thus insulating foreign investors from the vicissitudes of doing business under the same rules as local investors. The fact that international investment protection norms may lead to host states over-valuing the interests of foreign investors yet again shows that governments do not always respond to international sanctions and incentives by embracing good governance reforms. Not only is the over-valuing of foreign investors' interests unlikely to facilitate 'spill-over' of good governance practices into the domestic sphere so as to benefit host communities, but the overprotection of investors by insulating them from national laws and national courts is likely to hamper the emergence of national cadre of experts to diffuse and embed the norms of good governance. The genesis of reforms favouring the creation of legal enclaves for foreign investors also points to a significant role played by the international organisations and Western donors.

B. Withdrawal from the Investment Treaty Regime as a Form of Chilling Effect

Even in the early days of the investment arbitration boom, as the number of investment disputes against developing states surged, a note of caution was sounded that 'developing countries that are constantly paying damages to foreign investors for failing to provide a standard of treatment that is impossible for them to provide are unlikely to renew the treaty when it expires.'[125] Critics have also warned that reform is not the only possible response to investment treaty law and investment arbitration and that losing arbitral cases may result in dissatisfaction with the investment treaty regime.[126] As Guthrie observed, '[f]rustrations with unexpected or inconsistent arbitral interpretations of a BIT—a result of vague standards—can only heighten this discontent. The sense of discontent may in turn reduce support for the BIT and any related reforms.'[127]

An overview of recent trends in investment treaty practice shows that, indeed, host states tend to internalise lessons from their engagement with

[125] Nick Gallus, 'The Influence of the Host State's Level of Development on International Investment Treaty Standards of Protection' (2005) 6 *Journal of World Investment Trade* 711, 726.

[126] Benjamin K Guthrie, 'Beyond Investment Protection: An Examination of the Potential Influence of Investment Treaties on Domestic Rule of Law' (2012–2013) 45 *New York University Journal of International Law and Politics* 1151, 1197.

[127] ibid 1197.

the investment treaty regime differently. While some states—in particular developed economies—have embarked on treaty reform with the view to safeguarding the state's right to regulate and allay concerns relating to the investment treaty regime's lack of transparency and accountability, others have attempted to scale back the scope of their investment protection commitments by seeking a review of national legislation. Yet other states have focused on optimising the defence of state interests in investment arbitration as well as preventing investor-state disputes. Notably, there are states that made a decision to disengage from the international investment regime altogether.[128] As a recent UNCTAD report put it, 'unilaterally quitting IIAs sends a strong signal of dissatisfaction with the current system.'[129] The backlash against international investment law can manifest in '"intense", "sustained" and "aggressive" calls for the abandonment of a system or for the adoption of a radically alternative structure.'[130]

Such sense of profound dissatisfaction is clearly discernible in a withdrawal by a number of developing states from the investment treaty regime. On 2 May 2007 Bolivia submitted a notice of its denunciation of the ICSID Convention. Venezuela followed the suit on 24 January 2012. This denunciation process was triggered in February 2008 when the Venezuelan National Assembly openly condemned the case brought before ICSID by Exxon Mobil. The dispute was characterised by the national media as 'an action of economic and judicial terrorism carried out by the transnational Exxon Mobil and its accomplices' and was accompanied by calls for the government of Venezuela to withdraw from the ICSID system.[131] A similar step was taken by Ecuador on 6 July 2009. The Ecuadorian Constitution has been amended to incorporate a prohibition against resolving disputes through international arbitration.[132] In 2013, the government of Ecuador also founded the Ecuadorian Commission for a Comprehensive

[128] See eg David Ma, 'A BIT Unfair?: An Illustration of the Backlash Against International Arbitration in Latin America' (2012) *Journal of Dispute Resolution* 571; Anne van Aaken, 'Perils of Success? The Case of International Investment Protection' (2008) 9 *European Business Organization Law Review* 1 (discussing the consequences of overprotection, such as withdrawals from international investment instruments, refusals to honour awards, revising BITs, and abandoning investor-state arbitration).

[129] UNCTAD, 'Reform of the IIA Regime: Four Paths of Action and a Way Forward', IIA Issues Note No 3, June 2014, 4.

[130] David D Caron and Esmé Shirlow, 'Dissecting Backlash: The Unarticulated Causes of Backlash and Its Unintended Consequences' in Geir Ulfstein and Andreas Føllesdal (eds), *The Judicialization of International Law—A Mixed Blessing?* (Oxford, Oxford University Press, forthcoming).

[131] José Manuel García Represa, 'Regionalization Trends and Foreign Investment in South America: The Implications of the ALBA and UNASUR Initiatives' in N Jansen Calamita and Mavluda Sattorova, *The Regionalization of International Investment Treaty Arrangements* (British Institute of International and Comparative Law, London, 2015) 225, 239.

[132] Ma, 'A BIT Unfair?', 571.

Audit of Investment Protection Treaties and of the International Investment Arbitration System (*Comisión para la Auditoría Integral Ciudadana de los Tratados de Protección Recíproca de Inversiones y del Sistema de Arbitraje Internacional en Materia de Inversiones*—CAITISA).[133] Comprising government officials, legal experts and civil society representatives, the Commission was tasked with evaluating the legality, legitimacy and desirability of Ecuador's investment treaties. The Commission found that the investment treaties signed by Ecuador failed to deliver foreign direct investment, undermined the development objectives laid out in the country's constitution and its National Plan for Living Well (Buen Vivir), and failed to address significant social and environmental liabilities left by foreign investors. The Commission also noted the disproportionately high financial costs of investment treaties and investor-state arbitration for Ecuador. Following the Commission's recommendation, in May 2017 Ecuador announced its decision to terminate all its bilateral investment treaties.[134]

Russia has expressed its dissatisfaction with the investment treaty regime and investment arbitration by officially informing the Depository of the Energy Charter Treaty (ECT) on 20 August 2009 that it did not intend to become a contracting party to the ECT or the Protocol on Energy Efficiency and Related Environmental Aspects (PEEREA).[135] In June 2009, the South African Department of Trade and Industry launched a review of the policy framework relating to international investment agreements,[136] and later in 2010 the government announced its decision to terminate first-generation bilateral investment treaties, and to refrain from entering into investment treaties in future.[137] In July 2015 Indonesia notified the Netherlands of its decision to terminate their bilateral investment treaty and expressed its intention to terminate all of its 67 investment treaties with other states.[138] The latest instance of backlash took place in India in

[133] Gómez and Titi, 'International Investment Law and ISDS', 525.

[134] Cecilia Olivet, 'Why did Ecuador terminate all its Bilateral investment treaties?' www.tni.org/en/article/why-did-ecuador-terminate-all-its-bilateral-investment-treaties. The full report of CAITISA (in Spanish) is available at caitisa.org/index.php/home/enlaces-de-interes.

[135] Irina Pominova, 'Risks and Benefits for the Russian Federation from Participating in the Energy Charter: Comprehensive Analysis', Energy Charter Secretariat Knowledge Centre, 2014.

[136] 'Bilateral Investment Policy Framework Review', General Notice 961, in Government Gazette 32386 (7 July 2009).

[137] Engela C Schlemmer, 'An Overview of South Africa's Bilateral Investment Treaties and Investment Policy' (2016) 31 *ICSID Review* 167, 185.

[138] Ben Bland and Shawn Donnan, 'Indonesia to terminate more than 60 bilateral investment treaties', *Financial Times* (26 March 2014).

May 2016 when the government officially notified 47 treaty partners of its decision to completely overhaul the existing investment treaties.[139]

Despite the majority of states opting to continue with investment treaty practice and to address the existing dissatisfaction through reforming contentious treaty rules and procedures, the existence and steadily growing number of host states withdrawing from the regime clearly confounds the good governance narratives. Evidence from the rapidly evolving international and national practices amply illustrates that the impact of investment treaty law on host states may take a variety of forms, with some governments seeking to reduce their exposure to investment arbitration through changes in domestic laws, and other governments choosing to pre-empt the risk of investor-state disputes and their financial consequences by disengaging from the investment treaty regime altogether.

VI. INTERNALISING INVESTMENT TREATY PRESCRIPTIONS: WHY, AT WHOSE BEHEST AND WHAT COST?

A. Limited Learning and Internalisation: BITs that Do not Bite?

Contrary to the assumption that the growing exposure to investment arbitration would prompt host states to address the shortcomings in domestic governance frameworks through a comprehensive and systemic reform, the empirical findings from our case studies—when viewed together with other recent studies—suggest that host states do not always translate their 'learning' experience into concrete and meaningful measures to address the governance failures underpinning many investment disputes. The findings from all five case studies resonate with recent empirical examination by Poulsen of patterns of investment treaty-making in developing countries, which revealed that many government officials, including key stakeholders, 'had been unaware of the far-reaching scope and implications of BITs during the 1990s, when the treaties proliferated.'[140] Furthermore, Poulsen found that, even where the information about investment treaties and their liability implications was readily available, government decision-makers in developing states tended to ignore the experience of other countries and neglected to take investment treaties seriously until their first encounter with an investment arbitration claim in a respondent capacity.[141] Our case studies also support

[139] Deepshikha Sikarwar, 'India seeks fresh treaties with 47 nations', *The Economic Times* (27 May 2016).

[140] Poulsen and Aisbett, 'When the Claims Hit', 281–82.

[141] Poulsen, *Bounded Rationality*, 155.

the conclusion that the initial exposure to investment treaty claims indeed entails some learning about international investment law and its implications for the host state. However, the interviews also show that learning tends to remain confined predominantly to those officials who were involved, directly or indirectly, in the process of defending the government in a relevant investor-state arbitration case.[142] Government officials in other tiers of the government showed very limited or no awareness of investment treaties even after their country had to defend itself in investment arbitration on more than one occasion. It transpires that the awareness of investment treaty law and the standards of governance it imposes on host states is particularly low among government officials in local and regional executive bodies and the national judiciary.[143]

These findings have potentially significant implications: as observed in a recent UNCTAD report, 'disputes that reach the stage of arbitration can originate with measures taken by agencies or entities that at times do not have full understanding or knowledge of the commitments undertaken by central governments in IIAs.'[144] Recent qualitative studies of ICSID caseload show that the majority of government decisions leading to investor-state arbitrations are associated with actions taken by the executive agencies and that, beyond ministries, it was the conduct of subnational actors such as provincial, state and municipal authorities and agencies that dominated among the causes of investment disputes so far.[145] If government officials involved in making executive and judicial decisions vis-à-vis investors remain unaware of investment treaty law and its prescriptions even after the country has had to act as a respondent in a number of investment arbitration cases, significant doubts arise as to whether international investment law and its arbitration mechanism could lead to tangible changes in governance practices and culture within those agencies.

Our case studies also show that in some host states the actual exposure to international investment law disciplines in a respondent capacity has not only yielded at best 'partial' learning on the part of government officials, but also resulted in 'incomplete' translation of the lessons learnt into

[142] This finding resonates with Poulsen's observations about Mexico's learning from disputes such as *Metalclad*. He found that, at the time of his interviews, the learning process was confined 'within a small circle of technical staff'. Also, no regulatory agencies were aware of the treaties. Poulsen, *Bounded Rationality*, 147.

[143] See above Section III.

[144] UNCTAD, *Best Practices*, 12.

[145] Jeremy Caddel and Nathan M Jensen, 'Which host country government actors are most involved in disputes with foreign investors?', *Columbia FDI Perspectives* No 120, 28 April 2014, available at ccsi.columbia.edu/files/2013/10/No-120-Caddel-and-Jensen-FINAL-WEBSITE-version.pdf.

concrete changes in law and policy. This is despite significant financial cost incurred by the host government in defending themselves against investor claims. For instance, in *PSEG Global v Turkey*, the cost of the arbitration, including expenses and fees, totalled US$ 20,851,636.62, of which Turkey was ordered to pay 65 per cent, in addition to the US$ 9,061,479.34 it had to pay in compensation to the claimant investor.[146] In *Libananco*, despite the investor claims having been dismissed, Turkey's expenses amounted to US$ 35,702,417.76.[147] Similarly, in defending its interests in one case alone—*Metal-Tech v Uzbekistan*—the government of Uzbekistan incurred arbitration costs in the amount of US$ 7,985,954.95.[148] Contrary to the central premise of the good governance narratives, the financial pain of damages awards and arbitration costs has not prompted either country to question the root causes of investment disputes and to adopt systemic and comprehensive reforms with a view to avoiding future liabilities.

One possible explanation for the lack of concerted effort on the part of the Uzbek and Turkish governments to address domestic governance issues leading to investment disputes is that both countries might have perceived their experience of investment arbitration overall as positive. Some respondents in the Turkish case study pointed to the fact that a number of unmeritorious investor claims against the country were dismissed, thus leaving the government with an impression that the investment arbitration regime was overall balanced and no further reform was needed.[149] Some respondents also referred to an increasing rate at which investment arbitration was used by Turkish investors abroad, which the respondents believed contributed to the perception of the regime as being useful for Turkey.[150] The overall positive perception of international investment law may thus explain the lack of impulse to address home-grown governance issues at the heart of investment disputes brought against Turkey. A similar hypothesis can be made in relation to Uzbekistan's response to its first exposure to investment claims. At the time the case studies were completed, Uzbekistan had successfully defended itself in all but one of the resolved cases (the first arbitral award holding the government liable towards the claimant investor was made in 2015 in *Oxus Mining v Uzbekistan*).[151] Since Uzbekistan had enjoyed a period with no damages or significant arbitration costs ruling made against it, the government could arguably be seen as lacking a sufficient incentive to launch governance

[146] *PSEG Global Inc v Turkey*, Award and Annex, 19 January 2007, ICSID Case No ARB/02/5.

[147] *Libananco v Turkey*, Award, 2 September 2011, ICSID Case No ARB/06/8.

[148] *Metal-Tech Ltd v Republic of Uzbekistan*, Award, 4 October 2013, ICSID Case No ARB/10/3, para 414.

[149] Interviews MEN1, MEN2, MIT.

[150] Interview MIT.

[151] *Oxus Gold plc v Uzbekistan*, UNCITRAL, Award, 17 December 2015.

reforms so as to address the root causes of investor-state disputes and to prevent future liabilities. Similar observations were made by Poulsen in his empirical analysis of Sri Lanka, where the first investor-state arbitration award—even though made in favour of the investor-claimant—was perceived by Sri Lankan officials as a great success because the amount of damages awarded was small and one of the investor's key arguments on liability was denied.[152]

The fact that Turkey and Uzbekistan did not create any dispute prevention mechanisms may not necessarily be attributable to their satisfaction with the outcome of the investment disputes brought against them. For instance, Peru could be said to be in a comparable position in terms of a high proportion of cases where the government succeeded in defending itself in investor-state disputes. Yet unlike Uzbekistan and Turkey, Peru did put in place the Response System to prevent and manage investment disputes. The qualitative insights from the case studies in Turkey and Uzbekistan also point to internal capacity (or the lack of it) as a potentially significant factor underlying the host state's choice to refrain from any significant action to address domestic causes of investor-state disputes. The interviews suggest that the prevailing lack of awareness of true implications of investment treaty law, insufficient coordination between various agencies and officials within the government, and limited capacity to translate lessons learnt into concrete legal changes may play a significant part in shaping the ways host states respond to investment treaty law and its sanctions mechanism.

B. Dispute Prevention Versus Comprehensive Governance Reforms

The comparative analysis of how other developing states internalise their experience of investor-state arbitration also brings to the fore the question of whether awareness about investment treaty rules is not only necessary but also sufficient for preventing investor-state disputes. For international investment law to generate a positive spill-over effect on domestic governance by compelling the host states to change their lacking legal and bureaucratic practices, the host government should acknowledge and endorse the importance of such reforms, and possess the capacity to design and implement them. Since investor-state disputes have their roots in problems that investors encounter in their dealings with a variety of governmental bodies, a national monitoring and response mechanism should target all stages of government decision-making.[153]

[152] Poulsen, *Bounded Rationality*, 139, referring to his interviews with government officials discussing the consequences of *AAPL v Sri Lanka*.

[153] UNCTAD, *Best Practices in Investment*, 10.

Can the newly-established ombudsmen and investment promotion agencies be seen as evidence of host states learning from investor-state arbitration and seeking to pre-empt their exposure to investor claims? Peru's model of the 'response system' stands out in that it transcends the immediate concerns relating to optimal defence of the state interests in investment arbitration and acknowledges the importance of both raising the awareness among, and ensuring accountability of, public officials in different tiers and branches of government. Nevertheless, since it is usually the central government that is directly responsible for representing and defending the host state and for the payment of final arbitral awards, one could argue that the low levels of awareness among government officials in local and regional bodies may not a decisive factor: the central government can always intervene before the dispute has escalated into an arbitration case. It could be argued that for investor grievances to be resolved before arbitral proceedings are initiated, it is the *central* government that needs to be aware of and willing to rectify, in a timely fashion, the wrongdoing committed by (investment treaty-ignorant or incompetent) agencies at the lower tiers of government. One could contend that the lack of reformist impulse on the part of host governments is therefore not problematic: while sidestepping the need to raise awareness among government officials and reform their daily practices, these governments might prefer to deal with foreign investor disagreements when and as they turn into a conflict and come to the attention of the central government. Arguably, this approach focuses on dispute prevention and management rather than the more ambitious task of addressing causes of systemic failures of governance.

The disadvantage of placing emphasis on the prevention of investment disputes through timely intervention from a central government agency is that such pre-empting strategy is unlikely to bring about changes in daily practices of the host state's legal and bureaucratic institutions. Unless the prevention of investment disputes involves cascading down of the rules and policies aimed at improved governance, only foreign investors—in some cases—may be likely to benefit from such early detection and dispute management policies. The emphasis on prevention of investment disputes as opposed to transformation of a governance culture may have an effect similar to that of providing foreign investors with the opportunity to use international dispute settlement mechanisms and thus sidestep national remedies: by focusing exclusively on the pre-emption of investor-state disputes through intervention and settlement, the central government may be sidetracked from the broader need to transform legal and bureaucratic institutions and practices. For a host state to translate its lessons from investment arbitration into governance reforms, not only should public officials across various tiers of the government machinery be aware of investment treaty prescriptions but the host government as a whole must be committed to 'learning' and to a meaningful and systemic overhaul of the lacking governance institutions and practices.

With the exception of Peru, the fundamental shortcoming of the emerging national policies on prevention of investment disputes is the lack of a mechanism to ensure accountability of individual officials and agencies. While their primary objective is to facilitate an amicable resolution of investor-state disagreements, the investment promotion and dispute prevention agencies of Colombia, Kazakhstan, and Ukraine do not possess the requisite institutional power to ensure responsibility of government officials whose conduct leads to costly investor-state disputes. The interviews in Kazakhstan and Ukraine also suggest that presently the special units within the ministries of justice in both countries play a limited role in translating the lessons from investment arbitration disputes into concrete changes in national law and policy. Likewise, the recently established national investment ombudsmen and investment promotion agencies tend to opt for ad hoc, informal solutions to avoid lengthy legislative and bureaucratic changes. They do not possess effective institutional powers to propose and implement long-term and systematic reforms. Their current operational framework is underpinned by the idea of a centralised, tailor-made, 'door-to-door' support of individual investment projects through maintaining focal points of contact, rather than diffusing knowledge about investment treaty law and its governance prescriptions.

Finally, most of the existing dispute prevention and management models—even the comprehensive framework adopted in Peru—appear to be highly geared towards the protection of foreign investors and optimisation of the defence of state interests in investor-state arbitration, and as such are not designed to improve governance for all. When examined closely, Peru's response system appears to be preoccupied more with dispute management rather than long-term and *sustained* dispute prevention. This is also true of the ombudsman and investment promotion agencies founded in Ukraine and Kazakhstan. The institutional mandate of these organisations is to promote and protect foreign investors, often of a certain size and strategic importance to the host state economy.[154] The creation of separate regimes—legal enclaves—for foreign and domestic investors removes the incentive for foreign investors (and powerful domestic constituencies) to lobby for institutional reforms at a national level.[155] By prioritising foreign investment protection over a comprehensive change of national legal and bureaucratic landscape, such policy solutions do

[154] Interviews IK1 and UI1 stressed that only foreign investors of a strategic size and importance to the economy would be entitled to benefits of 'tailor-made, door-to-door protection'.

[155] Soumyajit Mazumder, 'Can I stay a BIT longer? The effect of bilateral investment treaties on political survival' (2016) 11 *Review of International Organisations* 477, 478.

little to meet interests of domestic business community and are therefore likely to hamper the emergence of legal and regulatory innovation that would benefit a broader range of domestic stakeholders.

Of all national approaches discussed so far, the Brazilian model treaty appears to be most promising due to its innovative alignment of the hitherto disparate agendas of investment promotion, dispute prevention, dispute settlement, and institutional governance for the implementation of investment protection commitments. Brazil's model is also notable for its (currently non-binding) commitment to involve a broader range of national stakeholders in shaping investment promotion and protection priorities.[156] As the model has been launched only recently, it is too early to predict its impact on national governance. The ultimate effectiveness of the Brazilian approach will hinge on how contracting state parties fulfil their treaty commitments to create an investment governance framework built on accountability, national treatment and pre-emption of disputes.

C. Internalisation and Resource Constraints

The interviews and comparative overview of domestic responses and reactions by developing countries to investment arbitration unveil a range of factors that may influence governmental choices in designing investment promotion and protection policies. One such factor is the cost of introducing and maintaining a comprehensive, systemic and robust dispute prevention and management framework. One of the biggest challenges faced by Peru in implementing its model was to make it widely known among government officials in various tiers and branches of the government. During the first years after the response system was launched, the government of Peru received support from UNCTAD to organise training of government officials.[157] However, making the response system known to the officials who do not necessarily form part of it but are involved with foreign investors necessitates a broader, far-reaching and costly capacity-building commitment.[158] The high costs of putting in place dispute prevention and management mechanisms brings to the fore the fact that the ability of host governments to internalise international investment rules and actively prevent their exposure to international liability by changing domestic governance practices can be severely circumscribed by human, financial and institutional constraints underpinning the lacking

[156] See eg Art 3.4.D. of the Brazil-Malawi IFCA (2015).
[157] UNCTAD, *Best Practices in Investment*, 37–38.
[158] ibid 37.

domestic legal and bureaucratic culture. This creates a vicious circle in which investment treaty law can play a controversial part: as developing states are held to monetary liability for failing to abide by good governance standards vis-à-vis foreign investors, the cash-strapped treasuries may face a difficult choice between paying significant damages awards or committing resources to the creation of effective mechanisms for prevention and management of investment disputes and improving domestic governance.

Resource constraints have long been recognised as one of the key impediments faced by external efforts to transform governance institutions and practices in developing states—the impediment which the good governance narratives of international investment law fail to address. If it were indeed the function of investment treaties and investor-state arbitration to foster improvements in legal and bureaucratic practices in developing countries, the international investment regime and its arbitration mechanism would effectively become the latest addition to a long queue of international institutions that have accumulated a certain track record of attempting to change domestic governance through external pressures and incentives. The effectiveness of externally-imposed domestic governance reforms has been scrutinised in much detail and generated volumes of academic literature. However, whilst the rule of law and good governance rhetoric seem to have been extrapolated from rule of law and development discourse into the investment treaty law context, the wealth of knowledge distilled by law and development scholars appears to be deliberately brushed aside by their counterparts in investment law. In particular, the good governance narratives appear to ignore or gloss over the existing consensus about the role of technical or resource-related constraints in precipitating failure of numerous rule of law projects over the last three decades. Many a developing country has found itself in a situation where

> despite the political will on the part of their leadership and citizens poor countries simply lack the financial, technological, or specialized human capital resources to implement good institutions generally, including legal institutions, thus impairing their development prospects (whatever one's conception of development), in turn making the poorer (in some relevant normative sense) and in turn further diminishing their ability to implement good institutions, hence a vicious downward spiral.[159]

Critics of international investment law have stressed that the expansive interpretation of investment protection rules, including the fair and

[159] Michael J Trebilcock and Ronald J Daniels, *Rule of Law Reform and Development: Charting the Fragile Path of Progress* (Cheltenham, Edward Elgar, 2008) 38–39.

equitable treatment standard, disproportionately affects developing countries.[160] Should developing countries be punished for a failure to ensure the standards of governance despite the fact that such failure is in no small measure caused by lack of human and economic capacity? The good governance narratives of international investment law tend to turn their blind eye to the fact that a failure to maintain transparency, stability, predictability and consistency is often the direct consequence of resource constraints which cannot be alleviated by merely imposing additional (and often considerable) financial liabilities on host states. The major fallacy of a central assumption underpinning the good governance rhetoric—that investment treaties and their remedial mechanisms incentivise host states to embark upon domestic legal reforms—lies in its simplistic and misguided belief that developing countries have the capacity to embrace domestic reforms but only need an external push to launch them. It disregards what law and development scholars have long acknowledged as one of the key endogenous factors hampering the success of externally-driven governance reform projects.

D. Internalisation and External Support

The fact that some countries chose to set up a formal dispute prevention and management framework whilst others refrained or failed to do so also points to the involvement of external financial and advisory assistance agencies as a prominent factor in shaping governmental approaches to reforming national investment governance frameworks. Even a brief glance at the genesis of the dispute prevention models adopted in Colombia, Kazakhstan, Peru and Ukraine shows the key role played by external entities such as the World Bank, EBRD, UNCTAD and the EU in the design and launch of the relevant policies. Interviews in Kazakhstan and Ukraine confirm that the impetus for these initiatives came from the external actors. The availability of capacity-building support thus emerges as a major factor in influencing national policy choices on investment protection and dispute settlement.

The fact that dispute prevention and management frameworks in Peru and Colombia have been founded with the aid of external actors resonates with international relations theories which link changes in government behaviour with the availability of resources. Long before investment arbitration has captured attention of the international scholarly community, Chayes and Chayes argued that the process of facilitating state compliance with international rules should involve *informing* states of international

[160] Kyla Tienhaara, *The Expropriation of Environmental Governance: Protecting Foreign Investors at the Expense of Public Policy* (Cambridge, Cambridge University Press, 2009) 213.

laws and *building* state capacity to comply.[161] When analysed from this angle, the fact that some developing states (such as Turkey and Uzbekistan) have not taken formal steps to prevent investment disputes need not necessarily be regarded as either their satisfaction with the regime or their deliberate defiance to act. Rather, such behaviour of contracting states parties can be a result of a lack of government commitment and capacity to make relevant changes in domestic laws.[162] As our interviews suggest, the ways developing countries respond to investment arbitration can be significantly influenced by a lack of awareness about international investment law and a lack of capacity to effectively 'learn' and to translate lessons from the government's involvement in investor-state arbitration into concrete changes. If host states are expected to respond to investment arbitration by refraining from behaviour that leads to investment disputes, it is essential that '[t]he issue of the party's capacity to carry out its obligations is examined and addressed, perhaps by some form of technical assistance or other resources if available'[163]—so as to raise the levels of awareness and to help reform the lacking governance institutions and practices at a domestic level.

As the impetus and financial support for reforms aimed at investor-state dispute prevention appears to have come from international organisations, a crucial question is whether these national policy developments should be regarded as a form of response by host states to investment treaty disciplines. Have the ombudsmen and investment promotion agencies been founded as a result of the host government's experience with investor-state arbitration and the ensuing desire to limit its exposure to potentially harmful financial consequences of future investment disputes? Are we truly witnessing what the proponents of good governance narratives would describe as learning by host states from their encounter with investment treaty law?

Both the analysis of national legislation and interviews show no links between the creation of investment ombudsmen and investment promotion agencies and investment treaty law. The interviewees representing these agencies had no awareness of investment treaties and investment arbitration cases. Our analysis suggests that these policy developments owe their origins to the investment liberalisation agenda actively pursued by international institutions and western donor organisations. Host state efforts to scale back their commitments of investment protection and

[161] Abram Chayes and Antonia Handler Chayes, *The New Sovereignty: Compliance with International Regulatory Agreements* (Cambridge MA, Harvard University Press, 1995) 25.

[162] See Mavluda Sattorova, 'Reassertion of Control and Contracting Parties' Domestic Law Responses to Investment Treaty Arbitration: Between Reform, Reticence and Resistance' in Andreas Kulick (ed), *Reassertion of Control over the Investment Treaty Regime* (Cambridge, Cambridge University Press, 2016) 71–72.

[163] Chayes and Chayes, *The New Sovereignty*, 110.

investment arbitration as well as their attempts to optimise and streamline the defence of state interests in arbitration can be clearly traced back to the respective governments' growing exposure to investment disputes. Those are 'nationally felt' responses. By contrast, the burgeoning national policies and institutions on investment promotion and dispute prevention have been brought into existence not by investment treaty law but rather by a broader, decentralised transnational machinery of international organisations, donors and reform entrepreneurs. The striking similarity of core features underpinning the recent reforms in Kazakhstan, Ukraine, Colombia, and even Peru and Brazil suggests the existence of an externally-authored blueprint.

This transnational network of influence and its dispute prevention and investment promotion agenda in developing countries raise a host of questions. Does the involvement of international organisations carry an enabling effect on national governance or is it effectively an exercise of control by external actors over developing governments preventing the latter from making their own choices with respect to investment protection, promotion and dispute settlement? Might externally-advocated models hinder the emergence of 'internally felt' norms and the production of new, innovative ways of interaction between developing states and the global investment protection regime? The very turn to the externally-sponsored initiatives concerning investment promotion and investment dispute prevention[164] raises the question whether the investment treaty regime is no longer deemed to be enough by its international protagonists. With its focus on retrospective sanctions for non-compliance, investment treaty law does little to foster the creation of domestically-situated frameworks to ease *the entry and operation* of foreign investors in host states. The fact that the international organisations are pushing for investment treaty protection whilst also advocating the parallel reforms on investment facilitation and dispute prevention at a national level could also be seen as tacit acknowledgement that investment treaty law does not automatically lead to 'learning' and improved governance in host states.

VII. CONCLUSION

This chapter has sought to evaluate the causal assumptions about the impact of investment treaty law on governance in host states. The intention

[164] The investment promotion and dispute prevention reforms akin to those implemented in Ukraine and Kazakhstan, Peru and Colombia appear to follow a blueprint presented in the recent UNCTAD report on investment facilitation. See UNCTAD, Global Action Menu for Investment Facilitation, September 2016. For a brief analysis, see Felipe Hees and Pedro Mendonça Cavalcante, *'Focusing on investment facilitation—is it that difficult?'*, *Columbia FDI Perspectives*, No 202, 19 June 2017.

was to go beyond analysing the formal characteristics of the investment treaty regime and to examine practical experiences of host states and government officials in developing countries. While acknowledging that the findings from the case studies reflect the particular experiences of the host states, they help unveil the hitherto invisible patterns of state behaviour and paint a more nuanced picture of the emerging patterns of state engagement with investment rule-making and dispute settlement.

One of the principal findings of this chapter is that the effect of investment treaty sanctions on government behaviour can be variously confounded by the lack of awareness about true implications of investment treaty law among government officials, insufficient coordination between various agencies and officials within the government, and inability or failure to translate lessons learnt into concrete legal changes. In particular, the claim that international investment law purportedly transforms governance in host states is belied by the emerging evidence which shows that, even after the states experienced a number of investor-state disputes, government officials in the executive and judicial organs have remained unaware of both the very existence of investment treaty law and of the fact that their acts or omissions affecting foreign investors may lead to investment arbitration disputes and potentially state liability. Furthermore, even when learning did occur, it has been confined to a limited group of individuals in key agencies and the lessons have not been translated into concrete measures to address the root causes of investment disputes.

The case studies also suggest that, even where a host government learns about investment treaty law from its encounters with investor-state arbitration in a respondent capacity, its response may not necessarily conform to what is predicted by the good governance narratives. In some cases, the governments choose to ignore and act contrary to legal advice on the implications of investment treaty law, which in turn belies an assumption that the exposure to investment treaty disciplines would make states more risk-averse. The interviews reveal that, despite having accumulated a certain learning experience, host states may continue to neglect the possible repercussions of their actions under investment treaty law. In some cases, dissatisfaction with their experience in investment arbitration may propel host states to scale back investment protection commitments in national laws or to withdraw from the investment treaty regime altogether.

Although the amount of empirical data is still limited and further longitudinal studies on a broader geographical scale are necessary, the emerging findings point to the growing importance of peering behind the unitary conception of state and identifying the factors which shape host state interaction with the investment treaty regime. There is a need for a greater focus on the perceptions and reality in developing countries, whose patterns of engagement in the making and implementation of investment treaty rules still remain under-explored. Some of the conclusions drawn from our case studies also raise novel questions that may apply to the broader array of states. For instance, the difference in the ways host states have responded to the imposition or threat of state liability under investment treaties and to the financial implications of investment arbitration suggests that the impact of investment treaty law is likely to vary significantly across states, and the deterrent effect of sanctions is likely to be diffused by a variety of endogenous and exogenous factors present in each individual case. One such factor appears to be the host state's capacity to translate its learning from the previous exposure to investment treaty arbitration into concrete changes at a national level. Drawing on the interviews as well as comparative analysis of national policy innovations in various developing states, this chapter concludes that financial consequences of the host state's involvement in investment arbitration alone are unlikely to provide a sufficient impetus for embracing a more risk-averse behaviour on the part of government organs and officials; more is needed to embed good governance precepts into the legal and bureaucratic culture of the host state.

External advisory and financial support appears to have played a significant part in shaping host states efforts to improve investment climate through the creation of dispute prevention and management agencies. Regrettably, these national agencies are presently geared towards protecting a certain category of foreign investors and do not have the competence to formulate and implement proposals for governance reforms. Most of the existing models also lack the mechanism to ensure accountability of government officials and agencies whose actions lead to investor-state disputes. Another unwelcome consequence of the relentless pursuit of foreign investment promotion agenda in host states is the emergence of legal enclaves for foreign investors. The prioritisation of foreign investment protection disadvantages domestic business actors and sidetracks host states from broader and more systemic governance reforms.

The findings from the case studies also point to the significance of a contextual examination of the effects of investment treaties on government behaviour and decision-making by identifying other (parallel or else) international projects and initiatives, such as the externally-sponsored programmes aimed at the improvement of investment climate in developing states. It may not always be possible to accurately disentangle the effects generated by these various international initiatives. However, interviews and comparative analysis of national regulatory landscape can be useful in tracing policy changes back to their source of influence. For instance, without such contextualisation, one might have been tempted to attribute the creation of an investment dispute prevention and management agency in Peru to Peru's desire to proactively embed its investment treaty commitments or to a post-hoc adjustment as a consequence of the country having experienced the bite of investment treaties.

Likewise, Brazil's new treaty has been described as revolutionary.[165] Yet the contextual examination of the reforms in both Brazil and Peru point in the direction of 'external authorship' rather than a domestic 'revolutionary' impulse. Only when situated within a broader context of various transnational influences bearing on national governments, can the actual impact of international investment law on host states be accurately measured and analysed.

[165] Anthea Roberts, 'The Shifting Landscape of Investor-State Arbitration: Loyalists, Reformists, Revolutionaries and Undecideds', EJIL: *Talk!* 15 June 2017.

4

The Role of Remedy Design in Inducing Host States to Comply with Investment Treaty Standards of Good Governance

I. DAMAGES AS A PRINCIPAL FORM OF RELIEF FOR AN INVESTMENT TREATY BREACH

THE NARRATIVES POSTULATING a virtuous effect of investment treaty law on governance in host states rest on a causal assumption that investment treaty rules, and in particular monetary remedies, prompt governments to act in a certain way.[1] The results of our empirical case studies suggest that holding states liable for a breach of investment treaty standards does not necessarily deter future breaches or otherwise foster changes in governance practices. As discussed in Chapter 3, the pain of monetary sanctions does not appear to act as a sufficient catalyst of domestic legal and bureaucratic reforms. The interviews with government officials reveal that host governments may at times ignore legal advice about the possible adverse financial consequences of investor-state disputes, and may choose to breach investment treaty rules when they find it expedient.[2] Neither has the actual imposition of liability made the respondent governments more risk-averse and compliant with investment treaty law. Thus, a crucial question is whether investment treaty rules on liability are *by design* capable of inducing host states to comply with treaty prescriptions on good governance. The nature and design of investment treaty rules on state liability are of fundamental importance for our understanding of the interaction between the investment treaty regime and domestic legal systems.

The unique feature of international investment law—and the source of much criticism—is its use of monetary remedies as a principal means of

[1] See Jonathan Bonnitcha, *Substantive Protection under Investment Treaties: A Legal and Economic Analysis* (Oxford, Oxford University Press, 2014) 45.
[2] See discussion in Chapter 3, Section IVA.

redress in investor-state arbitration.[3] As noted in a recent OECD study,[4] the prevalence of damages in investment treaty law is puzzling: monetary redress is rarely available to claimants challenging governmental conduct in either national legal systems or general international law (both favour non-pecuniary forms of relief).[5] National legal systems have traditionally restricted the use monetary damages as a remedy for governmental action and even more so for governmental omissions. The longstanding maxim of 'the King can do no wrong'[6] or 'le Roi ne peut mal faire'[7] continues to underpin rules governing state liability even in democracies.[8] In France, for instance, sovereignty and liability in damages were regarded as mutually exclusive notions.[9] Although the notion of state liability has since evolved and expanded, liability in the form of damages is still rather restricted.[10] Similarly, the reluctance to allow wider use of monetary remedies in English courts has been shaped by concerns over the constraints under which government agencies operate and the further effect that financial consequences of damages awards would entail.[11] In the words of Lord Browne-Wilkinson,

> it is not really in the interests of society as a whole if you spend your time concentrating on rights of individuals to damages—because that is what we are talking about, financial compensation—against public authorities who are charged with looking after society as a whole and doing their best to perform a social welfare function; the creation of ever more duties giving rise to financial compensation is actually counterproductive in a society.[12]

[3] See eg Margaret B Devaney, 'Remedies in Investor-State Arbitration: A Public Interest Perspective', *Investment Treaty News* (22 March 2013), International Institute for Sustainable Development.

[4] David Gaukrodger and Kathryn Gordon, 'Investor-state dispute settlement: A scoping paper for the investment policy community' (OECD Working Papers on International Investment, No 2012/3, OECD Investment Division) 26.

[5] See ibid. One notable exception is the *Francovich* liability under EU law, which allows individuals to claim damages where certain preconditions are met (*Francovich and Bonifaci v Italy*, Cases C-6/90 & C-9/90, [1991] ECR I-5357).

[6] In English law, for instance, although the Crown remains subject to the law, procedural requirements effectively delimited opportunities for redress in practice. See Duncan Fairgrieve, *State Liability in Tort. A Comparative Law Study* (Oxford, Oxford University Press, 2003) 8.

[7] ibid 3, see also Irmgard Marboe, 'State Responsibility and Comparative State Liability for Administrative and Legislative Harm to Economic Interests' in Stephan W Schill, *International Investment Law and Comparative Public Law* (Oxford, Oxford University Press, 2010) 382.

[8] For an overview of national traditions, see Marboe, 'State Responsibility', 382–99.

[9] Anne van Aaken, 'Primary and Secondary Remedies in International Investment Law and National State Liability: A Functional and Comparative View' in Schill, *International Investment Law*, 725.

[10] ibid 726.

[11] Fairgrieve, *State Liability in Tort*, 132.

[12] ibid 133.

The principal reasons for restrictive approaches to state liability in damages include fears over the paralysing effect on decision-making, budgetary burdens, and the risk of creating 'compensation culture' whereby claimants would be inclined to seek damages instead of using public law remedies such as injunction or specific performance.[13] National legal systems of developed states tend to emphasise the so-called 'primary' or 'judicial review' remedies that are non-pecuniary in their nature.[14] Unlike investment treaty law, where claimant investors can resort to multiple and often intersubstitutable causes of action, the opportunity to obtain redress against government agencies in administrative law of developed states is usually subject to strict conditions.[15]

In public international law remedies are not confined to pecuniary redress: international courts and tribunals may variously choose from specific performance, declaratory relief and restitution. As the International Law Commission (ILC) Articles on State Responsibility set out, the finding of an internationally wrongful act entails the respondent state's obligation: (a) to cease that act, if it is continuing; (b) to offer appropriate assurances and guarantees of non-repetition, if circumstances so require.[16] The responsible state is also under an obligation to make full reparation for the injury caused by the internationally wrongful act.[17] The notion of injury encompasses 'any damage, whether material or moral, caused by the internationally wrongful act of a State.'[18] The principal tenet of state responsibility in international law as elaborated by the Permanent Court of Justice in the *Chorzow Factory* case is that

> … reparation must, as far as possible, wipe out all the consequences of the illegal act and re-establish the situation which would, in all probability, have existed if that act had not been committed. Restitution in kind, or, if this is not possible, payment of a sum corresponding to the value which a restitution in kind would bear, the award, if need be, of damages for loss sustained which would not be covered by restitution in kind or payment in place of it—such are the principles which should serve to determine the amount of compensation due for an act contrary to international law.[19]

It is unsurprising that compensation remains the most commonly-sought remedy in international practice—recent analysis of practice of the

[13] van Aaken, 'Primary and Secondary Remedies', 729–30.

[14] Gaukrodger and Gordon, 'Investor-state dispute settlement', 26.

[15] See eg Law Commission, *Administrative Redress: Public Bodies and the Citizen* (2010) paras 2.44–2.48.

[16] Art 30.

[17] Art 31(1).

[18] Art 31(2).

[19] PCIJ, *Factory at Chorzow (Germany v Poland) (Claim for Indemnity) (Merits)* [1928] PCIJ Series A, No 17 47.

International Court of Justice has shown a greater compliance record for judgments and a less satisfactory one for provisional measures.[20] Yet specific performance and declaratory relief are also widely used.[21] Crucially, public international law does not offer an automatic waiver of the exhaustion of local remedies rule: prior to initiating an international dispute (and claiming monetary damages) the claimant is under an obligation to make recourse to remedies available under national laws of the respondent state.[22]

Why the prevalence of monetary remedies in investment treaty law? Historically, a foreign investor's right to claim damages in investment treaty arbitration was regarded as 'a relatively inexpensive commitment device'[23] through which contracting host states, in particular developing countries, would promise to refrain from arbitrary and unlawful behaviour vis-à-vis foreign investors. This would lower risks associated with investing in a host country, attract foreign investment and reduce the cost of capital for host states, thus accelerating their economic development.[24] As econometric studies have subsequently proliferated, showing little or no causal effect of investment treaties on the flow of foreign investment and economic development, new narratives emerged claiming that the use of monetary sanctions under investment treaties can also exert considerable pressure on host states 'to bring their domestic legal orders into conformity with their investment treaty obligations.'[25] By holding states liable for a breach of investment treaty obligations, arbitral awards act as '[a] powerful incentive to review and modernize their domestic legal systems.'[26]

However, the rise in the number of investor-state arbitration cases has also prompted profound concerns about the large sums awarded to claimant investors, the high cost of the arbitration process and the budgetary implications of these losses for host states, in particular developing countries. To comply with the arbitral awards, developing countries

[20] Freya Baetens and Marco Bronckers, 'Reconsidering financial remedies in WTO dispute settlement' (2013) 16 *Journal of International Economic Law* 281, 284–85; see further Constanze Schulte, *Compliance with Decisions of the International Court of Justice* (Oxford, Oxford University Press, 2004).

[21] van Aaken, 'Primary and Secondary Remedies', 732.

[22] Elettronica Sicula SPA (ELSI) (*United States of America v Italy*) (1989) ICJ Rep 15, para 50. See further CF Amerasinghe, *Local Remedies in International Law*, 2nd edn (Cambridge, Cambridge University Press, 2004).

[23] See Alan O Sykes, 'Public Versus Private Enforcement of International Economic Law: Standing and Remedy' (2005) 34 *Journal of Legal Studies* 631, 644.

[24] ibid 633.

[25] Stephan W Schill, 'System Building in Investment Treaty Arbitration and Lawmaking' (2001) 12 *German Law Journal* 1083, 1085.

[26] Rudolf Dolzer, 'The Impact of International Investment Treaties on Domestic Administrative Law' (2005) 37 *New York University Journal of International Law and Policy* 972.

could be forced to divert the already limited funds from important socio-economic objectives, such as investment in infrastructure, education and health.[27] Even in cases where the final award is in favour of the respondent state, developing countries have to cope with significant amounts in legal expenses and the costs of the arbitral proceedings.[28]

As developing countries continue to bear the brunt of investment arbitration awards,[29] the question inevitably arises as to whether good governance could at all be fostered through the externally imposed and crippling financial sanctions on host states. Indeed, the empirical data discussed in Chapter 3 shows that the imposition of monetary liability on host states does not deter them from breaching good governance prescriptions of investment treaties. Neither do financial sanctions appear to have an incentivising effect on host state behaviour. While arguing that investment treaty law and its remedial mechanism 'provides strong incentives to improve domestic institutions', the recent OECD study acknowledges, albeit in a footnote, that the efficacy of monetary sanctions in effecting change in domestic governance practices may be confounded by various factors. First, since remedies are imposed on host governments, the effect of what OECD refers to as 'monetary incentives' might not be felt by the individuals in charge of regulatory or judicial reform. Second, it is acknowledged that capture of the regulatory process by political and economic elites as well as lack of requisite human or financial resources might influence the state's capacity to respond to the monetary incentives.[30] Two key questions are: (1) can good governance be fostered through punishment? and (2) does the manner in which investment treaty remedies are designed and applied to facilitate greater state compliance with investment treaty prescriptions of good governance?

II. CAN STATE COMPLIANCE WITH GOOD GOVERNANCE STANDARDS BE FOSTERED THROUGH MONETARY SANCTIONS?

A fundamental problem of the good governance narratives of international investment law is an assumption that after experiencing the

[27] UNCTAD, Best Practices in Investment for Development. How to prevent and manage investor-State disputes: Lessons from Peru, Investment Advisory Series, Series B, No 10 (New York and Geneva, United Nations, 2011) 7.

[28] ibid 8.

[29] See eg the recent statistics showing the prevalence of developing countries among losing respondent states: 'Investor-State Dispute Settlement: Review of Developments in 2016' UNCTAD IIA Issue Note, No 1, 2017. See also Daniel Behn, Tarald Laudal Berge and Malcolm Langford, 'Poor States or Poor Governance? Explaining Outcomes in Investment Treaty Arbitration' (2017) *Northwestern Journal of International Law & Business* (forthcoming).

[30] Gaukrodger and Gordon, 'Investor-state dispute settlement', 14 at fn 17.

financial pain of damages awards, host states would be simultaneously deterred from breaching investment treaty rules and encouraged to incorporate them into their domestic law and practices. As Schill puts it, 'damages as a remedy sufficiently pressure States into complying with and incorporating the normative guidelines of investment treaties into their domestic legal order.'[31] Whilst the good governance rhetoric in investment treaty law seem to have been inspired by discourse on rule of law and development, the wealth of knowledge distilled by law and development scholars over the past decades appears to be deliberately brushed aside by their counterparts in investment law. In particular, scholars of international investment law tend to disregard a welter of studies produced by law and development and rule of law scholars scrutinising the effectiveness of external pressures in designing and implementing legal and political reforms. International institutions have traditionally resorted to a promise of financial assistance (rather than a threat of financial sanctions) in their rule of law and legal reform initiatives in developing states. For instance, since the 1990s, World Bank, along with other international financial institutions, such as the International Monetary Fund (IMF), began to condition its loans and development grants upon various levels of political, legal and economic reform.[32] Among other initiatives, World Bank deployed aid conditionality to pressure developing countries to improve their investment climates, with each country's performance to be measured against certain benchmarks and used in determining its eligibility for financial assistance.[33] Likewise, the IMF has long used aid conditionality in promoting the institutional reforms aimed at creating a 'business-friendly' environment in developing states.[34] Conditionality was also harnessed as a primary tool in the EU rule of law initiatives in the context of enlargement. In an effort to convince accession candidates to embrace certain standards of good governance, the EU adopted a strategy

[31] Stephan W Schill, *The Multilateralization of International Investment Law* (Cambridge, Cambridge University Press, 2009) 373.

[32] Frederick Rawski, 'Wold Bank Community-driven Development Programming in Indonesia and East Timor: Implications for the Study of Global Administrative Law' (2005) 37 *International Law and Politics* 919.

[33] See Amanda Perry-Kessaris, 'Prepare Your Indicators: Economics Imperialism on the Shores of Law and Development' (2011) 7 *International Journal of Law in Context* 401, 402; Tor Krever, 'Quantifying Law: Legal Indicators Projects and the Reproduction of Neo-Liberal Common Sense' (2013) 34 *Third World Quarterly* 131.

[34] Alexander E Kentikelenis, Thomas H Stubbs and Lawrence P King, 'IMF conditionality and development policy space, 1985–2014' (2016) 23 *Review of International Political Economy* 543, 560; see also Balakrishnan Rajagopal, 'From Resistance to Renewal: The Third World, Social Movements, and the Expansion of International Institutions' (2000) 41 *Harvard International Law Journal* 529, 574.

of reinforcement by reward, with rewards to be delivered in case of rule adoption and withheld in case of non-compliance.[35]

The policy of reinforcement by reward adopted in externally-sponsored governance reforms is arguably a far cry from the monetary sanctions of investment treaty law (even though some sources refer to the latter as 'monetary incentives'). Still, criticisms levelled at the use of conditionality by international institutions are instructive insofar as they highlight the limitations of financial pressures and incentives in fostering legal reform in developing states. For instance, as a number of critics pointed out, the effectiveness of conditionality in implementing domestic legal reforms was confounded 'by the reluctance of borrowing governments seriously to implement the whole range of reforms necessary to bring about equitable development'.[36] Analyses of the EU rule of law initiatives in the EU enlargement context also appear to concur that strict conditionality 'may contribute to the lack of mentality transformation, resulting in expedited legislative reforms and leaving no room for the internalisation of such reforms.'[37]

The deployment of conditionality in promoting reforms in developing states has also been criticised for its coercive nature. Even though, strictly speaking, conditionalities are often framed as financial incentives—as 'a promised benefit in exchange for some policy choice, rather than a punishment for some perceived failure'[38]—an element of coercion can be found in cases where reforms are effectuated under a threat of benefits being taken away.[39] Political science studies have found transformation through coercion to be less effective than initiatives based on persuasion:

> [r]ules that are transferred through social learning or lesson-drawing are much less contested domestically. Implementation is more likely to result in behavioural rule adoption and sustained compliance, while external incentives primarily privilege formal rule adoption as the least costly form.[40]

[35] See eg Frank Schwimmelfennig, Stefan Engert and Heiko Knobel, 'Costs, Commitment and Compliance: The Impact of EU Democratic Conditionality on Latvia, Slovakia and Turkey' (2003) 41 *Journal of Common Market Studies* 495.

[36] Ngaire Woods, 'Order, Justice, the IMF, and the World Bank' in Rosemary Foot, John Gaddis and Andrew Hurrell (eds), *Order and Justice in International Relations* (Oxford, Oxford University Press, 2003) 83.

[37] Firat Cengiz and Lars Hoffmann, 'Rethinking Conditionality: Turkey's European Union Accession and the Kurdish Question' (2013) 51 *Journal of Common Market Studies* 416, 429–30.

[38] Michael J Trebilcock and Ronald J Daniels, *Rule of Law Reform and Development: Charting the Fragile Path of Progress* (Cheltenham, Edward Elgar, 2008) 342.

[39] ibid.

[40] Frank Schimmelfennig and Ulrich Sedelmeier, 'Governance by conditionality: EU rule transfer to the candidate countries of Central and Eastern Europe' (2004) 11 *Journal of European Public Policy* 669, 674.

Furthermore, linking the provision of financial aid to rule of law and governance reforms has been condemned for its marketisation effect. In the words of Perry-Kessaris,

> '[t]he marketisation of legal systems leaves a mark on legal systems, those who produce them and those who use them. The first mark is left on our understanding of what law is for. When we think of legal systems as commodities, and investors as their main audience, we devalue, or even forget about, the other 'sacred' social functions of law.[41]

Conditioning financial assistance upon indicators of the country's success in improving its investment climate was also found to have led to cheating, or 'gaming' whereby states focused on improving indicators rather than seeking to improve the quality of their legal systems.[42] Our empirical case studies—and findings from qualitative analyses by others—also corroborate this view: the interviews with government officials in developing countries reveal that the use of financial incentives or sanctions to back up legal transformation does not facilitate the emergence of 'nationally felt' legal rules but instead tends to result a widespread scepticism and at times suspicion over the desirability of the proposed reforms for the host country.[43] As a consequence, externally advocated legal reforms are frequently seen as bargaining chips in financial negotiations with international financial institutions and donor organisations.

The use of monetary sanctions in the name of improved domestic governance is also incompatible with the investment treaty regime's historical mandate and raison d'etre—the promotion of economic development in host states. 'The gains of economic liberalisation should not be lost to its beneficiaries.'[44] Developing host states frequently pay a heavy social and economic price in the form of a variety of financial and other quantifiable

[41] Perry-Kessaris, 'Prepare your Indicators', 408.

[42] ibid 410.

[43] As one respondent in our case studies commented on compliance with investment treaty law, 'International institutions wanted us to sign the treaties, so it should be their headache how to implement them in practice.' (Interview TMZ). See Celine Tan observing that '… developing countries are increasingly required, through aid conditionalities, to adopt policies and institutional reforms which … in many ways, imitate the donors' structures of social and political organisation without due consideration of local circumstances or constraints.' Celine Tan, 'The New Disciplinary Framework: Conditionality, New Aid Architecture and Global Economic Governance' in Celine Tan and Julio Faundez (eds), *International Economic Law, Globalization and Developing Countries* (Cheltenham, Edward Elgar, 2010) 133. See also Akbar Rasulov, 'Central Asia and the Globalisation of the Contemporary Legal Consciousness' (2014) 25 *Law and Critique* 163, 170.

[44] Tan, 'The New Disciplinary Framework', 122.

concessions granted to investors, including tax exemptions, pollution permits and labour requirements.[45] As observed by Stiglitz,

> [e]ven if it could be established that BITs lead to increased investment, and even if that investment could be shown to lead to higher growth, as measured by increased gross domestic product ('GDP'), it does not mean that societal welfare will increase, especially once resource depletion and environmental degradation are taken into account.[46]

Add to this the need to pay out vast amounts in damages awards in cases where an investor succeeds in proving a breach of exacting 'good governance' standards of investment treaty law, questions arise as to whether the investment treaty regime might impede economic development, intensify poverty in host states—and delimit their ability to forge the requisite human and institutional capacity for good governance.

III. THE DESIGN OF INVESTMENT TREATY REMEDIES AND STATE COMPLIANCE WITH GOOD GOVERNANCE STANDARDS: A FUNCTIONAL ANALYSIS

If reinforcement by reward has largely failed in attaining a genuine transformation in legal and bureaucratic systems of developing states, the question arises as to the effectiveness and appropriateness of the strategy of reinforcement by punishment that lies at heart of the investment treaty regime. Can a threat and use of monetary sanctions be deployed to compel (or coerce) effectively host states into embracing good governance standards at a national level? The literature on law and development yet again offers a rich seam of findings. While there appears to be consensus that the success of financial sanctions as a mechanism to bring about policy change is 'at best uncertain',[47] the literature helpfully identifies a number of conditions for the effective use of sanctions. Among other things, effective monitoring mechanisms are likely to enhance compliance in a

[45] Kate Miles, *The Origins of International Investment Law: Empire, Environment and the Safeguarding of Capital* (Cambridge, Cambridge University Press, 2013) 91.

[46] Joseph E Stiglitz, 'Regulating Multinational Corporations: Towards Principles of Cross-Border Legal Frameworks in a Globalized World Balancing Rights with Responsibilities' (2008) 23 *American University International Law Review* 451, 455. See also Krista Nadakavukaren Schefer, 'Poverty and Investment Law: Starting the Discussion' (2014) 15 *Journal of World Investment and Trade* 908, 911, pointing out that 'Dam projects that require resettlement often affect the most disadvantaged and leave them with even less than before; foreign purchases of vast tracts of farmland can force local subsistence farmers to enter unequal relationships with the investor or leave; polluting industries and mining projects can have direct health effects on populations already struggling to survive.'

[47] Trebilcock and Daniels, *Rule of Law Reform*, 351.

variety of ways, for instance by 'improving dialogue between the relevant parties.'[48] Notably, sanctions need to be designed so as to exert pressure on specific decision-making elites or entities they control, or against specific activities.[49] As these findings suggest, remedies may produce the desired effect on state behaviour, but only if carefully designed and accompanied by effective communication and monitoring mechanisms.

When analysed in light of their historical underpinnings and current design, are investment treaty rules on remedies capable of serving as an incentive for host states to comply with investment treaty prescriptions of good governance? The right to claim damages is effectively a backward-looking remedy that focuses on redressing the effects of a wrong committed by a host government. By subjecting respondent states to the pain of financial sanctions, investment treaty rules on liability should arguably be able to deter *future* breaches the good governance standards enshrined in investment treaties.[50] Those who conceptualise investment treaty remedies as a deterrence mechanism and a catalyst of reforms also argue that the fiscal pressure of monetary damages for breaches of investment treaty law is likely to encourage (or pressure) host states to ensure ex ante compliance by good governance standards in their dealings with foreign investors, with improved governance practices eventually spilling over more widely into the domestic sphere and benefiting host communities.[51] For the purposes of our analysis, compliance is understood as a process that goes beyond the formal ratification of international treaty instruments and comprises ex ante internalisation of the norms contained therein as well as ex post adjustment of national legal framework in line with decisions of international adjudicatory bodies. The crucial question is: are investment treaty remedies (second order rules) designed in a way that would facilitate both ex ante and ex post state compliance with good governance standards (first order rules)?

Notwithstanding a large and growing body of scholarship engaging with various aspects of investment treaty remedies, the question of their design, functions and goals—and the impact on compliance—remains largely

[48] ibid.

[49] ibid.

[50] Sergio Puig, 'No Right Without a Remedy: Foundations of Investor-state Arbitration' in Zachary Douglas, Joost Pauwelyn and Jorge E Viñuales (eds), *The Foundations of International Investment Law: Bringing Theory into Practice* (Oxford, Oxford University Press, 2014) 235.

[51] See eg Benedict Kingsbury and Stephan W Schill, 'Investor-State Arbitration as Governance: Fair and Equitable Treatment, Proportionality, and the Emerging Global Administrative Law', Institute for International Law and Justice, NYU Law School, Working Paper 2009/6 (Global Administrative Law Series) 3, also Peter Muchlinski, Federico Ortino and Christoph Schreuer, 'Preface' in Peter Muchlinski, Federico Ortino and Christoph Schreuer (eds), *The Oxford Handbook of International Investment Law* (Oxford, Oxford University Press, 2008) vi.

unexplored. Nevertheless, useful insights can be drawn from scholarly debates about the relationship between remedies and compliance in GATT/WTO law. The primary remedy for a breach of WTO norms is the withdrawal (or modification) of an offending measure.[52] Compensation and suspension of concessions (also known as retaliation) are also available but not as an alternative to withdrawal; rather, claimants can resort to compensation and retaliation as temporary remedies in cases where the withdrawal of an inconsistent measure by the respondent state is not forthcoming.[53] One of the key goals of the WTO dispute settlement mechanism is that of 'inducing compliance with the primary norms underlying the multilateral trading regime'.[54] This emphasis on compliance manifests itself in the WTO DSU, where Article 3.7 explicitly states that the primary objective of the dispute settlement mechanism 'is usually to secure the withdrawal of the measures concerned if these are found to be inconsistent with the provisions of any of the covered agreements.'[55] In contrast with investment treaty law and its preoccupation with wiping out all the consequences of the illegal act and re-establishing the situation that would have existed prior to the occurrence of the breach, WTO rules are primarily concerned with achieving 'substantive compliance with prospective effect, at the expense of any injury that the breach may have caused during the time of non-compliance.'[56] The movement from GATT to WTO dispute settlement has only strengthened the cessation aspect of responsibility, with the reparation aspect having been 'all but suppressed.'[57]

Whereas the principal aim of withdrawal as a primary remedy for a breach of WTO law is indisputably to ensure compliance with multilateral trade rules, the goals of temporary remedies, such as compensation and retaliation, are not as clear-cut and have been the subject of scholarly debates. Some argue that both compensation and retaliation '[a]re

[52] Art 3.7 of the Understanding on Rules and Procedures Governing the Settlement of Disputes, Annex 2 of the Agreement Establishing the World Trade Organization, 1994.

[53] See ibid: 'The provision of compensation should be resorted to only if the immediate withdrawal of the measure is impracticable and as a temporary measure pending the withdrawal of the measure which is inconsistent with a covered agreement.'

[54] Yuval Shany, *Assessing the Effectiveness of International Courts* (Oxford, Oxford University Press, 2014) 195.

[55] ibid 195.

[56] Geraldo Vidigal, 'Re-assessing WTO Remedies: the Prospective and the Retrospective' (2013) 16 *Journal of International Economic Law* 505, 519.

[57] ibid 517. Pauwelyn also observes that retaliation was previously seen as a means to rebalance the original bargain or to compensate the injured state party, but is now regarded as a means to induce compliance or sanction the violation. See Joost Pauwelyn, 'The Calculation and Design of Trade Retaliation in Context: What is the Goal of Suspending WTO obligations?' in Chad P Bown and Joost Pauwelyn (eds), *The Law, Economics and Politics of Retaliation in WTO Dispute Settlement* (Cambridge, Cambridge University Press, 2010) 36.

designed to provide an incentive for a Member to remove any offending measure and bring its laws into compliance'[58] and not to 'punish a Member for having had the offending measure in the first place'.[59] Others contend that, historically, compensation and retaliation were viewed primarily as a means of rebalancing the situation, ie were focused on the injured state party; however, following the evolution of the quasi-conciliatory GATT into a highly judicialised WTO dispute settlement system there has been a 'gradual strengthening of the emphasis on rule compliance.'[60]

In contrast with GATT/WTO law, monetary relief—the remedy of damages—has traditionally been regarded as a principal form of redress and a primary means of enforcing substantive rules in investment treaty law. The question is: what is the goal of the remedy of damages in international investment law? Is it to induce compliance with substantive rules (including the good governance prescriptions) or to rebalance economic interests of parties to an investment dispute by compensating the aggrieved investor?

From an historical and doctrinal perspective, the long-standing emphasis on monetary redress and the fact that the latter has rarely been accompanied by other remedies suggests that the primary goal of the remedial mechanism in international investment law has been to rebalance the original bargain. The focus is thus on the injured party (a foreign investor) and on eliminating the negative economic consequences it incurred as a result of a violation by the state of its investment treaty commitments. Had the primary goal been to induce compliance, the investment treaty remedies would have been designed so as to focus on the breaching party, ie the host state, and on the need to punish it to deter future violations and induce it into acting in accordance with standards prescribed by international investment treaties. In light of this obvious prioritisation of the need to restore economic interests of aggrieved investors, one could argue that fostering state compliance, both ex ante and ex post, with investment treaty prescriptions has never been the primary goal of remedies in international investment law.

It could, of course, be argued that even though investment treaty remedies are primarily concerned with providing redress to the disaffected investor and not with rectifying the irregularities of host state behaviour, the negative financial consequences of damages awards would compel host states to identify and address the root causes of investment disputes and gradually adjust domestic legal orders in line with investment treaty

[58] Donald McRae, 'Measuring the Effectiveness of the WTO Dispute Settlement System' (2008) 3 *Asian Journal of WTO and International Health Law and Policy* 1, 8.

[59] ibid 8.

[60] Vidigal, 'Re-assessing WTO Remedies,' 107.

prescriptions of good governance. Yet the manner in which investment treaty remedies are designed and applied may in fact have the opposite effect on the host state behaviour. Not only are investment treaty remedies chiefly preoccupied with restoring the interests of an affected investor, but investment treaty rules in general are framed in way that allows host states to prefer the so-called efficient breach to compliance. The central premise of the theory of efficient breach is that an international treaty operates as an explicit contract between parties. Just as private parties to a contract benefit from mutual performance of their commitments, states generally benefit from the obligations undertaken under international treaties. However, just as is the case with private contracts, performance of international legal obligations may not always be seen by state parties as desirable.[61] Where the costs of state compliance with international treaty obligations exceeds the benefits, the state may find it more efficient to commit a breach than to comply.[62]

Without engaging in the debate as to whether efficient breach of investment treaty commitments should be permitted or is indeed desirable,[63] our aim here is to demonstrate that investment treaty norms are designed in a way that enables host states to breach their commitments when they believe the costs of compliance to exceed the benefits. As Brewster has convincingly argued, international dispute settlement mechanisms can act 'as a pricing mechanism, designed by negotiators to allow states to make use of the remedy regime as an alternative to performance.'[64] Where international norms attach a certain price to a breach, such rules can be seen as effectively permitting states to violate international law as long as the remedy is paid.[65] While the function of remedies—even of those aimed at rebalancing economic interests of an injured party—is to punish and disapprove, they can also operate as 'permission, even entitlement, to undertake certain actions' and a 'license to engage in behaviour at a certain cost.'[66] Designed so, international norms may facilitate breach, rather than deter it.

Brewster's argument that investment treaty norms can act as a pricing mechanism and enable host governments to choose a breach over compliance resonates with findings from our empirical case studies. Respondents

[61] Eric A Posner and Alan O Sykes, 'Efficient Breach of International Law: Optimal Remedies, "Legalized Noncompliance", and Related Issues' (2011–2012) 110 *Michigan Law Review* 243, 252. The authors go on to argue that performance should not always be required.

[62] ibid 258.

[63] See eg criticisms of the efficient breach theory, Baetens and Bronckers, 'Reconsidering Financial Remedies', 291–95.

[64] Rachel Brewster, 'Pricing Compliance: When Formal Remedies Displace Reputations Sanctions' (2013) 54 *Harvard International Law Journal* 259, 261.

[65] ibid 259.

[66] ibid 271–72.

from three different countries under examination suggested that a threat of monetary sanctions is unlikely to change a host government's decision to breach an investment treaty where such breach is seen as more expedient in economic and political terms.[67] One respondent recalled a situation where a high-ranking minister chose to proceed with a governmental measure that would violate the state's investment treaty commitments.[68] The said minister expressly ignored legal advice about the financial implications of the possible investment claim disputing the proposed measure, and justified his decision as being economically more important.[69]

Political economy and the psychology behind a government choosing to breach and pay are beyond the scope of this book. For the purposes of this chapter, the key question is whether the design of investment treaty norms enables host states to effectively opt out of compliance with good governance standards. Do investment treaties specifically require contracting states to adopt measures to foster and maintain good governance, or do they require the states to provide a set level of compensation for a failure to abide by good governance standards vis-à-vis foreign investors? Investment treaty law is effectively a pricing scheme.[70] One of the core investment treaty rules is an obligation to pay prompt adequate and effective compensation for expropriation. Investment treaty law does not demand that host states refrain from actions that may constitute direct or indirect expropriation; rather it acknowledges the sovereign right to expropriate or nationalise foreign investment but subjects the exercise of such right to legality requirements, including the obligation to compensate the affected investor. As Posner and Sykes put it, by pricing expropriation investment treaty law 'legalises' a behaviour that might otherwise be considered an international wrong.[71] Where the costs of breaching investment treaty provisions are less than the host state's gain from the same breach, the availability of monetary remedies may in fact render it considerably more attractive for the host state to choose breach over compliance.

Of course, it could be argued that expropriation rules are an exception and that other investment treaty norms act as unequivocal prescriptions of good governance rather than pricing mechanisms allowing states to depart from the good governance standards in exchange for compensating the disaffected investors. In contrast with the expropriation clause, the fair and equitable treatment standard—the primary source of good governance obligations in investment treaty law—is not couched in

[67] Interviews MEN1, DFI1, MUL, MUI.
[68] Interview MUI.
[69] ibid.
[70] Brewster, 'Pricing Compliance', 294.
[71] Posner and Sykes, 'Efficient Breach', 279.

permissive language.[72] A typical fair and equitable treatment clause requires that host states maintain a certain standard of conduct in their dealings with foreign investors. Yet because the traditional remedy for a breach of the fair and equitable treatment standard is monetary compensation, the standard operates in the same way as other liability rules.[73] As Bonnitcha has incisively observed, an arbitral tribunal's finding that a governmental measure has breached the fair and equitable treatment standard usually triggers a host state's obligation to pay compensation to the investor, not an order invalidating the measure that was found to fall short of the good governance standards.[74] Arbitral tribunals do not require respondent governments to bring their measures into compliance with good governance standards of investment treaties. As long as the benefits of breaching the transparency, stability and consistency requirements outweigh the costs of complying with these requirements, the host state is free to depart from the investment treaty prescriptions of good governance by complying with an investment arbitration award and compensating the investor. Undeterred by the existing investment treaty remedies design, host states can effectively opt out from the obligation to treat foreign investors in accordance with good governance standards. If investment treaty law does not act as a powerful enough factor to deter states from breaching good governance standards vis-à-vis foreign investors, it becomes all the more difficult to envisage how it could push states in the direction of compliance with good governance standards in wider domestic settings.

IV. COMPLIANCE AND OPTIMAL REMEDY DESIGN: PUNITIVE, NON-PECUNIARY, MULTI-TIERED?

Could investment treaty remedies be redesigned so as to facilitate host state compliance with good governance standards? Assuming that the goal of investor-state dispute settlement is to induce compliance and encourage or pressure host states to actively embrace and maintain good governance in their dealings with foreign investors (and beyond), investment treaty remedies would need to mete out a *higher* level of punishment than in cases where a key goal is to rebalance the economic interests of the parties by compensating the affected foreign investor.[75] In other words, awarding the investor with restitution or compensatory damages will not

[72] Bonnitcha, *Substantive Protection*, 59.

[73] ibid. See also van Aaken, 'Primary and Secondary Remedies', 746; Santiago Montt, *State Liability in Investment Treaty Arbitration: Global Constitutional and Administrative Law in the BIT Generation* (Oxford, Hart Publishing, 2009) 6.

[74] Bonnitcha, *Substantive Protection*, 45.

[75] Pauwelyn, 'The Calculation and Design of Trade Retaliation', 38–39.

likely suffice: if investment arbitration were to function as a mechanism of deterrence, arbitrators should be more willing (and allowed) to grant punitive damages 'to raise the cost of opportunistic behaviour on the part of the states.'[76] Sanctions should go beyond the actual harm borne by the investor-claimant.[77] As Brewster points out, remedies that comprise a punitive component 'can act as a sanction and revise upward the audience's beliefs about the mandatory nature of the treaty.'[78] Also known as exemplary damages, punitive damages represent 'sums awarded apart from any compensatory or nominal damages, usually … because of particularly aggravated misconduct on the part of the defendant.'[79] The principal rationales for punitive damages are to condemn and discourage certain behaviour.[80] In contrast with restitution and compensatory damages, punitive damages are granted chiefly to punish particularly wrongful conduct, not merely to compensate an injured party.[81]

Punitive damages, however, are not commonly granted under investment treaties. Some investment treaties expressly preclude arbitral tribunals from awarding punitive remedies.[82] Moreover, although the punitive component is likely to enhance the deterrent effect of investment treaty law and arguably prevent host states from opting out from compliance with good governance standards, the use of punitive damages is not desirable due to overarching policy considerations. Sanctioning investment treaty breaches by holding respondent host governments to punitive remedies will be starkly at odds with the investment treaty regime's principal raison d'etre—the promotion of economic development in host states, particularly in developing countries.

If the good governance standards enshrined in investment treaties were to be regarded as promises that the state parties are obligated to fulfil, and if the goal of investment treaty remedies were indeed to incentivise state behaviour consistent with the investment treaty regime's purported mission to foster good governance for all, then, bar punitive damages, another appropriate remedy would be specific performance.[83] By contrast

[76] Puig, 'No Right Without a Remedy,' 256.

[77] There is consensus among WTO scholars that to achieve rule-conformity by an otherwise non-complying state party, sanctions should go beyond the actual harm. See Shany, *Assessing the Effectiveness of International Courts*, 211; Pauwelyn, 'The Calculation and Design of Trade Retaliation', 38–39.

[78] Brewster, 'Pricing Compliance', 262.

[79] John Y Gotanda, 'The Unpredictability Paradox: Punitive Damages and Interest in International Arbitration' (2010) 7(1) *Transnational Dispute Management*, 2 (citations omitted).

[80] ibid.

[81] John Y Gotanda, 'Punitive Damages: A Comparative Analysis' (2004) 42 *Columbia Journal of Transnational Law* 391, 395–96.

[82] US model BIT 2012, Art 34(3); see also France-Mexico BIT 1998, Art 9.7.d(iv): 'An arbitral tribunal shall not order a Contracting Party to pay punitive damages.'

[83] See Brewster, 'Pricing Compliance', 275.

with damages awards, orders of injunctive relief and specific performance can effectively prevent host states from enjoying 'efficient breach' and opting out of compliance: '[b]oth injunctions and orders of specific performance are remedies that purport to constrain the manner in which a government may exercise its powers.'[84]

Yet specific performance and injunctive relief are not commonly sought and granted in investment treaty practice. In his seminal paper on the subject, Schreuer has examined jurisprudence of international courts and tribunals, as well as the *travaux preparatoire* behind the ICSID Convention to conclude that investment tribunals possess the power to grant non-pecuniary remedies such as specific performance and restitution *in integrum*.[85] Since the successive early drafts of the ICSID Convention were open to the use of remedies other than monetary redress, concerns were raised about practicability of enforcing awards granting such non-pecuniary remedies. As a solution, the Chairman, Mr Broches, proposed that only monetary awards would be enforceable under the Convention: although tribunals would still retain the power to order state parties to perform or refrain from certain actions, all that could be enforced would be the obligation to pay damages if the state did not comply with the award. The restriction of the award's enforceability to its pecuniary obligations does not, however, detract from the *res judicata* effect of the entire award and from the obligation of the relevant state parties under Article 53 to comply with the award.[86]

Presently, all arbitral awards rendered pursuant to the ICSID Convention are enforceable within the territories of the signatory states. In practice, however, the enforcement of damages awards can be more feasible because, unlike declaratory relief or specific performance, such awards can be executed even against the respondent state's will.[87] By contrast, the enforcement of an order of declaratory relief or specific performance would necessitate a further action on the part of the respondent state. Similarly, while the enforceability of non-ICSID awards granting non-pecuniary remedies is not expressly precluded by the New York Convention, a claimant-investor might face the absence of effective mechanisms to enforce an order of specific performance against the host state.[88]

Although not as effectively enforceable as damages awards, non-pecuniary remedies are available to claimant-investors, and investment arbitration tribunals are not precluded from granting specific performance

[84] Bonnitcha, *Substantive Protection*, 60.

[85] Christoph Schreuer, 'Non-pecuniary Remedies in ICSID Arbitration' (2004) 20 *Arbitration International* 325.

[86] ibid 325–26.

[87] See also van Aaken, 'Primary and Secondary Remedies', 734.

[88] Bonnitcha, *Substantive Protection*, 60.

in an effort to hold governments to their good governance commitments under investment treaties. Insofar as its capacity to induce governments into compliance with substantive prescriptions of investment treaty law is concerned, non-pecuniary relief appears to be a functionally more suitable alternative to the remedy of damages. The problem with limited enforceability of non-pecuniary remedies could arguably be resolved through the use of a multi-tiered redress. For instance, in a non-ICSID context, a tribunal in *Texaco v Libya* found that *restitutio in integrum* was the most suitable remedy for Libya's breach of its contractual undertakings with Texaco. The tribunal ordered the Libyan government to give full effect to the contracts concluded with the investor. That such remedy could be impossible and impracticable did not sway the tribunal's decision. It held that while the order of specific performance was the principal remedy, 'any possible award of damages should necessarily be subsidiary to the principal remedy of performance itself.'[89] The tribunal alluded to the fact that damages could be awarded in conjunction with specific performance. In ICSID jurisprudence, the most pertinent example of a two-tier remedy can be found in *Goetz v Burundi*.[90] The dispute concerned a withdrawal by the host government of a free zone certificate under which the claimant investor was entitled to tax and customs duty exemptions. After having established that the host government had acted in violation of its treaty commitments, the tribunal provided the respondent state with two options: the state was ordered to re-issue the certificate within the prescribed time period and, in case of a failure to comply with this order, to pay damages to the claimant-investor.[91] Here, damages were ordered only as a conditional remedy to be triggered by the respondent state failing to bring its measures in conformity with investment treaty standards.

The use of a multi-tiered or two-stage remedial process would supply the currently missing enforcement safeguards for arbitral awards of declaratory relief and specific performance. Multi-tiered remedies will also be more effective in signalling the importance of host state compliance with substantive commitments enshrined in investment treaty instruments, and prevent states from opting out of compliance where such conduct appears to be cost-efficient or otherwise expedient. Some investment treaties expressly allow one or more forms of relief to be sought and granted. For instance, Article 18 of the 2010 Austria-Kazakhstan BIT stipulates that

> Arbitration awards … may provide the following forms of relief: (a) a declaration that the Party has failed to comply with its obligations under this Agreement; (b) pecuniary compensation, which shall include interest from the

[89] *Texaco Overseas Petroleum Co and California Asiatic Oil Co v Government of the Libyan Arab Republic*, Award on the Merits, 19 January 1977, 53 ILR 389, 508.

[90] *Goetz v Burundi* (2000) 15 ICSID Review 457 (case report available at www.transnational-dispute-management.com/downloads/1859_case_report_antoine_goetz_v_burundi.pdf).

[91] ibid paras 135–37.

> time the loss or damage was incurred until time of payment; (c) restitution in kind in appropriate cases, provided that the Party may pay pecuniary compensation in lieu thereof where restitution is not practicable; and (d) with the agreement of the parties to the dispute, any other form of relief.

Although non-pecuniary remedies—used in their own right or in conjunction with damages—appear to be better suited for the task of facilitating state compliance with good governance prescriptions of international investment law, concerns about their use in investor-state arbitration go beyond the enforceability issues. Some fear that 'ordering a state to revoke a measure or ordering specific performance would infringe more on national sovereignty than a pecuniary award.'[92] For instance, in *Enron v Argentina*, the respondent contested the tribunal's jurisdiction to grant an injunction ordering the government to refrain from collecting taxes. The government contended that 'an ICSID tribunal cannot impede an expropriation that falls exclusively within the ambit of state sovereignty; that tribunal could only establish whether there has been an expropriation, its legality or illegality and the corresponding compensation.'[93] As van Aaken points out, states may also be reluctant to grant tribunals wide powers to use non-pecuniary relief as the latter might entail domestic political and constitutional challenges.[94] Holding host states to non-pecuniary obligations might pose legitimacy problems as national parliaments could be ordered (by unelected and unaccountable arbitral tribunals) to revoke or amend legislative acts produced through a democratic process.[95] It is perhaps for these reasons that non-pecuniary relief is not as widely used as damages. Besides, although the ICSID Convention permits the recourse to non-pecuniary redress, some investment treaties expressly restrict the available remedies to monetary redress. To name one such instance, Article 1135 of the NAFTA provides that a tribunal may award only monetary damages or the restitution of property.[96]

If investment treaty law was more receptive to the use of non-pecuniary remedies focusing on compliance rather than enabling host states to 'breach and pay', would that enhance the investment treaty regime's capacity to foster greater state compliance with good governance prescriptions of investment treaty law? As Schreuer observed, '[t]he fact that ICSID tribunals have granted pecuniary relief rather than ordered specific performance is not based on any fundamental restriction on their power to

[92] van Aaken, 'Primary and Secondary Remedies', 747.

[93] *Enron Corpn and Ponderosa Assets LP v Argentina*, Decision on Jurisdiction, 14 January 2004, 11 ICSID Reports 295, para 76.

[94] van Aaken, 'Primary and Secondary Remedies', 747.

[95] ibid.

[96] Art 26(8) of the Energy Charter Treaty also expressly provides the respondent state with the option of paying monetary damages in lieu of any other remedy granted. See also Japan-Peru BIT 2008, Art 18(19).

do so. Investors almost always seem to frame their claims in terms of monetary damages.'[97] In most investor-state disputes, the choice of remedy is dictated by a claimant-investor who may prefer to request non-pecuniary relief only in those situations where compliance by the state with investment treaty rules is in the investor's best economic interests, not because the investor is concerned about the long-term positive consequences of non-pecuniary remedies on host state behaviour and its compliance with good governance standards.

Such was the case in *Arif v Moldova*, where a dispute arose from the cancellation of a tender granting the investor permission to operate duty free concessions. After having found that the government's reversal of the tender to be in breach of investment treaty standards, the tribunal ordered the host government 'to make proposals to the investor for the restitution of its store, and proposals as to appropriate guarantees for a new lease.[98] The *Arif* award provides an apt illustration of how investors can at times find the non-pecuniary remedies more desirable than monetary relief. Yet the case also amply demonstrates that the investor had no interest in Moldova's efforts to adhere to good governance standards.[99] To date, most investor-claimants have shown little interest in demanding that a host state abides by good governance obligations under investment treaties. Arbitral tribunals may in some cases enjoy a certain degree of discretion in choosing the appropriate remedy; however, the ultimate choice will usually be determined by their mandate, which is to resolve the dispute as opposed to promoting good governance in host states. Although the ICSID Convention does not expressly preclude tribunals from granting non-pecuniary remedies, Article 48(3) requires that the award shall deal with every question submitted to the tribunal. The award of a two-state remedy is therefore possible only if a claimant-investor requests it: 'under the ICSID Convention a tribunal would exceed its powers in deciding on a non-requested remedy and put the award in danger of annulment.'[100] As it stands, the investor-state dispute settlement system continues to prioritise indemnification of investors over facilitating host state compliance with substantive investment treaty norms.

V. CONCLUSION

The overarching aim of this chapter was to highlight the inherent limitations in the design of investment treaty remedies as instruments through

[97] Schreuer, 'Non-pecuniary Remedies', 329.

[98] *Mr Franck Charles Arif v Republic of Moldova*, Award, 8 April 2013, ICSID Case No ARB/11/23, para 633.

[99] For a more detailed discussion, see Chapter 5, Section IIIBii.

[100] van Aaken, 'Primary and Secondary Remedies', 734.

which host states could be pressured to embrace good governance standards in their dealings with investors and beyond. The primacy of monetary remedies and the relatively limited space for non-pecuniary relief in investment treaty law points to the subordinate role that compliance plays in the hierarchy of the international investment regime's goals. Investment treaties and arbitration have traditionally been concerned with providing redress to disaffected investors, not with inducing host states to change the ways in which they govern. The very fact that the good governance narratives simultaneously claim 'incentivising' and 'deterrent' effect of investment treaty remedies on host state behaviour points to an inherent tension at the heart of such claims. Might investment treaty remedies incentivise host state breaches of treaty prescriptions of good governance and deter domestic governance reforms? In assuming a transformative impact of the monetary sanctions on host state conduct, the good governance narratives ignore the wealth of knowledge generated by law and development scholars, and in particular a growing consensus about the unsuitability of punitive financial mechanisms as a means of facilitating governance and rule of law reforms in developing states. As demonstrated by the experience of the World Bank, IMF and the EU in pushing for domestic legal and institutional reforms, the strategy of reinforcement by punishment may lead to expedited legislative changes but ultimately fails to ensure successful internalisation of such reforms and sustained compliance.

Investment treaty rules are also unlikely to foster host state compliance with good governance standards because they are designed as pricing mechanisms, as a licence to breach investment treaty norms as long as the host state pays the price—the damages award to a disgruntled investor. The scope for 'efficient breach' greatly undermines the feasibility investment treaty regime's good governance mission. So does the fact that investment arbitration tribunals are restricted in their ability to award remedies other than monetary relief. Although specific performance and injunctive relief are available, arbitral tribunals can resort to such remedies only if the investor specifically requests so. The capacity of investment treaty law to foster compliance with good governance standards is thus hampered by the institutional design of the investment dispute settlement mechanism and the key powers allocated to investors therein. Unless the existing desigh is radically transformed, investment treaty law is unlikely to be able pressure host states into ex ante compliance with good governance standards in their dealings with foreign investors, let alone compel them to embrace good governance more widely.

5

Investment Treaty Law and its Internal Capacity to Foster Good Governance in Host States

I. IS THE INVESTMENT TREATY REGIME COMPLIANT WITH GOOD GOVERNANCE STANDARDS?

AT THE CORE of the good governance narratives of international investment law lies the claim that, although legally enforceable only by foreign investors, strict investment protection standards create a 'spill over' effect that ultimately benefits national citizens and residents as the host country gradually develops better administrative practices to comply with international investment best practices.[1] The need to comply effectively with the rule of law and principles of due process imposed by investment treaties would arguably entail legal reforms and foster more legalistic and rule-oriented governance practices in host states.[2] While investment treaty law has been designed primarily to promote and protect foreign investment, domestic firms could arguably '[b]enefit from the halo effect provided by stronger constraints on arbitrary government action'.[3] Investment treaty law would signal to host state institutions and the national judiciaries 'what a proper, international and universal standard of governance is.'[4]

Yet does the investment treaty regime possess the necessary characteristics that would enable it to export the good governance standards into the domestic realm? If investment treaty law were to signal to host states what the universal standards of good governance are, it should be compliant with the good governance ideals in the first place. In more specific

[1] Roberto Echandi, 'What Do Developing Countries Expect from the International Investment Regime?' in Jose E Alvarez and Karl P Sauvant (eds), *The Evolving International Investment Regime: Expectations, Realities, Options* (Oxford, Oxford University Press, 2011) 13.

[2] ibid 14.

[3] World Bank, *World Development Report* (New York, Oxford University Press, 2005) 179.

[4] Thomas W Walde, 'The "Umbrella Clause" in Investment Arbitration. A Comment on Original Intentions and Recent Cases' (2005) 6 *Journal of World Investment and Trade* 183, 188.

terms, if holding the host states to stringent standards of conduct, such as the duty to maintain transparency, stability, consistency and predictability, were to induce host states to embrace such standards in the domestic sphere, the international investment regime should also be transparent, stable, consistent and predictable. It has been noted earlier that investment arbitration awards holding host states liable for a failure to comply with good governance standards were seen by many as a step too far: is it fair and just to hold developing states responsible for a failure to conform to good governance standards that even developed states might frequently fail to achieve?[5] A similar argument could be advanced with respect to the investment treaty regime's role in fostering good governance in host states: is it legitimate, fair, and effective to impose monetary sanctions on host states for lack of transparency, predictability, and consistency where both substantive investment treaty rules and investment dispute settlement mechanisms frequently fail to achieve the same?

II. LEGITIMACY AND 'COMPLIANCE PULL': (INSUFFICIENT) TRANSPARENCY AND COHERENCE OF INVESTMENT TREATY RULES AND ARBITRAL JURISPRUDENCE

An inquiry into the endogenous characteristics which determine the capacity of international investment law to bring about a change in domestic governance may offer new and useful insights for the presently largely unexplored question of state compliance with investment treaty norms. In the specific context of this study, one can distinguish three layers of compliance: pre-dispute compliance with good governance standards enshrined in investment treaty rules, post-dispute compliance with concrete arbitral prescriptions, and post-dispute adjustment of domestic governance norms and practices.[6] The rate of compliance with the concrete arbitral prescriptions stage may well be high, which is not surprising given the strength of the enforcement mechanism undergirding the investment treaty regime. In an effort to enforce arbitral awards, investors can go as far as resorting to judicial proceedings and discovery subpoenas seeking information about the respondent host state's banking assets and transactions abroad.[7] Compliance with arbitral awards may be involuntary and is frequently carried out against the respondent state's

[5] See Chapter 2, Section IICi.

[6] See further Mavluda Sattorova, 'Investment Treaties and Good Governance: Norm and Institutional Design, Internalisation and Domestic Rule-making' in August Reinisch, Mary E Footer and Christina Binder (eds) *International Law and …* (Oxford, Hart Publishing, 2016) 131.

[7] See *Republic of Argentina v NML Capital* 134 S Ct 2250 (2014).

will. Moreover, arbitral awards rarely if ever prescribe concrete changes in governance practices. Given these characteristics of the investment treaty regime, can it foster ex ante and ex post compliance by host states with investment treaty obligations which explicitly or implicitly require them to maintain good governance standards in daily practices of domestic bureaucratic and legal institutions?

Investment treaty law's capacity to foster state compliance with good governance prescriptions can be analysed through the lens of legitimacy. Legitimacy, as Thomas M Franck famously said, exerts a 'compliance pull'.[8] Many schools of thought seem to concur in viewing legitimacy as an important factor in generating state compliance with international law. Liberal institutionalist theory, for instance, admits that 'rules that are determinate and coherent—important components of legitimacy—are associated with greater compliance than those that are not.'[9] Legitimacy is also at the heart of the management theory of compliance by Chayes and Chayes, who argued that, among other causes, non-compliance is precipitated by 'ambiguity and indeterminacy of treaty language'.[10] The centrality of legitimacy in inducing state compliance with international norms is also a key feature of Harold Koh's theory of transnational legal process.[11] Just like the fairness framework of Thomas Franck and the management theory of Chayes and Chayes, the transnational legal process theory argues that the secret to better enforcement of international law is not coerced compliance, but voluntary obedience.[12] As further elaborated by Shaffer,

> Where the transnational legal norms are relatively clear, coherent, and accepted in practice, the transnational legal order is more salient and may be viewed in systematic terms. Where they are less so, the transnational legal order is more contingent and fragile, and thus, less likely to be effective in producing domestic legal and institutional change.[13]

Most of the normative theories of compliance tend to concur that legitimacy of an international norm hinges on three primary factors: (1) determinacy—'the ability of the text to convey a clear message, to appear transparent in the sense that one can see through the language

[8] See Thomas M Franck, 'Legitimacy in the International System' (1988) 82 *AJIL* 705.

[9] Robert Keohane, *Power and Governance in a Partially Globalized World* (London, Routledge, 2002) 120.

[10] Abram Chayes and Antonia Handler Chayes, *The New Sovereignty: Compliance with International Regulatory Agreements* (Cambridge MA, Harvard University Press, 1995) 10.

[11] Harold Hongju Koh, 'Why Do Nations Obey International Law' (1977) 106 *Yale Law Journal* 2599.

[12] ibid 2645.

[13] Gregory Shaffer, 'Transnational Legal Process and State Change' (2012) 37 *Law and Social Inquiry* 229, 236.

to the meaning';[14] (2) coherence—the rule must treat like cases alike and relate 'in a principled fashion to other rules of the same system';[15] and (3) procedural fairness—the rule must emanate from a fair and accepted procedure[16] and be 'closely connected to the secondary rules of process used to interpret and apply rules of international obligation.'[17] These criteria are aspirational—no existing legal system admittedly can meet all of them.[18] As put by Franck, legitimacy is 'a matter of degree.'[19]

Does international investment law possess the necessary characteristics to 'weigh the decision processes of states in the direction of compliance'[20]—to pull them towards embracing rule of law and good governance values? Are investment treaty provisions perceived to be legitimate enough to generate 'a compliance pull'? Analysis of investment treaty practice, investment arbitration jurisprudence as well as insights from the empirical case studies all suggest that international investment law, as it presently stands, lacks some of the vital characteristics necessary for the fulfilment of its promise to transform domestic governance in host states. Despite the recent reforms, the regime continues to fall short of transparency, coherence, and fairness.

A. International Investment Law and its Lack of Transparency

Whilst the advocates of investment treaty law stress the importance of transparency as an enabling factor in creating an investment-friendly regulatory environment in developing states, the role of regime transparency in facilitating host state compliance with investment treaty norms has received limited attention. Political science scholarship on state compliance with international law has long emphasised the prominence of transparency in facilitating greater adherence with treaty prescriptions. The notable example is the theory of managed compliance developed by Chayes and Chayes, which argues that transparency—understood as the availability of and access to information—'sets up a powerful dynamic for compliance with treaties' by facilitating coordination, providing state parties with reassurance, and by exercising deterrence against actors

[14] Franck, 'Legitimacy', 713.

[15] ibid 741.

[16] Chayes and Chayes, *New Sovereignty*, 127.

[17] Oona A Hathaway, 'Do Human Rights Treaties Make a Difference?' (2002) 111 *Yale Law Journal* 1935, 1959; Franck, 'Legitimacy', 41–46.

[18] Chayes and Chayes, *New Sovereignty*, 127.

[19] ibid.

[20] Thomas M Franck, *The Power of Legitimacy among Nations* (Oxford, Oxford University Press, 1990) 41.

contemplating non-compliance.[21] Procedural transparency—or the lack of it—is another angle from which the shortcomings of the good governance narratives of international investment law can be exposed and analysed. While investment treaty law requires that host states maintain transparency in their dealings with foreign investors, does it manifest an internal commitment to transparency in its own processes and procedures? From the early days of investment arbitration secrecy and confidentiality of arbitral proceedings have met with considerable criticism. Reflecting on the investor-state arbitration mechanism under the North American Free Trade Agreement (NAFTA), an article published by the New York Times in 2001 captured the growing concerns over the lack of transparency underpinning the operation of investment arbitration tribunals:

> Their meetings are secret. Their members are generally unknown. The decisions they reach need not be fully disclosed. Yet the way a group of international tribunals handles disputes between investors and foreign governments can lead to national laws being revoked and environmental regulations changed. And it is all in the name of protecting foreign investors under NAFTA.[22]

Even the staunch supporters of investment arbitration would not deny the fact that a strong emphasis on privacy and confidentiality has long been the hallmark of investor-state dispute settlement. Rules governing investor-state arbitration under the auspices of such institutions as the International Chamber of Commerce (ICC), the London Court of International Arbitration (LCIA), and the Stockholm Chamber of Commerce (SCC), as well as the UNCITRAL rules on ad hoc arbitration, were all designed for the resolution of commercial disputes and have traditionally favoured secrecy over transparency. Such in-house arbitration rules do not require cases to be registered, foreclose the participation of non-parties in the proceedings, and preclude the publication of the awards without the parties' consent.[23] Likewise, despite being considered as more transparent compared with other arbitration regimes, the ICSID arbitration rules too have long favoured the confidentiality and privacy of proceedings, particularly with regard to the publication of awards and allowing third party participation.[24]

Unsurprisingly, while conceived to facilitate speedy and efficient dispute settlement, the safeguards of confidentiality and privacy have been

[21] Chayes and Chayes, *New Sovereignty*, 136.

[22] Antony Depalma, 'Nafta's Powerful Little Secret; Obscure Tribunals Settle Disputes, but go too far' *New York Times* (New York, 11 March 2001).

[23] Alessandra Asteriti and Christian J Tams, 'Transparency and Representation of the Public Interest in Investment Treaty Arbitration' in Stephan W Schill (ed), *International Investment Law and Comparative Public Law* (Oxford, Oxford University Press, 2010) 790.

[24] Art 48(5) of the ICSID Convention precludes the Centre from 'publish[ing] the award without the consent of the parties'.

perceived by critics of the regime as something undermining the legitimacy of proceedings in investor-state arbitration.[25] One widely shared criticism of investment arbitration is that what may have been appropriate in the context of purely commercial dispute settlement becomes misplaced and illegitimate in arbitration involving a government of a sovereign state. Investment disputes may frequently be concerned with governmental regulations in the pursuit of various public policy objectives, such as the protection of environment and public health. Crucially, investment arbitration awards often entail significant financial consequences for the treasuries of respondent host states. These unique features of investment arbitration cast serious doubts over the applicability of norms and values governing commercial arbitration.[26]

It must be acknowledged that, in response to the growing concerns about the lack of transparency over the last two decades, there has been a burgeoning shift towards incorporating provisions to promote transparency and public participation in investment treaties and in rules governing investment arbitration. Enhancing transparency of investment arbitration—and of investment treaty law in general—has been considered as 'perhaps the single most important avenue for bringing the system more into line with principles of democratic governance under the rule of law'[27] and as a means of promoting good governance in host states.[28] To mention some developments, NAFTA parties have opened investment proceedings to a wider public. Article 1137(4) of NAFTA enables state parties to publish arbitral awards. The NAFTA Free Trade Commission has also recommended a standardised registration of claims.[29] In a similar vein, the 2006 revision of the ICSID Arbitration Rules features Article 37(2), which now confirms the possibility of submissions from non-disputing parties and limits the discretion of arbitral panels in determining the admissibility of the latter. ICSID Rule 37(2) has been praised as a significant step as it allows the tribunal to receive amicus briefs even without the consent of the parties.[30] An analogous provision is enshrined in the Free Trade Commission's Statement on Non-Disputing Party Participation.[31]

[25] Asteriti and Tams, 'Transparency', 792.

[26] See ibid.

[27] Stephan W Schill 'Editorial: Five Times Transparency in International Investment Law' (2014) 15 *Journal of World Investment and Trade* 363, 364.

[28] In addressing the UN General Assembly, Chairman of UNICTRAL Michael Scholl noted that '[t]ransparency lies at the very foundation of good governance'. See '*Newly Adopted Rules Play Fundamental Role in Good Governance, United Nations International Trade Law Body Tells Sixth Committee*', GA/L/3459, 14 October 2013.

[29] NAFTA Free Trade Commission, Statement on Notices of Intent to Submit a Claim to Arbitration, 7 October 2003.

[30] Kate Miles, *The Origins of International Investment Law: Empire, Environment and the Safeguarding of Capital* (Cambridge, Cambridge University Press, 2013) 374. Tribunals are still required to consult with the parties, but where certain preconditions are met the parties' wishes can be overridden.

[31] Statement on Non-Disputing Party Participation, 7 October 2003, para A1.

The burgeoning shift towards greater transparency can also be discerned in investment treaty practice of individual states. All of the investment treaties and investment chapters negotiated by the United States since 2002 contain a number of comprehensive provisions on public access to hearings and documents.[32] Similar changes have been embraced in Canadian investment treaty practice (with exception of a treaty concluded with China).[33] The North-American treaty innovations have been replicated outside the region, most notably in the 2007 Investment Agreement for the Common Market for Eastern and Southern Africa (COMESA) Common Investment Area, which features far-reaching provisions on all aspects of transparency, including third-party participation and publication of documents relating to arbitration.[34]

The move towards greater transparency, however, has been far from uniform, with the bulk of existing investment treaties making no or limited provisions on public access. For instance, the 2009 ASEAN Comprehensive Investment Agreement does not contain provisions on non-disputing party participation.[35] Similarly, there are no transparency provisions in investment agreements signed between ASEAN and Korea and China respectively.[36] The Chinese investment treaty practice has also been inconsistent: transparency provisions are absent from its treaties with Korea and Japan, whereas the 2012 treaty between China and Canada leaves the publication of pleadings and documents, as well as open hearings, to the discretion of the disputing states.[37]

At a multilateral level, a significant breakthrough has been made with the adoption of the United Nations Commission on International Trade Law (UNCITRAL) Rules on Transparency in Treaty-based Investor-State Arbitration and the subsequent opening for signature of the Mauritius Convention on Transparency. While representing a landmark shift towards enhancing the compliance of investment arbitration with good governance ideals, both the Transparency Rules and Transparency Convention have been criticised for leaving a number of loopholes enabling states and investors to continue to avoid disclosure.[38] Elsewhere, demands for greater transparency and inclusiveness have met with varying and at times limited degrees of success, as most aptly exemplified by reluctance

[32] Jansen N Calamita, 'Dispute Settlement Transparency in Europe's Evolving Investment Treaty Policy: Adopting the UNCITRAL Transparency Rules Approach' (2014) 15 *Journal of World Investment & Trade* 645, 656.

[33] ibid 657.

[34] ibid 660.

[35] ibid 661.

[36] ibid.

[37] ibid 664.

[38] Lise Johnson, 'The Transparency Rules and Transparency Convention: A good Start and Model for Broader Reform in Investor-State Arbitration' *Columbia FDI Perspectives* No 126, 21 July 2014.

of the SCC, the ICC, and the LCIA to embrace the reform.[39] Unsurprisingly, critics find this resistance by arbitral institutions ironic, given that investors frequently claim that investment treaties require state parties to adhere to the principles of openness and transparency.[40] On the whole, the global investment treaty regime and its dispute settlement mechanism continues to fall below the benchmarks of good governance which host states are expected to comply with in their dealings with foreign investors.

Significantly, the very process of reforming investment arbitration rules has exposed a considerable degree of resistance by developed states against a move towards greater transparency. Whilst supporting the view that investors should be able to claim damages for a lack of transparency in laws and regulatory practices of developing states, some traditional capital-exporting countries appear to have shown little enthusiasm for endorsing such rules in treaties that could be invoked against them. For instance, it has transpired that in the course of the debates over UNCITRAL proposals in 2010, not a single EU member state expressed support for transparency. Rather, in their formal submissions to UNCITRAL, 'the EU member states voiced considerable scepticism about the need for transparency in investor-state arbitration or the desirability of making transparency a default norm in investor-state cases in the absence of specific consent from the disputing parties.'[41] The 'great transparency debate' has thus revealed the lack of reciprocity underpinning the investment treaty regime: although investment treaty rules are deemed to be universally reciprocal in subjecting host governments, both in developed and developing states, to the exacting standards of good governance, the governments of developed states continue to demonstrate discomfort at the prospect of being bound by the same transparency norms that the investment arbitration regime seeks to impose on developing states.

Whereas the principal aim of procedural transparency is to enhance the legitimacy of international investment law, other aspects of transparency—such as reporting and data collection—have also been identified as significant factors in facilitating state compliance with international norms. Drawing on the analysis of international treaty regimes such as that of the International Labour Organization and the Montreal

[39] Nathalie Bernasconi-Osterwalder and Diana Rosert, 'Investment Treaty Arbitration: Opportunities to Reform Arbitral Rules and Processes', 11 (International Institute for Sustainable Development, January 2014).

[40] See eg David Schneiderman, *Resisting Economic Globalization: Critical Theory and International Investment Law* (Basingstoke, Palgrave Macmillan, 2013) 99–100.

[41] Calamita, 'Dispute Settlement Transparency', 672, referring to the United Nations Commission on International Trade Law, Working Group II, Settlement of commercial disputes: Transparency in treaty-based investor-State arbitration—Compilation of comments by Governments, 53rd session, 4–8 October 2010, A/CN.9/WG/WP.159/Add.2.

Protocol, Chayes and Chayes argued that reporting and data collection ought to be regarded as crucial prerequisites in generating information about treaty compliance and regime efficacy and enabling domestic actors to coordinate their independent activities in translating treaty norms into domestic laws and policies.[42] Importantly, it is through reporting procedures that the national bureaucracies become first engaged by the treaty regime: 'It is there that domestic officialdom begins to translate the treaty law into the daily work of administration and to define the level of commitment to it.'[43] As the experience of other international treaty regimes shows, reporting and data collection serve as a means of familiariasation with and internalisation of investment treaty laws by domestic actors.[44] However, at present the international investment regime does not provide effective institutional mechanisms for reporting and data collection that could facilitate such familiarisation with and internalisation of good governance prescriptions by national bureaucracies.

B. Lack of Coherence and Certainty in Investment Arbitration Jurisprudence

Most of the existing justifications for the creation of the investment treaty regime are explicitly or implicitly premised on the need to address the inadequacy of national remedies and international diplomatic solutions in resolving conflicts between foreign investors and host governments. National courts—particularly in developing states—are deemed too biased, corrupt, lacking expertise and controlled by the executive and therefore unable to provide fair, efficient and predictable outcomes.[45] Similarly, diplomatic protection is considered to be too politicised and offer only 'very uncertain and often ephemeral remedy'.[46] By contrast, international investment law arguably lays down clear and predictable rules to govern relations between investors and host states, thus benefiting not only foreign investors but also the host state population.[47] International investment law can purportedly compel host states to reform their

[42] Chayes and Chayes, *New Sovereignty*, 136.

[43] ibid.

[44] ibid 155–60.

[45] Rudolf Dolzer and Christoph Schreuer, *Principles of International Investment Law* (Oxford, Oxford University Press, 2008) 214–15.

[46] See Jeswald W Salacuse, *The Law of Investment Treaties* (Oxford, Oxford University Press, 2010) 53; A Broches, 'The Convention on the Settlement of Investment Disputes between States and Nationals of Other States' (1972) 136 *(II) Recueil Des Cours* 337.

[47] 'The expected key function of IIAs is to contribute to predictability, stability and transparency in investment relations': UNCTAD, World Investment Report 2015: Reforming International Investment Governance, 125.

governance practices by providing them with normative benchmarks and holding them responsible for a failure to act in a transparent, clear and consistent manner. Yet it is ironic that both investment treaties and investor-state arbitration have been strongly criticised for lack of clarity and consistency. The rapid proliferation of investment disputes over the last three decades has exposed numerous shortcomings both in the design of investment treaty standards and their interpretation in investment arbitration. Despite the claim that international investment law is evolving into a coherent and homogenous system of norms,[48] it is common knowledge that investment treaty obligations are vague and lead to inconsistent interpretations by arbitral tribunals.[49] In the words of van Harten,

> [i]nvestment treaties generally do not establish coherent, non-contradictory rules that are capable of being known and thus followed on a reasonably reliable basis, but rather a set of broadly-framed ideals that have in turn been assigned different and at times conflicting meanings when interpreted by arbitrators.[50]

These hallmarks of investment treaty law have generated profound concerns about a lack of predictability and ensuing uncertainty[51] as to the content of standards which host states are expected to maintain.

The lack of coherence is most aptly illustrated by arbitral practice on the fair and equitable treatment standard. It was in the course of establishing the substantive meaning and scope of the fair and equitable treatment standard that investment tribunals construed the notions of fairness and equity to mean a host state's obligation to provide a stable, transparent and consistent legal environment. Yet the very jurisprudence of investment tribunals on fair and equitable treatment as well as the formulation of the standard in investment treaty texts has attracted scathing criticism for lack of clarity, consistency, and predictability. As discussed in Chapter 2, due to its open-ended nature and lack of fixed content[52] arbitral interpretations of the fair and equitable treatment standard display little uniformity. A number of tribunals have construed fair and equitable treatment as a

[48] See Stephan W Schill, *The Multilateralization of International Investment Law* (Cambridge, Cambridge University Press, 2009).

[49] See Joachim Karl, 'International Investment Arbitration: A Threat to State Sovereignty' in Wenhua Shan, Penelope Simons and Dalvinder Singh (eds), *Redefining Sovereignty in International Economic Law* (Oxford, Hart Publishing, 2008) 237 (noting that 'a lack of consistency could make the outcome of arbitration proceedings unpredictable and thereby ultimately undermine the legitimacy of investor-state dispute settlement procedures'); see further Susan Franck, 'The Legitimacy Crisis in Investment Treaty Arbitration: Privatising Public International Law Through Inconsistent Decisions' (2005) 73 *Fordham Law Review* 1521.

[50] Gus Van Harten, 'Investment Treaty Arbitration, Procedural Fairness, and the Rule of Law' in Stephan W Schill, *International Investment Law and Comparative Public Law* (Oxford, Oxford University Press, 2010) 629.

[51] See David Schneiderman, 'Investment Rules and the New Constitutionalism' (2000) 25 *Law and Social Inquiry* 757, 775.

[52] Iona Tudor, *The Fair and Equitable Treatment in the International Law of Foreign Investment* (Oxford, Oxford University Press, 2008) 131.

standard autonomous from the customary international minimum, thus protecting investors against state conduct that displays 'a relatively lower degree of inappropriateness',[53] such as in cases where a legal environment in the host state lacked transparency, consistency and predictability. Such all-encompassing and far-reaching interpretation enables investors to challenge any type of governmental conduct that they deem unfair.[54] In some instances, the tribunal's failure to justify this expansive interpretation of investment treaty standards resulted in judicial review and setting aside of the relevant awards.[55] Other tribunals interpreted the fair and equitable treatment standard as an expression of the customary international law, and distanced themselves from a very broad definition given to the standard in previous arbitral cases.[56] The wording of the fair and equitable treatment standard in investment treaty instruments also significantly varies, opening them up to differing interpretations by investment tribunals.[57]

As a recent UNCTAD report has observed, the ensuing uncertainty within international investment law presents considerable challenges to host states and their agencies that interact with investors.[58] It has been pointed out that

> if the State and its subnational entities do not know in advance what type of conduct may be considered a breach of a treaty, then it cannot organise its regulatory and administrative decision-making processes and delegation in a way that ensures that its conduct will not incur liability under the [fair and equitable treatment] standard.[59]

The lack of clarity, consistency and predictability of investment treaty law is in fact

> antithetical to several of [rule of law] requirements: that decisions not be made in an arbitrary or ad-hoc manner, that rules be understandable, and that rules (in this case as interpreted by tribunals) not change so frequently as to make it difficult to plan behaviour around them.[60]

[53] *Saluka Investments BV v Czech Republic*, Partial Award, 17 March 2006 (PCA—UNCITRAL) para 293.

[54] UNCTAD, 'Reforming International Investment Governance', 137.

[55] *United Mexican States v Metalclad Corpn* [2001] 89 BCLR 3d 359, para 58.

[56] See eg *El Paso Energy International Company v Argentina*, Award, 31 October 2011, ICSID Case No ARB/03/15, paras 342–43; see also *MTD Equity v Chile* (Decision on Annulment, 21 March 2007) paras 66–67; *Cargill Inc v Mexico*, Award, 18 September 2009, ICSID Case No ARB(AF)/05/02, para 294; *Feldman v Mexico*, Award, 16 December 2002, (2003) 18 ICSID Review 488, para 133.

[57] 'Fair and Equitable Treatment: A Sequel', UNCTAD Series on Issues in International Investment Agreements II (New York and Geneva, United Nations, 2012) 17.

[58] ibid 12.

[59] ibid.

[60] Benjamin K Guthrie, 'Beyond Investment Protection: An Examination of the Potential Influence of Investment Treaties on Domestic Rule of Law' (2012–2013) 45 *New York University Journal of International Law and Politics* 1151, 1196.

Unless investment treaty law ensures the clarity and internal coherence of its message—unless host states know what standards they will be held to, investment treaty prescriptions of good governance cannot be effectively internalised and transposed into the daily practices of national institutions.

III. INTERNATIONALISATION OF INVESTMENT LAW AND ITS (DISEMPOWERING) EFFECTS ON GOVERNANCE IN HOST STATES

A. Investment Arbitration as a Substitute for National Institutions: Suppressing Domestic Demand for Reforms?

Can the institution of investor-state arbitration, with its predominantly externalised, decentralised and frequently ad hoc nature, provide the necessary bedrock of support to facilitate effective and consistent embedding of good governance and rule of law values in the legal and bureaucratic practices of host states? The interpretation of investment treaties as instruments to foster good governance in host states is confounded by the historical emphasis the investment treaty regime's forefathers and the founders of the ICSID Convention placed on transferring the resolution of investment disputes from the (weak, biased and incompetent) domestic institutions to (competent, effective and independent) international panels. International investment law and its enforcement mechanism were conceived as a substitute for the lacking domestic legal institutions of host states.[61] Recent debates over the local remedies exhaustion and the role of domestic courts in adjudicating investment disputes in Australia and the EU have made it clear that investment treaty law and in particular the institution of investor-state arbitration were created and continue to function as an alternative to domestic judicial bodies and not as a means of bringing about change on a national level in developing states.[62] The primary concern for advocates of the international investment regime is not

[61] Commentary on the ICSID Convention has almost invariably stressed its role in the depoliticisation of investor-State dispute settlement by offering moving matters from the control of domestic institutions to independent third-party panels. Most scholars are in agreement as to the intention behind the creation of international investment treaty law and its remedial mechanism, such intention being mostly to offer an alternative to domestic structures. See eg Christoph Schreurer, Loretta Malintoppi, August Reinisch and Anthony Sinclair, *The ICSID Convention: A Commentary*, 2nd edn (Cambridge, Cambridge University Press, 2009) 352; Campbell McLachlan, Laurence Shore and Matthew Weiniger, *International Investment Arbitration: Substantive Principles* (Oxford, Oxford University Press, 2007) 128.

[62] See Mavluda Sattorova, 'Return to the Local Remedies Rule in European BITs?: Power (Inequalities), Dispute Settlement, and Change in Investment Treaty Law' (2012) 39(2) *Legal Issues of Economic Integration* 223.

to improve governance in host states but rather to limit foreign investors' exposure to domestic legal structures and practices by offering investors the possibility of exiting the domestic legal regime and using international remedies.

The historical emphasis on the internationalisation of remedies for foreign investors, as opposed to promoting change at a national level, seems to invite a conclusion that the good governance objective was never in the minds of treaty drafters but has become a popular banner inasmuch as it offered an additional justification for the recent expansion of the investment treaty regime and its increasingly intrusive reach. Indeed, a historical analysis of the investment treaty regime exposes a noticeable circularity of the good governance argument: the weaknesses and shortcomings of domestic legal systems in developing states have been traditionally cited as a rationale for insulating foreign investors from domestic institutions and practices.[63] However, as this international mechanism came of age (and rather worryingly for some, demonstrated its growing reach), the separateness of the international and national domains is now being downplayed and emphasis is instead made on the spill-over effects of international investment protection norms on domestic institutions and practices. The language of insulating foreign investors from national realities is being replaced with the rhetoric that foregrounds investment treaties as instruments for transformation of governance at a national level.

It could, of course, be argued that, even though initially created as a substitute for lacking and ineffective domestic regimes and not intended as a catalyst of regulatory reform in host states, international investment law has subsequently developed into a mechanism that can foster positive transformations at a national level. In other words, the idea of fostering good governance and strengthening the rule of law in host states may not have been an original shared goal of investment treaty instruments but rather is an unintended (and desirable) side effect. As summarised by Schultz and Dupont, 'in substituting foul play in domestic litigation with hypothetically non-dysfunctional international adjudication, investment arbitration seeks to improve the regulatory quality of investment protection in the host state, bringing it to firmer adherence with the rule of law.'[64]

[63] Aron Broches, 'The Convention on the Settlement of Investment Disputes between States and Nationals of Other States' (1997) 136 *Recueil des Cours de l'Academie de Droit International* 337, 343; Salacuse, *The Law of Investment Treaties*, 358; Dolzer and Schreuer, *Principles*, 214–15.

[64] Thomas Schultz and Cédric Dupont, 'Investment Arbitration: Promoting the Rule of Law or Over-empowering Investors? A Quantitative Empirical Study' (2014) 25 *EJIL* 1147, 1161.

Yet questions have been raised whether by effectively insulating foreign investors from the shortcomings of domestic regimes and by replacing the latter with an arguably stronger and more effective international alternative, the investment treaty regime reduces the incentive for host states to carry out legal reforms and to improve domestic governance institutions and practices. By allowing foreign investors to escape the allegedly dysfunctional local institutions, investment treaties 'relegate locals—including domestic businesses, who may be the lifeblood of domestic investment—to the mercies of these inadequate institutions.'[65] Furthermore, owing to its substitution strategy, international investment law does not ameliorate but may in fact entrench weaknesses of domestic legal orders.[66] The availability of the investor-state dispute settlement regime at an international level, as Ginsburg has convincingly argued, makes it easier for host governments to attract international investment without having to improve domestic governance mechanisms and practices.[67]

The good governance narratives seem to assume that the availability of international alternatives to national institutions would spur some form of regulatory competition within host states whereby domestic courts, for instance, would be pushed to compete for the business of resolving commercial disputes and thus improve their quality.[68] The fallacy of this assumption lies in its untested premise that, along with other domestic institutions, local courts internalise the benefits of adjudication. In fact, the existence of international avenues of dispute resolution may diminish national judicial incentives to improve the quality of domestic adjudication by depriving key actors of a need to invest in such improvement.[69] 'Unless domestic judiciaries internalise the benefits of institutional quality, they will not be concerned with the loss of 'business' to international competitors such as arbitral bodies.'[70]

[65] Mark Halle and Luke Eric Petersen, 'Investment provisions in Free Trade Agreements and Investment Treaties: Opportunities and Threats for Developing Countries', Asia-Pacific Trade and Investment Initiative UNDP Regional Centre in Colombo December 2005, available at www.snap-undp.org/elibrary/Publications/InvestmentProvisions.pdf.

[66] See Tom Ginsburg, 'International Substitutes for Domestic Institutions: Bilateral Investment Treaties and Governance' (2005) 25 *International Review of Law and Economics* 107, 121.

[67] ibid. See also David Gaukrodger and Kathryn Gordon, 'Investor-state dispute settlement: A scoping paper for the investment policy community' (OECD Working Papers on International Investment, No 2012/3, OECD Investment Division), available at www.oecd.org/daf/investment/workingpapers, 14.

[68] Ginsburg, 'International Substitutes for Domestic Institutions', 119. Aranguri also produced regression analysis to conclude that signing an investment treaty has a little impact on the rule of law in signatory states and that a foreign investor's success in an investor-state disputed under the treaty is likely to have negative (albeit statistically insignificant) impact on the rule of law in the host state. Cesar Aranguri, 'The Effect of BITs on Regulatory Quality and the Rule of Law in Developing Countries', NYU Investment Law Forum, Spring 2011 (online).

[69] Ginsburg, 'International Substitutes for Domestic Institutions', 119.

[70] ibid 121.

Evidence from our empirical case studies tends to corroborate these arguments. In particular, the interviews among representatives of the national judiciary not only point to a pervasive lack of awareness about international investment arbitration but also reveal a prevailing tendency among the host states to treat investment protection in isolation from other matters falling within the purview of national courts. For instance, the interviews in Kazakhstan, Ukraine, and Uzbekistan suggest that in addition to guarantees of access to international investment tribunals, foreign investors are often granted various privileges at a national level, including the opportunity to resort to expedited dispute resolution through investment ombudsmen.[71] There is also evidence of informal privileges, such as in the cases where the governments instructed the courts to ensure that 'foreign investors are always treated well'.[72] Particularly instructive also are the recent efforts by the government of Kazakhstan to create a special economic and jurisdictional zone in Astana, where investment disputes would be adjudicated by special courts applying foreign law and equipped by foreign judges.[73] Rather than creating conditions to foster competition between national courts and international tribunals, the prioritisation of foreign investment protection by host states appears to result in the fragmentation of the national judicial and regulatory landscape and the emergence of legal enclaves with special decision-making bodies responsible for insulating foreign investors from the vicissitudes of dealing with national law and institutions.[74] Instead of encouraging a comprehensive reform of national governance institutions and practices, host governments appear to be driven towards the 'good governance for foreign investors' solutions.

The focus on privileges for foreign investors not only obviates the need for a broader reform or 'good governance for all', but also seems to further entrench the sense of scepticism and even cynicism over the role of international law and institutions in bringing about positive change at a national level. As our interviews in Kazakhstan, Ukraine and Uzbekistan reveal, host government officials are aware of the fact that preferential treatment of foreign investors creates incentives for local business ventures to use corporate structuring and 'disguise as foreign investors'.[75] As one interviewee put it, '[m]ost so-called foreign investment projects are actually business ventures owned by local oligarchs who take advantage of better protections international and national law offers

[71] See Chapter 3.
[72] Interview THS, also interview KHS.
[73] Interview MFA1.
[74] For more discussion, see Chapter 3.
[75] Interviews VHS, also MZ, MUL.

to foreign investors.'[76] Another interviewee, from a different country, made a similar point: '[l]ocal business leaders are increasingly turning to international law to ensure the safety of their investments. They are interested in structures that would insulate them from national law and national courts.'[77] Externalisation of foreign investment protection and the ensuing insulation of foreign investors from the realities of national governance institutions and practices deprives both host states and other national stakeholders of an incentive to push for comprehensive governance reforms. Instead of fostering a broader transformation of national attitudes towards the rule of law and good governance, international investment law is seen as an avenue favouring a certain privileged category of business actors.

These effects of externalisation of investment protection and dispute settlement once again demonstrate a failure of the good governance narratives of international investment law to acknowledge and engage with the existing knowledge on the role of political economy-based impediments in rule of law and governance reforms. There is consensus in the law and development literature that a long-term and a more sustainable alternative to external (and coercive) pressures is to create domestic demand for reform.[78] With its strategy of substituting national structures with international alternatives, international investment law suppresses rather than stimulates domestic demand for reform as host governments opt for over-protection of investors and local businesses opt to 'dress' as foreign investors to insulate themselves from (lacking) domestic governance institutions and practices. Alongside other international institutions and agencies forming part of a broader transnational network of influence,[79] international investment law contributes to entrenching a (misplaced) belief in superiority and effectiveness of external, foreign expertise and of external, foreign laws. Rather than building domestic capacity, the externalisation and internationalisation of foreign investment protection appears to have an emasculating effect on national actors and institutions, hampering the emergence of local, internally-felt demand for, and commitment to, good governance.

[76] Interview MUL, also echoed in interviews MUH, MUD, and VHS.

[77] Interview GM.

[78] John Hewko, 'Foreign Direct Investment: Does the Rule of Law Matter?' Carnegie Endowment for International Peace Rule of Law Series, Democracy and Rule of Law Project, Working Paper No 26, April 2012, 24; see also Michael J Trebilcock and Ronald J Daniels, *Rule of Law Reform and Development: Charting the Fragile Path of Progress* (Cheltenham, Edward Elgar, 2008) 354, and Frederick Rawski, 'Wold Bank Community-driven Development Programming in Indonesia and East Timor: Implications for the Study of Global Administrative Law' (2005) 37 *International Law and Politics* 919.

[79] See above Chapter 3.

B. Embedding Good Governance Prescriptions in National Law and Practices: What Role for National Courts?

Since one of the purposes of investor-state arbitration is 'to avoid the use of local courts',[80] national judicial bodies are not merely deprived of economic and political incentives to compete with international tribunals and enhance the quality of their governance outputs, but they are also effectively prevented from otherwise embedding international standards of good governance in the legal and bureaucratic practices of host states. Political science scholarship has long stressed the role of embeddedness in promoting compliance with international rules. As observed by proponents of liberal institutionalist theory, when international legal commitments are embedded in domestic legal systems, it is no longer necessary for governments and in particular national executives to take positive action to ensure enforcement of international judgments.[81] Rather, enforcement is expected to be attained through domestic courts and executives bodies 'who are responsive to judicial decisions.'[82] Hence, 'other things being equal, the more firmly embedded an international commitment is in domestic law, the more likely is compliance with judgements to enforce it.'[83]

Other theories of compliance, among them notably the theory of transnational legal process, have also stressed the importance of embedding and norm internalisation as a precondition of compliance. Koh has argued, for example, that 'self-enforcing patterns of compliance' are generated through internalisation of international norms in domestic structures through executive, legislative and judicial action. It is through repeated participation in the transnational legal process—the interaction between transnational legal actors and national epistemic communities—that states comply with international law. In Koh's view, '[t]rue compliance is not so much the result of externally imposed sanctions … as internally felt norms.'[84] Social science theories of governance also point in the direction of iterative interaction between external and internal actors; after all, governance is defined as 'the creation of a structure or an order which *cannot be externally imposed* but is the result of the interaction of a multiplicity of governing and each other influencing actors.'[85]

80 Christoph Schreuer, 'Calvo's Grandchildren: The Return of Local Remedies in Investment Arbitration' (2005) 4 *Law and Practice of International Courts and Tribunals* 1.

81 Robert O Keohane, Andrew Moravcsik, and Anne-Marie Slaughter, 'Legalized dispute resolution: interstate and transnational' (2000) 54 (3) *International Organization* 457, 476.

82 ibid 476.

83 ibid 478.

84 Harold Koh, 'How Is International Human Rights Law Enforced?' (1998) 74 *Indiana Law Journal* 1397, 1407; see also Hathaway, 'Do Human Rights Treaties Make a Difference', 1961.

85 Gerry Stoker, 'Governance as theory: five propositions' (1993) 50 (155) *International Social Science Journal* 17.

i. Waiver of Local Remedies and Lack of National Judicial Involvement in Investor-State Dispute Settlement

Does international investment law facilitate the iterative interaction between international institutions and domestic counterparts? Does it foster the translation of externally-imposed norms into internally-felt norms and practices of good governance? The recent trends in investment arbitration practice demonstrate the enduring emphasis on primacy of international, not national, remedies. Waiver of the local remedies exhaustion—a unique feature and cornerstone of the investment treaty regime—is a primary factor explaining the presently limited scope for national courts in embedding the good governance prescriptions. Historically, courts in developing states were deemed too biased, corrupt, lacking expertise and controlled by the executive to provide a fair and efficient forum for the resolution of disputes between investors and the host government. To address these concerns, the ICSID Convention established a framework whereby a foreign investor could exercise its right of direct access to independent third-party arbitration, such right possessing the status of an exclusive remedy in lieu of recourse to national courts. Although premised upon the idea of formal equality between contracting states, the waiver of local remedies in favour of third-party arbitration in the ICSID Convention was conceived as a means of mitigating disparities between the expectations of foreign investors investing in host states and the deficiency of judicial institutions and remedies that capital-importing states could offer. While the signatory states were free to retain the exhaustion of local remedies as a precondition for the investor's recourse to ICSID arbitration, only a few availed themselves of such an opportunity. Bilateral investment treaties have almost uniformly waived local remedies. With the exception of a few notable attempts to re-introduce local remedies through the backdoor,[86] investment tribunals have enforced what has become a customary waiver of local remedies, enabling investors to steer clear of national courts and to obtain redress and enforce their rights through investor-state arbitration. As a consequence of this transfer of adjudicatory powers to international tribunals, national courts are removed from 'the transnational iterative process'. Lack of vertical interaction between international tribunals and national courts prevents the latter from exercising an instrumental role in embedding good governance standards in domestic legal orders.[87]

[86] Such as through the so-called rule of judicial finality: see further *Loewen v United States*, Award, 26 June 2003 (2003) 42 ILM 811, paras 143–56.

[87] See Diane Desierto, 'ASEAN's Constitutionalization of International Law: Challenges to Evolution under the New ASEAN Charter' (2011) 49 *Columbia Journal Transnational Law* 268, 316, highlighting the importance of national judiciaries in norm embedding in the context of ASEAN.

It should be noted that, when granting investors access to international arbitration, many of the first generation investment treaties have envisaged other forms of participation by national courts in investor-state dispute resolution. For instance, some investment treaties require that domestic remedies be used (even if not exhausted) before investment arbitration can be instigated. A pertinent example is Article 10 of the Argentina-Germany BIT, which states that

> [a]t the request of one of the parties to the dispute if no decision on the merits of the claim has been rendered after the expiration of a period of eighteen months from the date on which the court proceedings referred to in para. 2 of this Article have been initiated, or if such decision has been rendered, but the dispute between the parties persists.

While the obvious aim of this requirement appears to be to enable national courts to redress any wrongdoing suffered by a foreign investor in a host state—and thus arguably to enable national courts to embed and enforce good governance standards in domestic legal settings—in practice the provision 'has been honoured mainly through its non-application.'[88] Two often-cited examples are *Maffezini v Spain*[89] and *Siemens v Argentina*,[90] where the claimant investors were allowed to rely on the most-favoured nation treatment clause to avoid the application of the requirement of prior recourse to national courts. Those supporting the primacy of investment arbitration over national adjudication argue that 'the requirement to attempt a settlement in the host State's domestic courts for a certain period of time looks like a half-hearted revival of the local remedies rule' and that 'it does not seem to serve any useful purpose.'[91] It must be conceded that the time periods most treaties provide for the use of domestic courts—the typical example being 18 months—are often not long enough to yield a meaningful outcome.[92] These arguments, however, only highlight the flaw in the good governance justifications of investment treaty law by yet again exposing the fact that investment treaty norms, as construed and applied by investment tribunals, are not concerned with the transformation of domestic governance but rather prioritise the protection of foreign investments by providing them with expedited means of dispute resolution *outside* the domestic legal systems.

Of recent arbitral cases, the reasoning adopted by the *Urbaser v Argentina*[93] merits attention as it highlights the inherent lack of concern

[88] Schreuer, 'Calvo's Grandchildren', 4.

[89] *Maffezini v Spain*, Decision on Jurisdiction, 25 January 2000, (2001) 40 ILM 1129, para 38.

[90] *Siemens AG v Argentina*, Decision on Jurisdiction, 3 August 2004, ICSID Case No ARB/02/8, para 82.

[91] Schreuer, 'Calvo's Grandchildren', 4.

[92] ibid.

[93] *Urbaser v Argentina*, Decision on Jurisdiction, 9 December 2012, ICSID Case No ARB/07/26.

for domestic governance reforms in host states and the current futility of investment treaty regime's good governance promise. To justify its failure to comply with the 18-month rule prior to initiating investment arbitration, the investor invoked the MFN clause and contended that the latter could be used to import more favourable procedural provisions from other treaties. The investor did instigate domestic judicial proceedings but initiated international arbitration before the expiry of the prescribed 18-month period (its domestic suit was still in the evidentiary phase at the time of the hearing at ICSID—the investor claimed that it would have been impossible for the local courts to resolve the dispute within 18 months.).[94] Whilst acknowledging that the disputed provision indeed clearly required resort to domestic courts as a precondition for resorting to international arbitration, the *Urbaser* tribunal questioned whether the investor's non-compliance with the domestic litigation requirement deprived the host state 'of a fair opportunity to address the dispute within the framework of its own domestic legal system'.[95] The tribunal deployed the notion of bilateralism, which in its view should guide the interpretation of the domestic litigation requirements:

> In the context of the 18 month rule, this principle of bilateralism holds that the Host State is precluded from insisting on the investor's obligation to resort to domestic courts if the investor is not able to fulfil such obligation because of the unavailability of courts capable of handling such disputes that may reasonably contemplate on adjudication on the substance of the dispute within 18 months.[96]

The tribunal held that since a decision on the substance of an investor-state dispute before the local courts could not be possibly reached within the 18-month period, 'a proceeding that can in no reasonable way be expected to reach that target is useless and unfair to the investor.'[97] Hence, the investor's disregard for the requirement did not act as a jurisdictional impediment to its investment arbitration claim.

The reasoning of the *Urbaser* tribunal aptly illustrates the fallacy of the good governance narratives of investment treaty law insofar as investment arbitration tribunals are portrayed as agents of diffusion of good governance norms. Just as its numerous predecessors, the *Urbaser* tribunal effectively reduced the 18-month domestic litigation requirement to an ultimately irrelevant formality. By definition, most developing—and developed—countries would arguably fall short of offering the judicial system capable of swift resolution of disputes. One could argue that the 18-month requirement is part of the due process framework of

[94] ibid para 81.
[95] ibid para 129.
[96] ibid para 148.
[97] ibid para 202.

investment treaties—due process for all. Resorting to the futility argument, as the *Urbaser* tribunal effectively did, allows investors to sidestep procedural requirements expressly set by treaties. Contrastingly, host states are not allowed to similarly sidestep procedural safeguards without incurring investment treaty sanctions. Investment arbitration practice offers numerous examples showing that where a host state fails to fully abide by due process, no matter how futile and perfunctory the compliance with such requirements might be, it is still likely to be held in breach of due process.[98] Furthermore, if the domestic litigation requirements are persistently disapplied due to national judicial avenues being regarded as allegedly ineffective, one could question whether such persistent removal of investor-state disputes from the purview of domestic courts would have a positive transformational impact on governance in host state. By precluding the involvement of national judicial bodies in the process of investor-state dispute settlement, investment tribunals effectively hamper the process of learning and internalising good governance standards by domestic actors and institutions.

The domestic litigation requirements are not the only treaty provisions which envisage some degree of involvement by host state courts in the settlement of investor-state disputes. There are also provisions on waiting periods whereby a right to initiate investor-state arbitration is granted on the expiry of a certain period of time during which parties to a dispute are expected to settle disagreements amicably.[99] However, arbitral tribunals have so far tended to allow investors to bypass such requirements. For instance, in *SGS v Pakistan* the tribunal was faced with the Pakistan-Switzerland investment treaty providing for a 12-month consultation period, after which the investor could initiate ICSID arbitration. The claimant investor did not comply with the waiting period, arguing that the requirement was not a prerequisite for its exercise of right to access investor-state arbitration but rather a mere recommendation aimed at avoidance of arbitration. The investor also argued that even if the requirement was adhered to, any negotiation would have been futile.[100] The tribunal noted that previous practice had tended to treat the waiting periods as 'directory and procedural rather than as mandatory and jurisdictional in nature.'[101] It concluded that non-compliance with

[98] See eg *Técnicas Medioambientales Tecmed, SA v United Mexican States*, Award of 29 May 2003 (2003) 23 ILM 133 para 173, and *Rumeli Telekom AS and Telsim Mobil Telekomunikasyon Hizmetleri AS v Republic of Kazakhstan*, 29 July 2008 (ICSID Case No ARB/05/16) paras 614–18. See also *Amco Asia Corporation v Republic of Indonesia*, Resubmitted Case, Award, 31 May 1990 (ICSID Case No ARB/81/1) paras 174–78.

[99] See eg Art VI of the US-Czech BIT.

[100] SGS *Société Générale de Surveillance SA v Pakistan*, Decision on Objections to Jurisdiction, 6 August 2003 (2003) 42 ILM 1290, paras 130–31.

[101] ibid para 184.

the requirement ought not to be treated as an impediment to the investor's access to arbitration.[102]

The involvement of domestic courts in investor-state dispute settlement can also be mandated by an underlying contractual instrument. For instance, where an investor-state dispute concerns a breach of contract, the domestic forum choice clauses in such a contract may require the dispute to be submitted for resolution by host state courts before it can be referred to investment arbitration.[103] Some scholars have argued that a contractual forum selection clause made in favour of domestic courts should not be binding on an international investment tribunal[104] and that where competing jurisdictions exist, it would be preferable for the entire dispute to be heard by the forum with the most comprehensive jurisdiction, namely, an investor-state tribunal.[105] Lest an investor-state tribunal's jurisdiction over the dispute become an empty shell, it has been argued, the arbitration option provided by an investment treaty should prevail over the domestic forum choice in an investment contract.[106] Yet again, in deciding on the matter of competing jurisdictions some tribunals have dismissed the relevance of domestic forum choice clauses, allowing investment arbitration to prevail over domestic adjudication.[107] Investment treaty law, particularly as manifested in arbitral awards rendered to date, has been resolutely concerned with removing investment disputes entirely from the national judicial realm, effectively precluding host state courts from playing a part in the process of learning from, and embedding, good governance standards in national legal settings.

ii. National Judicial Action to Enforce Good Governance Standards May Constitute a Breach of Good Governance Standards

Not only are national courts effectively prevented from transposing international good governance prescriptions into domestic practices, but judicial attempts to abide by good governance may controversially be condemned as a breach of investment treaty rules, resulting in the finding

102 ibid.

103 See eg SGS *Société Générale de Surveillance SA v Philippines*, Decision on Objections to Jurisdiction and Separate Declaration, 29 January 2004, ICSID Case No ARB/02/6.

104 See Stephan W Schill, 'Enabling Private Ordering: Function, Scope and Effect of Umbrella Clauses in International Investment Treaties' (2009) 18 *Minnesota Journal of International Law* 1, 66–67.

105 Schreuer, 'Calvo's Grandchildren', 11–12.

106 ibid.

107 See for instance, the award in *Eureko BV v Poland*, Partial Award and Dissenting Opinion, 19 August 2005, 12 ICSID Reports 335, where the respective tribunal allowed the claimant-investor to rely on the contract in establishing their disputed rights and but effectively ignored the same contract's forum selection clause referring contentious matters to the jurisdiction of local courts. For criticism, see Zachary Douglas, *The International Law of Investment Claims* (Cambridge, Cambridge University Press, 2009) 372–75.

of the host state liable before the investor. The case of *Arif v Moldova*[108] provides a stark illustration of the internally contradictory set of obligations imposed by international investment law on host states. The investor-claimant won a tender to set up and run a network of five duty-free stores at the border with Romania. The dispute arose after Moldovan courts had found illegality in actions of Moldovan airport authorities. In particular, the Moldovan judiciary found that the airport authorities failed to follow a competitive tender process required by the law, thereby preventing the foreign investor's competitors from participating in a tender for the right to operate duty-free shops. Disgruntled by this national judicial ruling, the investor initiated investor-state arbitration. The investment tribunal acknowledged that the courts of Moldova had acted in what was an exemplary manner by transition economy standards. Yet the courts' effort to restore the rule of law by pronouncing on the illegality of the administrative action was found to be in violation of Moldova's investment treaty commitments. In the tribunal's view, a breach manifested itself in the fact that the executive branch encouraged the investment but the judicial branch subsequently found the executive action to be illegal.[109] This inconsistent treatment of the investor by the two branches of the Moldovan government was found to constitute a violation of the fair and equitable treatment standard. The executive branch was found to have committed a further treaty breach when it enforced the national court's orders against the investor so as to restore legality and compliance with national laws.[110]

The case of *Arif v Moldova* epitomises an internal contradiction in international investment law and its purported good governance mission. On the one hand, weak domestic governance—including the lack of domestic remedies—can lead to host state liability, including under the effective means standard and other investment protection standards.[111] On the other hand, the availability of such remedies and their utilisation by national courts could also expose host states to liability, as attempts to restore legality in domestic law by national courts could be held in a breach of investment treaty law. This leaves host states in a situation where any judicial attempt to rectify the original wrongfulness in executive conduct may be seen not only as superfluous but also in violation of investment treaty provisions. Can suppressing domestic judicial oversight of domestic executive action foster the rule of law and good governance?

[108] *Mr Franck Charles Arif v Republic of Moldova,* Award, 8 April 2013 (ICSID Case No ARB/11/23).

[109] ibid para 547.

[110] ibid para 547(f).

[111] See above Chapter 2, Section IIC.

How can investment treaty prescriptions of good governance be embedded and implemented in domestic legal orders if restoring the rule of law by judicial bodies can itself be condemned and sanctioned as an investment treaty breach? If host states cannot simultaneously respect the rule of law prescriptions of investment treaties and maintain legality and integrity in the functioning of national institutions, the contribution of investment treaty law to the creation of rule-orientated governance practices is highly questionable.[112]

IV. GOOD GOVERNANCE AS A TWO-WAY STREET: DEALING WITH INVESTOR MISCONDUCT IN TREATY PRACTICE AND ARBITRATION

A. Impact of Investor Misconduct on Governance in Host States

Another critical shortcoming of the existing investment treaty regime, which detracts from its capacity to foster compliance with good governance standards and can discourage rather than encourage positive change in host states, is its lop-sided nature and the resulting ambiguity of normative values that it stands for and is able to export into host countries. Of particular interest here is the failure of international investment law to balance investor rights with investor responsibilities, particularly in the context of corruption and other instances of investor involvement in illegal acts. Well-evidenced and extensively discussed elsewhere in the literature, the cases of misconduct by foreign investors and their complicity in illegal actions by governmental agencies in host states is an illustration of how investments can affect local communities not by eliminating inadequate governance practices but rather by entrenching them. Consequently, both the credibility and viability of the good governance mission of international investment law hinges on how investor misconduct is addressed by investment treaties and investment arbitration practice.

Our empirical case studies, particularly the interviews with government officials in Ukraine, highlighted the scale of concerns over foreign investors' complicity in corruption. On the one hand, the majority of respondents concurred in identifying corruption in the government as a major obstacle for doing business in Ukraine. Many of the recent externally-sponsored governance reform initiatives are aimed at countering

[112] See also Todd Tucker, 'Investment Agreements versus the Rule of Law?' UNCTAD-IPFSD-Forum Discussion Paper 9, 9 October 2013, 3: '[i]f states cannot simultaneously respect arbitral norms and facilitate the integrity of institutions that support development, one of the key justifications for IIAs—their contribution to economic development—can be brought into question.'

corruption so as 'to make life easier for investors'.[113] On the other hand, a number of interviewees pointed to widespread awareness of the involvement of foreign investors in corruption and other forms of illegal behaviour. As one respondent has put it, '[f]oreign investors need stability and predictability. They had that during the rule by Yanukovich. They would pay, say, 10% and everything would be sorted. At present, however, everything is stably and predictably bad.'[114] This response resonates with findings presented in other studies on the relationship between investment and democratic governance. As one such study has noted, '[f]or a commercial company trying to make investments, you need a stable environment. Dictatorships can give you that.'[115] Four interviewees mentioned the collusion between foreign investors and government officials in the pharmaceuticals business, or the so-called pharma mafia.[116] One interviewee said that 'foreign investors are well known for their lobbying and otherwise influencing the government to get the outcome they want, for instance a hands-off regulation of a relevant industry.'[117] These responses confound the assumptions that foreign investment fosters good governance as 'powerful foreign investors can lobby host governments either directly or through their home governments, or push for reform by demanding appropriate changes during the negotiation of investment contracts'.[118] The emerging evidence suggests that foreign investors are just as likely to entrench poor governance through their contribution to normalising corruption, bribery and regulatory capture.

The instances of foreign investor complicity in corruption are also well-documented in investment arbitration awards. One notable example from the early investment arbitration practice is *World Duty Free v Kenya*, where the claimant investor made no secret of a bribe it offered to the government in order to obtain permission for a duty-free concession in Nairobi and Mombasa international airports.[119] The investor submitted that the then president of Kenya solicited a personal donation amounting to US$2 million, and that making the payment was part of 'protocol in Kenya', by

[113] Interview AC. See also the description of a mission of Business Ombudsman Council of Ukraine, available at boi.org.ua/en/about.

[114] Interview DFI.

[115] Christopher L Avery, 'Business and Human Rights in a Time of Change' in Menno Kamminga and Saman Zia-Zarifi (eds), *Liability of Multinational Corporations under International Law* (Leiden, Kluwer Law International, 2000) 27; see also Walid Ben Hamida, 'Investment treaties and democratic transition: Does investment law authorise not to honor contracts concluded with undemocratic regimes?' in Stephan W Schill, Christian J Tams and Rainer Hofmann (eds), *International Investment Law and Development: Bridging the Gap* (Cheltenham, Edward Elgar, 2015) 314.

[116] Interviews MUL, MZ, MP, AC.

[117] Interview MUL.

[118] Guthrie, 'Beyond Investment Protection', 1170.

[119] *World Duty Free Co Ltd v Kenya*, Award, 4 October 2006, ICSID Case No ARB/00/7.

which the investor had to abide if he wished to obtain a contract.[120] The contract was granted but some three years later the relationship between the investor and the government soured, culminating in a claim brought by the investor against Kenya before an ICSID tribunal. The investor's testimony of the facts surrounding his 'personal donation' to Kenya's highest standing official provides some minute details of the transaction, including the fact that part of the payment had to be taken in cash in a case directly to the President:

> I understood that [the intermediary] had received the cash worth US$500,000. ... He had then arranged for this to be exchanged into Kenyan Shillings (KSh). He brought the KSh in cash to my meeting with HEDAM in a brown briefcase. When we entered the room where the President received us, he put the briefcase by the wall and left it there. After the meeting we collected the briefcase from where we had left it. On the departing journey I looked in the briefcase and saw that the money had been replaced with fresh corn.[121]

Investment arbitration awards offer numerous examples of investor complicity in bribery and corruption.[122] As of 2013, allegations of corruption were made in at least 28 investor-state arbitration cases.[123] It is true that 'due to their actual or perceived wealth, foreign companies are often the target of host state corruption in the developing world.'[124] Descriptions of this kind, however, present investors as victims of corruption and underplay the fact that by supplying bribes, investors contribute to the worsening of the already weak governance in host states and thus hamper rather than stimulate rule of law reforms.

Similarly, some authors have argued that the impact of investor complicity in bribery would vary depending on the investor's country of origin. For instance, one such narrative argues that

> [a] foreign investor from a country with a tradition of corruption and weak enforcement institutions may have a different view of, and contribution to make to, legislative and institutional reform [in a host state] than an investor from a country at the opposite end of the enforcement and corruption spectrum.[125]

Likewise, in the specific context of the impact of foreign investment in Central Asia, concerns have been raised over the growing Russian and Chinese involvement in the region, such involvement being marked by

[120] ibid para 66.

[121] ibid para 130.

[122] For a comprehensive analysis of arbitral jurisprudence, see Aloysius P Llamzon, *Corruption in International Investment Arbitration* (Oxford, Oxford University Press, 2014).

[123] ibid 100.

[124] Cameron A Miles, 'Corruption, Jurisdiction, and Admissibility in International Investment Claims' (2012) 3 *Journal of International Dispute Settlement* 329, 330.

[125] Hewko, 'Foreign Direct Investment', 6. See also John Hewko, 'Foreign Direct Investment in Transitional Economies: Does the Rule of Law Matter?' (2002) 11 *East European Constitutional Review* 71, 72.

'a lack of transparency and a reluctance or inability to accompany investment with support for institutional improvement.'[126] Such investments may arguably even 'derail Western-supported institutional and governance reforms in the region.'[127] Such narratives raise a host of important issues.

Characterising foreign investors complicit in bribery and other forms of corruption merely as victims of demands from government officials in developing countries with poor governance is not only belied by growing evidence from investment arbitration cases as well as national enforcement proceedings, but is also confounded by a wealth of empirical insights from law and development literature. Empirical studies have shown that investors frequently

> depend upon informal mechanisms, rather than the legal system, in order to structure and implement their economic activities. It is therefore possible that some foreign investors might prefer to perform their economic activities with limited reference to the legal system of the host state …[128]

Furthermore, rather than actively countering corruption in host states, foreign investors have been known to 'find unclear legislation and a weak, opaque, unpredictable and corrupt system were at times highly desirable'.[129] It transpires that in developing states with weak governance foreign investors magnify the problems of state capture and procurement bribes.[130] As one author put it, '[f]oreign investors are generally not altruistic organizations, and their interests may not always coincide with those of society as a whole or with those of domestic investors.'[131]

The most widely-used definition of corruption—as the abuse of entrusted power for private gain—too understates the role of private business actors in perpetrating corrupt acts. As Rose pointed out in her recent study of international anti-corruption norms, such a definition is skewed because of its focus on the role of the public rather than the private sector in perpetrating such acts.[132] The less one-sided approach to defining corruption, she argues, would be to characterise the latter as 'the abuse of entrusted power for private gain *or* the exercise of improper influence over those entrusted with power.'[133]

[126] Martha Brill Olcott, 'Asia's Overlooked Middle' (Carnegie Endowment for International Peace, 17 June 2009).

[127] Martha Brill Olcott, 'China's Unmatched Influence in Central Asia' (Carnegie Endowment for International Peace, 18 September 2013).

[128] Amanda Perry, 'Effective Legal Systems and Foreign Direct Investment: In Search of the Evidence' (2000) 49 *ICLQ* 779, 788.

[129] Hewko, 'Foreign Direct Investment', 10.

[130] Guthrie, 'Beyond Investment Protection', 1151.

[131] Hewko, 'Does the Rule of Law Matter', 72.

[132] Cecily Rose, *International Anti-Corruption Norms: Their Creation and Influence on Domestic Legal Systems* (Oxford, Oxford University Press, 2015) 7.

[133] ibid.

The fact that corruption in the foreign investment context is not merely a problem of demand has become evident in recent years after a number of developed states moved towards a stricter enforcement of national anti-corruption laws. The most prominent example is the United States, where the introduction of strict criminal sanctions targeting US firms abroad was said to have placed the latter in a competitive disadvantage vis-à-vis their competitors from others states where similar criminalisation was not the order of the day.[134] Spalding has argued that a stringent enforcement of anti-corruption laws in the US significantly increases the costs of investing in developing countries, and tends to cause a decrease in US investment abroad.[135] In striking contrast, Chinese companies do not incur these added costs because their legal regime does not impose penalties on the methods of doing business that U.S. progressivism proscribes.'[136] Spalding's chief concern is that an increasingly robust enforcement of anti-corruption legislation in the US delimits the ability of US investors to invest abroad. Consequently, a void is created, filled by companies from countries with less stringent anti-corruption laws—companies that are able to conduct business without fear of violating laws concerning corruption and human rights.[137] A similar concern is echoed in Rose-Ackerman's argument that

> … the growing importance of multinationals from countries outside the 1990s 'anti-corruption consensus' poses a challenge. On the plus side, these firms increase competitive pressures on firms based in wealthy countries, but on the negative side, their use of corrupt tactics increases the pressure on all firms to follow suit.[138]

While such claims tend to characterise investors from emerging and transition economies as more prone to corruption than their competitors from developed countries, they can also be seen as implicitly and tacitly acknowledging the fact that prior to the move towards stricter enforcement of anti-corruption laws in countries such as the US, investors from the latter countries had in the past engaged in corruption for purposes of entering and maintaining their commercial position in host states and

[134] Joost Pauwelyn, 'Different Means, Same End: The Contribution of Trade and Investment Treaties to Anti-Corruption Policy' in Susan Rose-Ackerman and Paul Carrington (eds), *Anti-Corruption Policy: Can International Actors Play a Constructive Role?* (Carolina Academic Press, 2013) 247–65.

[135] Andrew Brady Spalding, 'The Irony of International Business Law: U.S. Progressivism and China's New Laissez Faire' (2011) 59 *UCLA Law Review* 354, 358.

[136] ibid 358–59.

[137] ibid 359.

[138] Susan Rose-Ackerman, 'Anti-Corruption Policy: Can International Actor Play a Constructive Role?' John M Olin Centre for Studies in Law, Economics, and Public Policy Research Paper No 440, 1.

are now prevented from doing so by their home governments. As further confirmed by evidence from investment arbitration cases, investors from developed countries have shown no lesser proclivity for corruption than their counterparts from emerging economies.[139] Some of the most infamous publicised instances show that in Western corporations bribery and other forms of corruption have been so widely practised as to become 'a business model.'[140] For instance, an investor-state arbitration case in *Siemens v Argentina* revealed that the corporation's corrupt practices both in Argentina and globally were systematic and widespread.[141] The findings from the US FCPA investigations against former Siemens executives unveiled that between 1996 to 2007 the corporation paid US$100 million in bribes to Argentine officials (including two presidents and cabinet ministers).[142] Bribes were paid to obtain the contract for a US$1 billion national identity card project, to return the contract into force after it was terminated by the Argentine government, and yet again later to suppress the evidence that the terminated contract had been obtained through corruption.[143] These payments were made through consultants and shell companies and improperly characterised in the corporate accounts as 'consulting fees' or 'legal fees.'[144]

While investors from the countries with weaker governance (and less effective anti-corruption legislation) may indeed be less deterred from committing corrupt acts when making and operating their investments abroad, increasingly plentiful and irrefutable evidence emerging from domestic enforcement of anti-corruption laws in countries such as the US and Germany, as well as from investment arbitration case law, affirms that: (1) investors from developed countries also remain prone to corruption; and (2) regardless of its origins, foreign investment—due to its proclivity for corruption—may have a negative, rather than positive impact on domestic governance and the rule of law reforms in developing host states. As Hirsch observed, 'international investments are not only affected by socio-cultural factors, they often influence the socio-cultural features of

[139] For instance, in a dispute against Azerbaijan, the representative of the claimant-investor testified that he had 'provided funds to bribe officials in Azerbaijan in early 2006.' *Azpetrol v Azerbaijan*, Award, 8 September 2009, ICSID Case No ARB/06/15, para 6.

[140] 'Siemens and the battle against bribery and corruption', *The Guardian* (18 September 2013) www.theguardian.com/sustainable-business/siemens-solmssen-bribery-corruption.

[141] Luke Eric Peterson, 'Siemens Pleads Guilty to Breach of Foreign Corrupt Practices Act' *Investment Arbitration Reporter* 17 December 2008.

[142] Llamzon, *Corruption*, 124.

[143] ibid 124–25.

[144] Peterson, 'Siemens, and its Argentine Subsidiary', see also *The Guardian*, 'Siemens and the battle against bribery and corruption' (noting that Siemens 'even had a handy accounting euphemism for its bribes: 'nützliche Aufwendungen,' or 'useful money').

the involved communities.'[145] There is a growing recognition in the literature of the importance of foreign investment 'as a channel for the diffusion of knowledge, technology and management practices.'[146] The actual impact of investment treaty law on governance in host states would hinge on the stance the regime takes on investor behaviour. If investment treaty instruments and arbitral tribunals applying them in investor-state disputes turn a blind eye to illegality committed by an investor in host states, including instances of bribery and complicity in other forms of illegal acts, the investment treaty regime is not only far from exerting positive influence on domestic governance culture and practices but can arguably be seen as being complicit in encouraging and perpetuating inadequate and undesirable patterns of behaviour by governments and foreign investors.

B. Countering Investor Misconduct in Investment Arbitration

Does international investment law make provision to ensure accountability of investors? The bulk of existing investment treaty instruments do not contain provisions expressly addressing corruption, or for that matter, any other form of investor misconduct. One of the criticisms frequently levelled against the investment treaty regime is its asymmetric nature—the fact that most investment treaties create investor rights, but not investor obligations.[147] Faced with evidence of investor misconduct, some arbitral tribunals have creatively resorted to other treaty provisions to fill the void created by investment treaties' silence on the issue of investor obligations. For instance, a number of tribunals held that investments made in breach of domestic laws of the host state ought not to benefit from investment treaty protection.[148] In doing so, the tribunals have relied on treaty clauses that require investments to be in accordance with host state law. In some treaties, the requirement that investment be in accordance with host state laws is part of the treaty clause defining investment. For instance, the Italy-Morocco BIT defines the term investment as

> all categories of assets invested, after the coming into force of the present agreement, by a natural or legal person, including the Government of a Contracting

[145] Moshe Hirsch, 'The Sociology of International Investment Law' in Zachary Douglas, Joost Pauwelyn and Jorge E Viñuales (eds), *The Foundations of International Investment Law: Bringing Theory into Practice* (Oxford, Oxford University Press, 2014) 146.

[146] ibid.

[147] See generally Andrew Newcombe and Lluis Paradell, *Law and Practice of Investment Treaties: Standards of Treatment* (Alphen aan den Rijn, Kluwer Law International, 2009) 64.

[148] For an overview of investment arbitration practice see Stephan W Schill, 'Illegal Investments in Investment Treaty Arbitration' (2012) 11 *Law and Practice of International Courts and Tribunals* 281.

> Party, on the territory of the other Contracting Party, *in accordance with the laws and regulations of the aforementioned party.* (emphasis added)

There are also investment treaty instruments in which the implicit requirement that investments comply with host state law is built into the obligations undertaken by host states with regard to admission and treatment of investments. One such example is the Spain-El Salvador BIT which stipulates that '[e]ach Contracting Party shall promote the realization of investments in its territories by investors of the other Contracting Party and shall admit such investments *in accordance with its laws.*' This provision was relied upon by a tribunal in *Inceysa v El Salvador*, where an investor committed fraud in the bidding process for a state contract.[149] The tribunal held that protection under the treaty was limited to legally acquired investments, thus rendering investments obtained through fraud and misrepresentation to fall outside the scope of the treaty.[150]

There is also yet another category of cases where arbitral tribunals held illegal investments to be ineligible for investment treaty protection despite the fact that the applicable treaty contained no express requirement of legality. For example, in *Plama v Bulgaria*, the host state argued, in its defence, that there was no eligible investment as the claimant investor had failed to disclose its true financial position and structure at the time of investing. Although the tribunal did not accept this argument as an objection to its exercise of jurisdiction, it examined the question of misrepresentation as part of deciding on the merits of the case. It held that since the investment was a result of 'deliberate concealment amounting to fraud',[151] the question was whether the investment protections under the Energy Charter Treaty (ECT) could apply to such an investment. Even though the treaty did not contain an express legality requirement, the tribunal held that such an investment was outside the scope of the treaty's protective ambit. The tribunal drew on the introductory note to the Energy Charter Treaty which provided that 'the fundamental aim of the ECT is to strengthen the rule of law on energy issues,' and held that the treaty should therefore be interpreted consistently with this aim.[152] It concluded that the 'substantive protections of the ECT cannot apply to investments that are made contrary to law'.[153]

[149] *Inceysa v El Salvador*, Award, 2 August 2006, ICSID Case No ARB/03126.

[150] ibid, paras 255–57.

[151] *Plama Consortium Ltd v Bulgaria*, Award, 27 August 2008, ICSID Case No ARB/03/24, para 135.

[152] ibid para 139.

[153] ibid. See also *Yaung Chi Oo Trading v Myanmar* Award, 31 March 2003, (2003) 42 ILM 540, 58, holding that even in the absence of a specific treaty provision there existed a 'general rule that for a foreign investment to enjoy treaty protection it must be lawful under the law of the host State.'

Other tribunals went as far as reading the legality requirement into jurisdictional preconditions laid out by the ICSID Convention. The pertinent example is *Phoenix Action v Czech Republic*, where the tribunal held that compliance with host state law was not only prescribed by the investment treaty applicable in a dispute before it but was also implicitly required by Article 25(1) ICSID.[154]

Another notable instance where the tribunal has addressed the issue of corrupt investment despite the underlying contractual instrument providing no express guidance on the matter is the award in *World Duty Free v Kenya*. As mentioned earlier, it was the investor who admitted bribing the host state officials.[155] Drawing on prior judicial decisions and international anti-corruption conventions, the tribunal concluded that bribery was contrary to international and Kenyan public policy. Quoting a 1963 ICC award by Judge Lagergren, the tribunal reiterated that corruption was 'an international evil' contrary to 'good morals and international public policy common to the community of nations'.[156] It concluded that investment claims tainted by corruption forfeit 'any right to ask for assistance of the machinery of justice'.[157] The tribunal resorted to the doctrines of *ex turpi causa non oritur actio* and *ex dolo malo non oritur action* before concluding that investor claims based on contracts of corruption or on contracts obtained by corruption cannot be upheld.[158]

Not all arbitral tribunals, however, have been prepared to consider the relevance of investor misconduct in determining the outcome of investor-state disputes. In *Fakes v Turkey*, for instance, the tribunal refused to take into account the fact of illegality tainting the claimant investor's case in deciding the latter's eligibility for investment treaty protection. It held that

> … the principles of good faith and legality cannot be incorporated into the definition of [Article 24(5)(1)] of the ICSID Convention without doing violence to the language of the ICSID Convention: an investment might be 'legal' or 'illegal', made in good faith or not, it nonetheless remains an investment.[159]

Likewise, in *Fraport v Philippines*, the dissenting arbitrator suggested that interpreting 'in accordance with host state law' provisions as a requirement that an investor must ensure compliance with any law—no matter how trivial the law or the violation—would create an 'Achilles Heel of

[154] *Phoenix Action Ltd v Czech Republic*, Award, 9 April 2009, ICSID Case No ARB/06/5, para 134.

[155] *World Duty Free Co Ltd v Kenya*, para 130.

[156] ibid para 148.

[157] ibid, quoting the 1963 award by Judge Lagergren in ICC Case No 1110, (1994) *Arbitration International* 277.

[158] ibid para 157.

[159] *Saba Fakes v Turkey*, Award, 12 July 2010, ICSID Case No ARB/07/20, para 112.

investment arbitration' and make investment treaty protection dependent on the claimant passing a full legal compliance audit.[160]

Of particular concern here are the cases where arbitral tribunals were hesitant in sanctioning investor involvement in corruption. For instance, in *Wena Hotels v Egypt*[161] a dispute arose from Egypt's failure to prevent the seizure of the investor-owned hotels and the withdrawal of the investor's hotel operating licence. Egypt argued that the claim should be dismissed because the investor had bribed a senior government official to obtain hotel leases.[162] The tribunal admitted that, if proved, the allegations of undue influence by the investor over the government officials would provide a ground for dismissal of the investor's claim.[163] However, the tribunal also noted that even if there had been illegality involved in obtaining hotel leases, Egypt failed to present evidence of any investigation by Egyptian authorities in the matter. Given that the government had been made aware of the allegations of corruptions but decided not to prosecute the concerned government officials, the tribunal was reluctant to immunise Egypt for liability.[164] Notwithstanding its corrupt behaviour, the investor was allowed to benefit from investment treaty law and obtained a damages award.[165] Such treatment of investor corruption seriously undermines the narratives which present international investment law as a vehicle for the rule of law reform and fostering good governance in host states.

The reluctance shown by some tribunals to prevent investments tainted by illegality and corruption from enjoying the benefits of investment treaty protection can be explained by the fact that the other party to an investment dispute is a host government whose own record of compliance with domestic and international norms may often be far from ideal, and who, in the context of corruption, often represents the demand side of corruption and uses the latter opportunistically as a defence against investor claims.[166] There is consensus that 'combatting corruption effectively requires a series of both supply and demand measures.'[167] In cases where the investor is shown to have been involved in corrupt activities, dismissing its claims—the so called zero-tolerance approach—would arguably

[160] *Fraport AG Frankfurt Airport Services Worldwide v Philippines*, 16 August 2007, ICSID Case No ARB/03/25, Dissenting Opinion of Mr Bernardo M Cremades, para 37.

[161] *Wena Hotels Ltd v Arab Republic of Egypt*, Award, 8 December 2000, (2002) 41 ILM 196.

[162] ibid para 76.

[163] ibid para 111.

[164] ibid para 116.

[165] ibid.

[166] See eg *Metal-Tech Ltd v Republic of Uzbekistan*, Award, 4 October 2013, ICSID Case No ARB/10/3, where the respondent state used evidence of bribery as defence.

[167] Daniel Litwin, 'On the Divide Between Investor-State Arbitration and the Global Fight Against Corruption' (2013) 10(3) *Transnational Dispute Management* 5–6.

leave the demand side unaddressed and even implicitly condoned.[168] Some investment treaty lawyers have been vocal in expressing their opposition to a 'zero tolerance' rule, contending that it is 'an inflexible and onerous sanction on investors' and that it might lead to corrupt government officials being rewarded twice—first by keeping the bribe proceeds, and, second, by avoiding investment treaty sanctions.'[169] Letting host states off the hook might even encourage 'the misuse of corruption as a cynical defensive tool by host States who stand to benefit from the corrupt acts of their own officials.'[170] Finally, a zero-tolerance approach to corruption is said to undermine the general welfare of non-parties to the arbitration.[171]

What these narratives tend to ignore is the fact the host state population is not going to benefit from investment arbitration awards which grant protection to investors notwithstanding their corrupt practices. Rather, host state communities would be disadvantaged twice: once by having to shoulder the financial burden of the award holding the state liable towards such investors, and by having to endure the long-term consequences of corrupt practices perpetuated through foreign investors' complicity. The fundamental conceptual flaw in the existing conceptualisations of corruption is that illegality is seen to be carried out jointly by two actors—the host state and the investor. As Bonnitcha presciently argues, an alternative—and one should add, a more nuanced—approach would be to conceptualise the host state as 'a site of contestation between different groups'.[172] The host state does not benefit from corruption: '[b]ribes are not paid into the public revenue' and the host state 'suffers a significant loss when assets and other valuable legal entitlements are transferred into private hands the less than their real value through corrupt transactions.'[173]

It must be acknowledged that what is missing in the countries suffering from endemic government corruption is a *culture* of legitimate and transparent business practices and the political will to encourage such practices by enforcing national anti-corruption laws.[174] But investors' contribution to perpetuating the existing illicit business practices in host states should not be dismissed or rewarded as it helps to maintain the status quo and even exacerbates it. There is a fundamental flaw in the argument that allowing corrupt investors to claim damages in cases where the state has

168 Kevin Lim, 'Upholding Corrupt Investors' Claims Against Complicit or Compliant Host States—Where Angels Should *Not* Fear to Tread' in Karl P Sauvant (ed), *Yearbook on International Investment Law & Policy 2011–2012* (Oxford, Oxford University Press, 2013) 619.

169 ibid.

170 Llamzon, *Corruption*, 290.

171 Lim, 'Upholding Corrupt Investors' Claims', 620.

172 Jonathan Bonnitcha, 'Investment Treaties and Transition from Authoritarian Rule' (2014) *15 Journal of World Investment and Trade* 965, 1000.

173 ibid.

174 Lim, 'Upholding Corrupt Investors' Claims', 622.

condoned or demanded bribes from investors is 'a more effective method of combating corruption and enhancing the rule of law.'[175] How can the rule of law be strengthened through international law enabling investors to continue a never-ending circle of corruption by supplying bribes to public officials? Enabling investors to harness the investment treaty regime in an effort to recover their losses in cases tainted by corruption entirely undermines the portrayal of international investment law as a mechanism facilitating economic development and good governance in host states.

Furthermore, the argument that considers investors' participation in bribery to be of lesser importance than that of the host government has at times gone as far as positing that, unlike the host state which can be internationally responsible for bribery and corruption, corrupt investors cannot be considered to have violated international law. This, it has been argued, stems from the fact that the private investors do not have a requisite international legal personality to be held responsible for an international wrong.[176] Such arguments yet again demonstrate a structural imbalance at the very core of international investment law and certain strands of investment law scholarship: the investor is seen as deserving and indeed needing an international legal standing to benefit from extensive treaty privileges and protections vis-à-vis host states, but when the issue of investor responsibilities comes to the fore investors are seen as (conveniently) lacking an international legal personality.

While policy solutions to investor corruption should not overlook host state complicity and only 'demonise the corrupt investor',[177] neither should investor complicity and participation in corrupt practices be swept aside as irrelevant, less still be rewarded with the chance to recuperate losses. A more balanced approach would be to address both the supply and demand side of the corruption problem, and to ensure that neither investors nor host governments are allowed to use investment treaty law to benefit from their corrupt behaviour. Such approach was taken by the tribunal in *World Duty Free v Kenya*. The tribunal condemned the state's engagement in corrupt practice, and its failure to prosecute the crime, as well is its use of corruption as a defence against the investor's claim.

> It remains … a highly disturbing feature in this case that the corrupt recipient of the Claimant's bribe was more than an officer of state but its most senior officer, the Kenyan President; and that it is Kenya which is here advancing as a complete defence to the Claimant's claims the illegalities of its own former President. Moreover, on the evidence before this Tribunal, the bribe was apparently solicited by the Kenyan President and not wholly initiated by the Claimant. Although the Kenyan President has now left office and is no longer

[175] ibid.
[176] ibid 631.
[177] ibid 678.

> immune from suit under the Kenyan Constitution, it appears that no attempt has been made by Kenya to prosecute him for corruption or to recover the bribe in civil proceedings.[178]

The tribunal, however, was equally scathing in condemning the investor's behaviour. It pointed out that the investor was 'steeped in illegal conduct in paying the bribe to the Kenyan President.'[179] Whilst acknowledging that corruption was rife in Kenya, the tribunal stressed that prior to paying the bribe, the investor had a free choice whether or not to invest in Kenya and that, on the facts of the case, he chose to pay the bribe without being oppressed, coerced or otherwise subjected to undue influence in making his decision.[180] In such circumstances, 'it would be an affront to public conscience to grant the plaintiff the relief which he seeks because the court would thereby appear to assist or encourage the plaintiff in his illegal conduct or to encourage others in similar acts'.[181] The tribunal thus highlighted the wider repercussions which the upholding of the investor's claim would have for Kenyan people and the international community in general.

C. Investment Treaty Rules on Investor Misconduct

The capacity of international investment law to promote better governance practices in host states certainly hinges on whether and to what extent investment tribunals are enabled—by virtue of express treaty provisions—to foreclose the investor claims tainted by corruption whilst also ensuring that such measures do not confer benefits on corrupt host governments by shielding them from investment treaty sanctions. 'The ability of international courts and tribunals to attain the goals prescribed by their mandate is decisively influenced by their jurisdictional powers and the rules on admissibility that are available to for them to apply.'[182] It is baffling and concerning in equal measure that, despite investment arbitration practice having generated a considerable body of decisions illustrating the shortcomings of existing treaty drafting patterns, most of the new generation investment treaties continue to remain silent on the issue of corruption and on the matters relating to investor misconduct in general.

178 *World Duty Free v Kenya*, para 180.
179 ibid para 178.
180 ibid.
181 ibid para 161.
182 Yuval Shany, *Assessing the Effectiveness of International Courts* (Oxford, Oxford University Press, 2014) 67.

One noteworthy exception is the CARIFORUM-EU Economic Partnership Agreement.[183] This agreement features clauses expressly addressing the behaviour of investors. First, the agreement prescribes the contracting state parties to cooperate and take any necessary domestic measures to ensure that investors are forbidden from and held liable for bribing public officials.[184] Furthermore, the chapter on transparency requires the state parties to take measures to stem the corruption of local and foreign public officials, as well as measures establishing specified acts of bribery or corruption as criminal offences, the commission of which is liable to sanctions, and to endeavour to take measures to protect informants.[185] While the agreement should be commended for pioneering the incorporation of provisions on corruption in investment treaty texts, the wording of the relevant provisions is likely to detract from their effectiveness in dealing with cases of corruption in investor-state arbitration. One principal shortcoming of the approach taken by the agreement's drafters is its focus on host states rather than investors and the fact that such provisions have limited if any enforceability in investor-state arbitration.

A bolder and arguably more effective solution would be to adopt an approach proposed in the IISD Model investment agreement, which features a standalone clause on investor corruption.[186] Rather than focusing exclusively on host states and national anti-corruption measures, Article 13 of the model text is framed as a set of obligations by which investors must abide:

> (A) Investors and their investments shall not, prior to the establishment of an investment or afterwards, offer, promise or give any undue pecuniary or other advantage, whether directly or through intermediaries, to a public official of the host state, for that official or for a third party, in order that the official or third party act or refrain from acting in relation to the performance of official duties, in order to achieve any favour in relation to a proposed investment or any licences, permits, contracts or other rights in relation to an investment.
>
> (B) Investors and their investments shall not be complicit in any act described in Paragraph (A), including incitement, aiding and abetting, and conspiracy to commit or authorisation of such acts.

[183] Economic Partnership Agreement Between the CARIFORUM States and the European Community, 30 October 2008, [2008] OJ L 289/I/3. See further Chantal Ononaiwu, 'Regional Investment Treaty Arrangements in the Caribbean: Developments and Implications' in N Jansen Calamita and Mavluda Sattorova, *The Regionalization of International Investment Treaty Arrangements* (British Institute of International and Comparative Law, London, 2015) 205.

[184] Art 72 CARIFORUM-EU EPA.

[185] Art 48 CARIFORUM-EU EPA.

[186] Howard Mann, Konrad von Moltke, Luke Peterson and Aaron Cosbey, IISD Model International Agreement on Investment for Sustainable Development (April 2005, International Institute for Sustainable Development).

In addition to expressly proscribing corrupt investment practices, the IISD model agreement subjects investors to a host of other obligations, ranging from a duty to comply with the host state laws to a post-establishment commitment to undertake activities in line with environmental, human rights and labour standards.[187] However, the approach advocated in this model is yet to be implemented in an actual investment treaty, and the majority of existing treaties continue to fall short of providing a meaningful mechanism for preventing the negative impact of investor misconduct on host states and their communities.

The fact that the recently revised and arguably more progressive treaty texts fail to expressly address corruption tends to undermine the good governance promise of international investment law and cast doubt on whether the promotion of good governance in host states is truly one of its objectives. The little concern shown by investment arbitration for combatting investor corruption becomes particularly salient given that other international regimes, including the WTO, have demonstrated their commitment to fostering good governance beyond symbolic declarations on the importance of anticorruption measures. Avoidance of corrupt practices is now expressly mentioned in the preamble of the revised Agreement on Government Procurement, as well as being stipulated in the form of an obligation binding upon contracting member states.[188] The wording of the relevant provisions lends support to an interpretation whereby they create not only an obligation to prevent corruption but also a cause of action to challenge corrupt acts.[189] Likewise, the World Bank has supported numerous anti-corruption initiatives to help governments develop national laws governing procurement activities.[190] The lack of a comparable effort by the ICSID and other arbitral bodies to address the supply side of corruption is therefore all the more concerning.

The reluctance shown by drafters of new generation treaties to incorporate express provisions imposing obligations on investors can be partly explained by the fact that, traditionally, investment treaties were conceived as agreements between host states, with investors being the beneficiaries, not the bearers of substantive and procedural guarantees. The inclusion of

[187] ibid, Arts 11 and 12.

[188] Art IV provides the positive obligation of Parties to ensure that each 'procuring entity shall conduct covered procurement in a transparent and impartial manner that (c) prevents corruption'. WTO Agreements: Revised Agreement on Government Procurement, entered into force April 2014.

[189] See Krista Nadakavukaren Schefer, Mintewab Gebre Woldesenbet, 'The Revised Agreement on Government Procurement and Corruption' (2013) 47 *Journal of World Trade* 1129, 1154.

[190] See Ibrahim FI Shihata, 'Corruption—A General Review with an Emphasis on the Role of the World Bank' (1997) 15 *Dickinson Journal of International Law* 451.

investor obligations into treaty texts might therefore be seen as too radical a step, and meet with a degree of resistance on the part of treaty drafters and negotiators. Nevertheless, it is still possible to harness certain treaty provisions as legal deterrents against investor misconduct without framing such provisions as investor obligations. One such drafting solution would be to add more specificity and content to the existing 'in accordance with host state law' clauses. For instance, in order to address the current lack of consistency and predictability as to when illegality should act as a ground for denying treaty protection to investments tainted by corruption or other misconduct, Yackee has proposed to expand the 'in accordance with host state laws' provisions in the following manner:

> In order to enjoy the protections granted by this treaty, an otherwise covered investment must be made and operated in accord with the international principle of good faith, without fraud or deceit, and in accord with the material laws and regulations of the State party in whose territory the investment is made. In addition, any investment procured or operated, in whole or in part, through the corruption of public officials shall not be covered by the provisions of this treaty.

The advantages of the drafting solution proposed by Yackee are manifold. First, the provision is not framed as an express obligation imposed on the investor but rather as a pre-condition for the enjoyment of benefits which the investor can be entitled to under the treaty. It does not change drastically the nature of investment treaties, and, at present, might therefore be seen as more feasible in the short term than the bolder proposals to include expressly-stated investor obligations. The proposed drafting also implies a continuous investor obligation to act in good faith rather than being focused on the initial period of making investment.[191] Such formulations would curb inclinations by arbitral tribunals to give a narrow interpretation to the duty to comply with host state laws, and are therefore more in line with the purported good governance mission of investment treaty law. Although it does not revolutionise the existing approaches to investor responsibilities, the proposed approach goes some way towards addressing the deep-seated structural imbalance within international investment law. What remains to be seen is whether host states—especially the traditional champions of investment treaties—would take up this or similar proposals in amending their treaties and concluding new agreements. Unless investment treaties make an express commitment to combating investor corruption, both the legitimacy of the investment treaty regime and its capacity to foster good governance in host states will remain highly contestable. A failure to address lack of investor accountability in international investment law is not only inconsistent with the

[191] Yackee, 'Investment Treaties and Investor Corruption', 743.

investment treaty regime's internal commitment of the ideals of rule of law and good governance, but it may also further reinforce the emerging perceptions of investment treaties 'as an act of collusion between often corrupt and despotic governments in developing countries and western states serving the interests of their corporate constituencies.'[192]

V. CONCLUSION

Does international investment law possess the necessary characteristics to fulfil its promise of good governance in host states? Analysis of investment treaty practice and arbitral jurisprudence, as well as the emerging empirical data, all point to 'the paradox of a system that purports to uphold standards of good governmental conduct … yet fails to engender such values within its institutional structure.'[193] The investment treaty regime often fails to adhere to the good governance and rule of law standards it expects host states to maintain in their dealings with foreign investors. Despite the recent emergence of alternative visions of how international investment law should operate, the regime continues to fall short of the requirements of transparency, coherence, and fairness.

The feasibility (and internal consistency) of the good governance promise of international investment law is also undermined by structural flaws in the design of investment treaty rules and investor-state arbitration. Since the very existence of investor-state arbitration is premised on the need to allow foreign investors to escape national law and courts, judicial bodies in host states are not merely deprived of incentives to improve the quality of their governance outputs, but they are also effectively denied the opportunity to embed international standards of good governance in the legal and bureaucratic practices of host states. As the empirical evidence and analysis of developments at a national level demonstrate, the persistent focus on the internationalisation of foreign investment protection and the tendency to over-value the protection of foreign investors is likely to have an emasculating effect on national actors and institutions, doing little to foster the emergence of an internally-felt demand for good governance and the requisite reform of domestic institutions and practices.

The legitimacy, fairness, and effectiveness of the investment treaty regime—and its capacity to weigh government decision-making in the

[192] Mattias Kumm, 'An Empire of Capital? Transatlantic Investment Protection as the Institutionalization of Unjustified Privilege' (2015) 4(3) *ESIL Reflections*.

[193] Celine Tan, 'Reviving the emperor's old clothes: the good governance agenda, development and international investment law' in Stephan W Schill, Christian J Tams and Rainer Hofmann (eds), *International Investment Law and Development: Bridging the Gap* (Cheltenham, Edward Elgar, 2015) 170.

direction of compliance with good governance norms—are further undermined by the currently ambiguous stance the regime takes on investor responsibilities. Evidence from the case studies as well as investment arbitration practice demonstrate that rather than fostering good governance through lobbying host governments and otherwise pushing for reform, foreign investors at times contribute to weak governance by partaking in corruption, bribery and regulatory capture. With a few notable exceptions, investment treaties continue to provide investors with rights but no responsibilities. Likewise, despite some tribunals having stressed the importance of denying international protection to investments tainted with illegality, there is a significant current within the international arbitration community that favours the vision of investors as victims of corrupt governments and thus downplays their role in normalising and entrenching weak governance in developing states. Instead of inspiring a belief in international law as a force for positive change at a national level, the failure to counter investor misconduct in international investment law is likely to reinforce the existing scepticism towards the rule of law, and further entrench the existing perception of international treaties as a protective mechanism for a select privileged group of actors.

6

International Investment Law and its Anti-participatory Animus

In the modern nation-state, power is 'billeted' and powers are 'bounded'; in global space, power is diffused to networks of private and public actors, escaping the painfully established controls of democratic government and public law. This is a world that is not only 'inherently less-permeable to democratically-grounded values and conceptions of the public interest or collective good, but also less capable of generating the public policy outcomes people want'.[1]

I. THE INVESTMENT TREATY REGIME AND ITS DISREGARD FOR THE POLITICAL AND SOCIAL INTERFACES OF DEVELOPMENT

NEOLIBERAL THEORIES, FROM which international investment law draws its justifications, have traditionally stressed the primary role of markets in economic growth.[2] However, such theories are guilty of showing little concern 'for law as a guarantor of political and civil rights or as protector of the weak and disadvantaged.'[3] The more recent studies in law and development are underpinned by a growing recognition of the need for a reconceptualisation of development that would de-centre the focus on economic growth and instead also encompass the pursuit of human development—'of which income is only an aspect, and equal consideration should be paid to political, social, and legal development.'[4] Understood as a freedom, development should 'enhance people's capabilities and to enable individuals to lead the life they choose to live.'[5] This, in turn, points to the importance of greater local participation in the

[1] Carol Harlow, 'Global Administrative Law: The Quest for Principles and Values' (2006) 17 *EJIL* 187, 212 (citations omitted).

[2] See eg Stephan W Schill, 'Fair and Equitable Treatment, the Rule of Law, and Comparative Public Law' in Stephan W Schill, *International Investment Law and Comparative Public Law* (Oxford, Oxford University Press, 2010) 177–81.

[3] David M Trubek and Alvaro Santos, 'Introduction: The Third Moment in Law and Development Theory and the Emergence of a New Critical Practice' in David M Trubek and Alvaro Santos (eds), *The New Law and Economic Development: A Critical Appraisal* (Cambridge, Cambridge University Press, 2006) 2.

[4] ibid 7.

[5] ibid.

design and implementation of economic reforms, and avoidance of blueprints advocating 'one size fits all' approaches.[6]

Successive efforts by international institutions and donor agencies to promote rule of law and governance reforms in developing countries have long been criticised for their excessive state-centrism and misguided efforts to mechanistically transplant institutional models from one setting to another.[7] Such efforts ignore the reality that in many developing countries

> [s]tate institutions are less important to social control than tribal or other structures. Legal rules are made not by and for the whole society but by small elites or power groups, and in any case are often not observed, nor are state courts very independent or very important.[8]

In the absence of an internal commitment to rule of law reform, governments are unlikely to be sensitive to state-level pressure mechanisms, such as sanctions and all forms of conditionality.[9] For rule of law and good governance reforms to succeed, it is vital to nurture a robust domestic constituency so that 'a broadly representative range of social, economic and political interests come to see their interests and values as aligned with the promotion and preservation of the rule of law.'[10] It is increasingly acknowledged that optimal institutional reforms 'will often be importantly shaped by factors specific to given societies, including history, culture, political traditions and institutional culture' and this implies greater emphasis should be made on the role of '"insiders" with detailed local knowledge.'[11] There is also growing consensus that an emerging 'global norm of good governance' should encompass such principles as accountability and an individual right of participation.[12]

Unlike the recent advances in law and development scholarship, however, the good governance narratives of international investment law view the improvement of domestic governance primarily as an instrument to achieve economic growth,[13] with governments expected to serve as major agents of change. In doing so, these narratives disregard the political and

[6] ibid.

[7] Benedict Kingsbury, 'Global Administrative Law in the Institutional Practice of Global Regulatory Governance' in Hassane Cissé, Daniel D Bradlow, and Benedict Kingsbury, *International Financial Institutions and Global Legal Governance* (World Bank Publications, 2011) 26.

[8] ibid.

[9] Michael J Trebilcock and Ronald J Daniels, *Rule of Law Reform and Development: Charting the Fragile Path of Progress* (Cheltenham, Edward Elgar, 2008) 354.

[10] ibid.

[11] ibid 12.

[12] Frederick Rawski, 'World Bank Community-driven Development Programming in Indonesia and East Timor: Implications for the Study of Global Administrative Law' (2005) 37 *International Law and Politics* 919, 942.

[13] See eg Stephan W Schill, *The Multilateralization of International Investment Law* (Cambridge, Cambridge University Press, 2009) 377, arguing that '… investment treaties aim at binding states into a legal framework that gives them an incentive and a yardstick for transforming their legal systems into ones that are conducive to market-based investment activities and provide the institutions necessary for the functioning of such markets.'

social interfaces of development. This is unsurprising given the historical origins and current mandate of the investment treaty regime.[14] The obvious contradiction within the good governance narratives of international investment law is that investment treaties are said to be aimed at changing 'the political dynamic of reform of domestic dispute resolution and policy making institutions'[15] and promoting 'democratic accountability and participation'[16] in host states whilst simultaneously insulating foreign investors from any such political changes and, importantly, suppressing any meaningful input by other stakeholders in shaping treaty rules and jurisprudence. This chapter seeks to contest the good governance narratives of international investment law by situating them within an ongoing debate over the indifference and even resistance of international investment law and its institutions towards political and social enablement in host states. It will argue that international investment law is unlikely to foster good governance so long as it remains inimical to the ideals of promoting democracy, participation, and the political and socio-cultural rights of citizens. The regime's animosity to these ideals is manifested in both its processes and outcomes: the process of making investment treaty rules and their application in investor-state arbitration.

II. FOREIGN INVESTORS AND THE DOMESTIC POLITICAL PROCESS

The proponents of good governance narratives of international investment law argue that investment arbitration promotes democratic accountability and participation alongside the protection of rights and other deserving interests.[17] Yet the practice of investment arbitration has generated profound concerns about the regime's lack of commitment to democracy, accountability and openness. These concerns are particularly strongly manifested in an ongoing debate about the clash between investment protection and host states' freedom to regulate in the public interest. It has been argued that by allowing foreign corporations to challenge regulatory acts of the host state, investment treaties and their investor-state arbitration mechanism constitute an 'inherent assault on democracy' and effectively mean 'unelected transnational corporations can dictate the

[14] See eg Kenneth J Vandevelde, *Bilateral Investment Treaties: History, Policy, and Interpretation* (Oxford, Oxford University Press, 2010) 1–19.

[15] David Gaukrodger and Kathryn Gordon, 'Investor-state dispute settlement: A scoping paper for the investment policy community' (OECD Working Papers on International Investment, No 2012/3, OECD Investment Division) 13.

[16] Benedict Kingsbury and Stephan W Schill, 'Investor-State Arbitration as Governance: Fair and Equitable Treatment, Proportionality, and the Emerging Global Administrative Law', Institute for International Law and Justice, NYU Law School, Working Paper 2009/6 (Global Administrative Law Series) 8.

[17] ibid.

policies of democratically elected governments.'[18] Recently, the actual and potential reach of investment arbitration—and its constraining effect on the exercise by states of their regulatory powers—was starkly illustrated in cases such as *Vattenfall*, involving Germany's nuclear power-phase out, and *Philip Morris v Australia*, where an investor challenged an Australian regulation on plain tobacco packaging.[19] International investment treaties are increasingly seen as instruments creatively deployed by foreign business actors to insulate '[k]ey aspects of economic life from the pressures of majoritarian politics.'[20] Concerns have also been raised whether measures in pursuit of public interest adopted by democratically elected governments should be adjudicated by foreign, unelected and unaccountable arbitrators in a process largely governed by commercial principles and lacking public input.[21] In the words of Choudhury, 'a system that curtails democratic principles—by, for example, removing issues that directly affect citizens to a system that is inaccessible and structurally isolated from public input—creates a democratic deficit.'[22]

The international investment regime's 'anti-participatory animus'[23] is also manifested in a long-standing tension between the right of political participation and international investment protection rules. The right of individuals to participate in the conduct of public affairs is articulated in the Universal Declaration of Human Rights and incorporated in the International Covenant on Civil and Political Rights and all regional human rights treaties.[24] The key function of political participation is to

[18] Lee Williams, 'What Is TTIP? And Six Reasons Why the Answer Should Scare You' *The Independent* (6 October 2015) www.independent.co.uk/voices/comment/what-is-ttip-and-six-reasons-why-the-answer-should-scare-you-9779688.html.

[19] So troubling was this inroad by investor-claimants into the area of public health decision-making that international bodies such as the World Health Organization are now offering capacity building programmes to ensure that government officials are aware of potential challenges that new public health regulations may face under international investment law. See eg World Health Organisation, 'Key considerations for the use of law to prevent noncommunicable diseases in the WHO European Region', Report of an intensive legal training and capacity-building workshop on law and noncommunicable diseases, Moscow, 30 May–3 June 2016.

[20] David Schneiderman, *Constitutionalizing Economic Globalization: Investment Rules and Democracy's Promise* (Cambridge, Cambridge University Press, 2008) 101.

[21] Barnali Choudhury, 'Recapturing Public Power: Is Investment Arbitration's Engagement of the Public Interest Contributing to the Democratic Deficit?' (2008) 41 *Vanderbilt Journal of Transnational Law* 775, 779.

[22] ibid 784.

[23] Tim Wood, 'Political Risk or Political Right? Reconciling the International Legal Norms of Investment Protection and Political Participation' (2015) 30(3) *ICSID Review* 665, 673.

[24] See International Covenant on Civil and Political Rights (ICCPR) (opened for signature 16 December 1966, entered into force 23 March 1976) 999 UNTS 171; American Convention on Human Rights (opened for signature 22 November 1969, entered into force 18 July 1978) 1144 UNTS 123, Art 23.1; Arab Charter on Human Rights (opened for signature 15 September 1994, entered into force 15 March 2008) Art 24; African Charter on Human and Peoples' Rights (opened for signature 27 June 1981, entered into force 21 October 1986) 1520 UNTS 217, Art 13(1).

guarantee persons' right to 'exercise power as members of legislative bodies or by holding executive office' directly[25] and the right to exert 'influence through public debate and dialogue with their representatives or through their capacity to organise themselves'.[26] Indirect political participation ranges from top-down interest groups to bottom-up social movements and manifests itself in such civil and political rights as free association and free assembly.[27] Political participation is not merely a human right but also the embodiment of a 'political ideal inspiring that right': democratic governance.[28]

As investment arbitration practice shows, in international investment law the right to political participation has been seen not as a good governance ideal but rather as a threat to the security and financial viability of a foreign investment—as a form of political risk from which a foreign investor should be insulated. Many an investment dispute arose from the local community protesting against the ways in which a foreign investment project was being carried out, such protests eventually resulting in the host government taking measures to stop or otherwise address the contentious aspects of the foreign investor's conduct.[29] The application of investment treaty rules to the relevant governmental measures (and finding such measures to be in breach of investment treaty rules) has led some critics to argue that, rather than promoting democracy and good governance, the international investment protection regime reveals 'ambivalence, if not outright disdain, for the product of democratic processes ... Democratic processes are considered, for the most part, to be untrustworthy constituents of social change.'[30]

The argument frequently raised in justification for shielding the investors from economic consequences of the exercise by individuals of their right to political participation—and for insulating the investors from consequences of governmental regulations in pursuit of a public interest—is that 'non-nationals are more vulnerable to domestic legislation: unlike nationals, they will generally have played no part in the election or designation of its authors despite their interests being at stake.'[31] Since

[25] UN Human Rights Committee (HRC), ICCPR General Comment No 25: Article 25 (Participation in Public Affairs and the Right to Vote) The Right to Participate in Public Affairs, Voting Rights and the Right of Equal Access to Public Service (12 July 1996), Doc ICCPR/C/21/Rev1/Add 7, para 6.

[26] ibid para 8.

[27] ibid para 25.

[28] Wood, 'Poltical Risk', 673.

[29] See eg *Metalclad Corpn v Mexico*, Award, 25 August 2000, ICSID Case No ARB (AF)/97/1, (2001) 40 ILM 36; *Técnicas Medioambientales Tecmed SA v Mexico*, Award, 29 May 2003, 10 ICSID Rep 130; *Glamis Gold Ltd v United States*, UNCITRAL, Award, 14 May 2009, *Biwater Gauff (Tanzania) Ltd v United Republic of Tanzania*, Award, 28 July 2008, ICSID Case No ARB/05/22.

[30] Schneiderman, *Constitutionalising Economic Globalization*, 114.

[31] *Tecmed v Mexico*, para 122, quoting *James v United Kingdom*, Application No 8793/79 (1986) Series A No 98, para 63. In particular, the *Tecmed* tribunal stressed that 'the foreign investor has a reduced or nil participation in the taking of the decisions that affect it, partly because the investors are not entitle[d] to exercise political rights reserved to the nationals of the State, such as voting for the authorities that will issue the decisions that affect such investors'.

foreign investors are neither part of domestic political constituency nor are benefactors of the public policies being pursued, they are said to be entitled to protection from policy changes which domestic counterparts do not enjoy.[32] The underlying 'publicness' of a disputed governmental action and of the civic opposition to the investment have thus been seen by arbitral tribunals as factors 'exemplifying the need for more stringent investor-protections.'[33]

The portrayal of foreign investors as 'victims of opportunistic politicians'[34]—and the ensuing arguments in favour of shielding investors from the effects of domestic political process—are confounded by the fact that it is not uncommon for foreign corporations to influence politics in host states, including through lobbying.[35] Foreign investors are known to have exercised considerable political influence over governmental decision-making, and can often be authors as well as benefactors of domestic regulatory policies. A stark illustration of foreign investor influence over domestic policy-making can be found in a report on the erosion by British American Tobacco (BAT) of public health legislation in Uzbekistan. Following the privatisation of the tobacco industry in 1994 BAT established its production monopoly in a market which was described as 'unique in the world in terms of its singularly unexploited advertising and promotional environment' and where 'trade and consumer loyalty could be established rapidly as advertising costs were cheap enough to allow multinationals almost unrestricted market spend.'[36] Before completing its investment, BAT learnt that the Uzbek Ministry of Health had prepared a potentially highly-effective piece of tobacco control policy that would have outlawed tobacco advertising and smoking in public places and introduced health warnings.[37] In its response to the decree, BAT described the policy as a '"deal stopper" that infringed its agreement with the Uzbekistan government' and sought its reversal or deferral.[38] BAT sought to counter the adoption of the policy by depicting it as jeopardising foreign investment in Uzbekistan, and threatening the health ministry that it would lead to 'the immediate demise of the domestic cigarette industry'.[39] BAT also

[32] Andreas Kulick, *Global Public Interest in International Investment Law* (Cambridge, Cambridge University Press, 2012) 248.

[33] Kate Miles, *The Origins of International Investment Law: Empire, Environment and the Safeguarding of Capital* (Cambridge, Cambridge University Press, 2013) 115.

[34] Muthucumaraswamy Sornarajah, *The International Law on Foreign Investment* (Cambridge, Cambridge University Press, 2004) 78.

[35] See eg David Schneiderman, 'Investing in Democracy? Political Process and International Investment Law' (2010) 60 *University of Toronto Law Journal* 909, 915.

[36] Anna B Gilmore, Jeff Collin, Martin McKee, 'British American Tobacco's erosion of health legislation in Uzbekistan' (2006) 332 *British Medical Journal* 355, citing D Sims, *Marketing report Uzbekistan. Field visit 6/10/93 to 15/10/93*. Guildford Depository: British American Tobacco, Bates No 203465873-93.

[37] ibid 356.

[38] ibid 356.

[39] ibid.

denied the health effects of smoking as described in the decree, suggesting that 'smoking has not been proven to actually cause' diseases.[40] It characterised the proposed policy as 'seriously interfering with … commercial freedom' and pointed instead to voluntary codes adopted in some countries as an example of 'the industry's responsible approach in working with governments to agree advertising standards'.[41] Consequently, the intended bans on advertising tobacco were replaced by a code drafted by the tobacco industry, and the ban on smoking in public space, including colleges and universities, was scaled back to healthcare facilities, early education establishments and schools.[42] Reports suggest that such influence by multinational tobacco firms over public health policy-making has not been confined to Uzbekistan but could be traced in other countries.[43]

Evidence from our empirical case studies also exposes the fallacy of the narratives that portray foreign investors as victims of regulatory change, deprived of the opportunities to influence government policies and therefore entitled to additional international protections to insulate their investments from the political process in host states. As discussed earlier, the interviews have highlighted the widely-known instances of collusion between foreign investors and government officials in certain sectors of the host state economy.[44] The responses reveal a growing perception that 'foreign investors are well known for their lobbying and otherwise influencing the government to get the outcome they want, for instance a hands-off regulation.'[45] Likewise, investment arbitration awards in cases involving allegations of corruption amply demonstrate that a certain category of foreign investors are prone to exercising improper influence over those entrusted with power.[46] Investors are not always bystanders: there are well-publicised instances of foreign corporations variously seeking to influence the domestic political process and attempting to insulate themselves from the latter.

III. DEVELOPING COUNTRIES AND THE MAKING OF INTERNATIONAL INVESTMENT LAW: LACK OF PARTICIPATION AND INCLUSIVITY

The anti-participatory animus of international investment law can also be discerned in the process through which international investment rules are created and modified. Is the investment treaty-making process inclusive,

40 ibid.
41 ibid.
42 ibid.
43 See eg K Alechnowicz and Simon Chapman, 'The Philippine tobacco industry: "the strongest tobacco lobby in Asia"' (2004) 13 *Tobacco Control* (Supplement 2).
44 See Chapter 4, Section II.
45 Interview MZ.
46 See Chapter 4, Section II.

participatory and generally conducive to fostering the ideals of democracy, participation and individual freedoms? Does the international investment regime sufficiently enable developing countries to make a tangible input in the process of formation, reform and application of investment rules? Despite recent efforts to reform the regime, it still fails to accommodate processes for consultation, deliberation and dialogue, including with the actors who ultimately bear the costs and benefits of investment rules—the citizens of contracting states and their representatives.[47]

A. Lack of Input by Developing States into the Making of Customary International Rules on Investment Protection

History shows that a reluctance to embrace the ideals of participation and inclusivity lies at the very foundation of the contemporary investment treaty regime. During the colonial period, assets of foreign investors were protected through a combination of bilateral agreements, concession contracts and, most importantly, political and military pressure.[48] The fall of the imperial order brought about the need for a new legal framework governing foreign investment. Some of the major precepts of customary rules on investment protection that emerged during that period, in particular the absolute guarantee of prompt, adequate and effective compensation for expropriation and sanctity of contract, were neither widely practiced in domestic legal systems of Western states nor endorsed by developing countries.[49] Western capital-exporting countries faced a significant difficulty to persuade the newly-independent developing countries to endorse these customary international norms in multilateral settings.[50] The vociferous opposition by an overwhelming number of developing states to the customary rules on expropriation was premised not only on the fact that the contested norms were the product of colonialism and therefore no longer suited the new economic and political realities, but also the historically incontrovertible truth that developing countries had no input into the creation of customary international law. In the words of Denza and Brooks, developing countries thus asserted their 'right to throw off the yoke of economic colonialism and

[47] Jurgen Kurtz, 'Building Legitimacy through Interpretation in Investor-State Arbitration' in Zachary Douglas, Joost Pauwelyn and Jorge E Viñuales (eds), *The Foundations of International Investment Law: Bringing Theory into Practice* (Oxford, Oxford University Press, 2014) 257, 263.

[48] See eg Santiago Montt, *State Liability in Investment Treaty Arbitration: Global Constitutional and Administrative Law in the BIT Generation* (Oxford, Hart Publishing, 2009) 31–48.

[49] See generally Rudolf Dolzer, 'New Foundations of the Law of Expropriation of Alien Property' (1981) 75 *AJIL* 553.

[50] For instance, Latin American states refused to include the international minimum standard into multilateral agreements during the interwar years. See eg Montt, *State Liability*, 51–55.

rules of international law fashioned before their admission to the family of nations.'[51]

The disagreement between developing and developed states over the continuing validity of the customary norms on the protection of foreign investment eventually culminated in the pronouncement of the New International Economic Order (NIEO) and the adoption of the 1974 Charter of Economic Rights and Duties of States.[52] Yet these efforts by developing states to reshape investment protection rules met with formidable resistance from developed countries, which persisted in denying the validity of the NIEO instruments as a source of international law.[53] Western jurists argued that these resolutions had no legal effect and were 'merely empty assertion or aspiration'.[54]

Similarly, efforts to deny the validity of these instruments as sources of international law were made in arbitral practice.[55] The resulting void in international law was subsequently filled with a growing number of bilateral investment treaties, which ironically reintroduced the Hull rule of prompt, adequate and effective compensation through the back door, alongside other far-reaching investment protection guarantees.[56] These treaties by and large followed the so-called OECD template which in turn had been inspired by the 1959 Abs-Shawcross Draft Convention, named after its authors, a German banker Herman Abs and a British lawyer and diplomat, Lord Shawcross. Although the efforts by the OECD to produce a multilaterally endorsed investment instrument ultimately failed, the draft convention became a blueprint for a rapidly growing number of investment treaties between developed and developing countries. Some claimed that this blueprint merely sought to 'reaffirm the more elementary and generally accepted principles of international law';[57] others regarded some of its prescriptions to be 'a far-reaching departure from the law as it stands'.[58]

[51] Eileen Denza and Shelagh Brooks, 'Investment Protection Treaties: United Kingdom Experience' (1987) 36 *ICLQ* 908, 909.

[52] The Charter manifested 'the unbridgeable chasm … between the developed countries on one side and the developing and socialist countries on the other.' Andreas F Lowenfeld, 'Investment Agreements and International Law' (2003) 42 *Columbia Journal of Transnational Law* 123, 124.

[53] See eg Wil D Verwey and Nico J Schrijver, 'The Taking of Property Under International Law: A New Legal Perspective?' (1984) 15 *Netherlands Yearbook of International Law* 3.

[54] Rosalyn Higgins, 'The Taking of Property by the State: Recent Developments in International Law' (1982) 176 *Recueil des Cours* 259, 292.

[55] Arbitrator Dupuy in *Texas Overseas Petroleum Co & California Asiatic Oil Co v Libyan Arab Republic* (1978) 17 ILM 1, 24.

[56] Denza and Brooks, 'Investment Protection Treaties', 913, noting that investment treaties were designed 'to provide important support for those standards of customary international law which had seemed to be slipping away' and to take 'political steam out of the whole subject of the treatment of foreign investment.'

[57] Hartley Shawcross, 'The Problems of Foreign Investment in International Law' (1961-1) 102 *Recueil des Cours* 335, 361–62.

[58] Georg Schwarzenberger, 'The Abs-Shawcross Draft Convention on Investments Abroad: A Critical Commentary' (1960) 9 *Journal Public Law* 147, 155.

B. Developing Countries and the Making of the Contemporary Investment Treaty Norms

Even though developing countries somewhat inexplicably entangled themselves in a vast network of bilateral investment agreements containing an array of substantive and procedural safeguards going well beyond the scope of customary international norms on investment protection, the recent study by Poulsen reveals that initially the idea of concluding investment treaties met with considerable scepticism on the part of developing countries.[59] Some developing countries expressed their disagreement with the very idea of investor-state arbitration. For instance, representatives from 19 Latin American member states of the World Bank voted against the ICSID Convention on the ground that 'investment arbitration was contrary to the accepted legal principles of our countries.'[60] When a bilateral investment treaty with the UK was proposed, Kenya requested whether the British negotiators could offer a 'new and less obviously pro-British draft.'[61] The negotiation of US treaties too often took shape of 'an intensive training seminar conducted by the United States, on U.S. terms, on what it would take to comply with the U.S. draft.'[62]

The very existence of model investment treaties—and their prevalence among developed countries[63]—lends support to the argument that developing countries are frequently seen by negotiators as lacking capacity and authority to insist on their own treaty design. Developing countries often end up as rule-takers, signing investment treaties that may only marginally depart from the developed state partner's model agreement.

Poulsen's investigation also reveals that developed countries who advocated bilateral investment treaties acted in the knowledge that such instruments were not in the interests of developing states. For instance, evidence from political archives shows that German bureaucrats had expressed concerns that developing countries would regard attempts by developed states to create a treaty-based investment protection regime 'as continuation of an imperialist and colonialist policy' and consider it 'as an intervention in their sovereignty.'[64] Likewise, UK officials were clear that bilateral investment treaties which they sought to conclude with developing countries represented an 'attempt to "freeze" customary

[59] Lauge N Skovgaard Poulsen, *Bounded Rationality and Economic Diplomacy: The Politics of Investment Treaties in Developing Countries* (Cambridge, Cambridge University Press, 2015).

[60] Poulsen, *Bounded Rationality*, 57; also Antonio R Parra, *The History of ICSID* (Oxford, Oxford University Press, 2012) 67.

[61] Poulsen, *Bounded Rationality*, 61–63.

[62] Jose Alvarez, 'Remarks' (2012) 86 *ASIL Proceedings* 550, 552.

[63] With some minor exceptions, it is developed states that follow model treaties in their international investment relations with other countries. See eg Chester Brown (ed), *Commentaries on Selected Model Investment Treaties* (Oxford, Oxford University Press, 2013).

[64] Poulsen, *Bounded Rationality*, 55, referring to the Federal Archives.

international law as understood by HMG in our favour'.[65] The British High Commissioner for Singapore voiced his concern that the treaties would involve Singapore affording guarantees to British investors 'with nothing in return.'[66] Overall, British officials were conscious that while the treaty regime were 'very much in our interests, it might not serve the interests of developing countries equally well.'[67]

Despite being aware that investment treaties offered very few—if any—benefits to developing states, government advisors from the developed capital-exporting states actively deployed bilateral negotiations as well as multilateral platforms to promote investment treaties. Although developing countries were not directly coerced into signing investment treaties, their dependence on debt relief and foreign aid, in particular in the aftermath of the 1980s debt crisis, rendered them vulnerable to policy advice and guidelines emanating from international financial institutions. For instance, the Multilateral Investment Guarantee Agency, although established with the aim of providing political risk insurance for investment projects in developing countries, took an active part in promoting investment treaties through its exercise of policy-advisory functions, including guidelines proposing the incorporation of specific investment protections in national foreign investment laws and the signing of treaties as 'obvious complements to domestic reform.'[68]

Another key player in actively advocating investment treaties has been UNCTAD. Even after its first publicly-available econometric analysis acknowledged no impact of bilateral investment treaties on investment flows, UNCTAD continued to encourage developing countries to sign such treaties. Since 1990s, UNCTAD 'promoted the process by bearing the costs of travel, full board, and lodging for developing country officials as well as organising the necessary facilities and substantive support.'[69] On some occasions, the so-called negotiation rounds involved a number of fully-finalised BITs following the OECD templates signed between various countries during a single meeting.[70] The message that UNCTAD and other treaty negotiators pushed home in promoting pre-drafted investment treaty templates was that such treaties could be effective in attracting investment in conjunction with domestic governance reforms, and that Western treaty templates were 'good enough' and easy to adopt.[71]

65 ibid 64, quoting from the FCO archives.
66 ibid 68.
67 ibid.
68 ibid 79, 76.
69 ibid 92; see also Olof Karsegard, Pedro Bravo and Hubert Blom, (2006) Final In-Depth Evaluation Report, September 2000–July 2005: UNCTAD Work Programme on Capacity Building in Developing Countries on Issues in International Investment Agreements (New York, United Nations, 2006).
70 Poulsen, *Bounded Rationality*, 93–94.
71 ibid 109.

The effect of these concerted efforts by developed country advisers and international organisations was the emergence of an extensive web of bilateral investment agreements that emulated the carefully-designed Western templates, with developing countries frequently failing to appreciate the consequences of the treaties. These treaties were not the product of national policy choice reflecting the 'internally-felt' commitment to sanctity of contract, protection of private property and de-politicisation of investor-state disputes. Rather, when signing investment treaties developing countries acted as rule-takers, making no tangible input into shaping treaty standards that would subsequently bind (and bite) them.

Even now, when a number of developed countries have embarked on recalibration of their investment treaties (due to the invocation of investment treaties against them), developing states continue to be minimally involved in the process.[72] With the exception of a few developing states that have announced their withdrawal from the investment treaty regime or major modification of their investment treaties,[73] the majority of developing states have so far opted for minor changes and refrained from any significant overhaul of their investment treaty practice. Others have attempted to reassert control over investment protection and dispute settlement but only through changes in domestic legal frameworks rather than investment treaties.[74] Yet another group of states opted for preserving the status quo.

The recent empirical studies, including those conducted by this author, suggest that many developing countries continue to be afflicted by lack of sufficient legal capacity to take a more meaningful and assertive input in the process of formation and change of investment treaty norms.[75] Although necessary expertise can be amassed through experience, empirical studies suggest that career rotations, high staff turnovers in ministries, and lack of inter-agency coordination militate against the emergence of a sufficiently robust class of national investment treaty negotiators.[76] These empirical insights resonate with findings from recent political science studies which demonstrate that lack of capacity—and of bargaining power—frequently places developing countries at a disadvantage in exercising influence over investment treaty design. The reality is that

[72] Antonius Hippolyte, 'Aspiring for a Constructive TWAIL approach towards the International Investment Regime' in Stephan W Schill, Christian J Tams and Rainer Hofmann (eds), *International Investment Law and Development: Bridging the Gap* (Cheltenham, Edward Elgar, 2015) 197.

[73] For instance, India, Indonesia and South Africa have announced a radical overhaul of their investment treaties, while Venezuela and Ecuador denounced their investment treaty commitments. For more discussion, see Chapter 3.

[74] See above Chapter 3, Section IV.

[75] Poulsen, *Bounded Rationality*, 194.

[76] ibid 195: 'Frequent rotation of developing country bureaucrats is common, and it undermines their ability to gain sufficient knowledge of the intricacies and complexities of investment treaty arbitration'. See also my findings from case studies in Chapter 3.

> … the home government consistently pursues its universal design preferences, and the resulting treaty typically conforms to its wishes, provided that its relative bargaining power is sufficient. … BITs, and the terms within them, are particularly susceptible to global power dynamics. For one, most treaties are signed by pairs of states in which one state is to some degree more powerful than the other.[77]

These arguments find some support in our case studies. In one of the countries we analysed, the interviewees involved in drafting and negotiating investment treaties confided that while they have been working on their own model treaty (aided by international advisory institutions), there was a sense that such model might be of limited use as '[m]ost countries who want to sign an investment treaty with us insist on using their model treaty … For example, if Japan wants to sign a treaty with us, we will have to adopt their model rather that insisting on ours.'[78]

How can developing countries address the lack of capacity to be able to draft and negotiate their investment treaties with other partners on a more equal footing? Poulsen suggests that under-resourced developing countries 'could call upon developed countries, or groups of developing countries, to fund one or more independent advisor centres on investment law, as recently initiated in Latin America.'[79] Yet the feasibility or indeed desirability of such an approach is doubtful. To what extent would reliance on developed countries for building national expertise facilitate the empowering of developing states and help them to meaningfully participate in the investment treaty-making process? As the history of the investment treaty regime shows, external advice has frequently produced outcomes favouring the interests of developed economies and international organisations.[80]

[77] Todd Allee and Clint Peinhardt, 'Evaluating Three Explanations for the Design of Bilateral Investment Treaties' (2014) *World Politics* 47, 62. See also Celine Tan, 'Navigating New Landscapes: Socio-legal mapping of plurality and power in international economic law' in Amanda Perry-Kessaris (ed), *Socio-legal Approaches to International Economic Law: Text, Context, Subtext* (Abingdon, Routledge, 2013) 21, arguing that 'the susceptibility of states to the authority of international economic regulatory regimes—that is, their ability to influence and be influenced by the agenda of international economic law—depends on their relative power.'

[78] Interview IDM2.

[79] Poulsen, *Bounded Rationality*, 194–95.

[80] See eg Celine Tan, 'The New Disciplinary Framework: Conditionality, New Aid Architecture and Global Economic Governance' in Julio Faundez and Celine Tan (eds), *International Economic Law, Globalization and Developing Countries* (Cheltenham, Edward Elgar, 2010) 133 observing that '… developing countries are increasingly required, through aid conditionalities, to adopt policies and institutional reforms which do not just reflect the economic and geostrategic priorities and interests of powerful donor states but also, in many ways, imitate the donors' structures of social and political organisation without due consideration of local circumstances or constraints.' See also Akbar Rasulov, 'Central Asia and the Globalisation of the Contemporary Legal Consciousness' (2014) 25 *Law and Critique* 163, 170, pointing to a growing perception in some developing states that the stream of reform-related external advice is 'a vehicle not just for "bad economics" but also "bad statescraft" and grounded in an atrociously poor understanding of the local institutional landscape and informal governance sector.'

Our empirical studies also show a potentially disempowering effect of external advisory support on developing countries. For instance, both in Kazakhstan and Ukraine our interviews show that reliance on external advisory support leads to the sense of dependency on, and inherent superiority of, foreign expertise, shifts the focus away from the need to build an internal capacity—and diminishes a belief in the very possibility of creating the domestic cadre of experts. As one interviewee explained, '[f]oreign experts and foreign laws will look more convincing. It is important that we use "brands" which foreign investors will trust.'[81] Unless the way external advisory initiatives operate is dramatically changed, they are unlikely to facilitate a more inclusive rule-making process. Other pathways need to be considered to facilitate greater input by developing states into the shaping of investment treaty rules. Such pathways range from setting up coalitions with each other to enlisting the support of domestic stakeholders in developed countries, including civil society groups.[82]

C. Developing Countries' Input into Shaping Investment Arbitration Jurisprudence

Have developing countries been able to make a meaningful input into shaping investment arbitration jurisprudence? It is beyond doubt that arbitrators exert considerable influence on investment arbitration practice—and on the principles and interpretative stances crystallised through such practice. Although there is no formal rule of binding precedent in investment arbitration,[83] arbitrators 'often feel somewhat constrained by their previous awards when deciding new cases and are conscious that what they say in one case could have an impact upon future cases and appointments.'[84] Investment tribunals are law-makers to the extent that their awards become part of 'the corpus of normative materials that counsel and tribunals will take into account in future proceedings.'[85] As Miles puts it, individuals appointed to decide on the merits of investor-states dispute 'comprise an epistemic community responsible for knowledge-creation within international investment law.'[86] Arbitrators' individual approaches

[81] Interview AFM1.

[82] Poulsen, *Bounded Rationality*, 201.

[83] 'That a special jurisprudence is developing from the leading awards in the domain of investment arbitration can only be denied by those determined to close their eyes'. Jan Paulsson, 'International Arbitration and the Generation of Legal Norms: Treaty Arbitration and International Law' (2006) 5 *TDM*, available at www.transnational-dispute-management.com.

[84] Anthea Roberts, 'Clash of Paradigms: Actors and Analogies Shaping the Investment Treaty System' (2013) 107 *AJIL* 45, 53.

[85] Alec Stone Sweet, Michael Chung, and Adam Saltzman, 'Arbitral Lawmaking and State Power: An Empirical Analysis of Investment Arbitration' (17 February 2017), available at ssrn.com/abstract=2919723, 4.

[86] Miles, *The Origins of International Investment Law*, 343.

to framing, interpreting and applying investment treaty provisions are inevitably shaped by their background, training, and interests.[87] In particular, the background of arbitrators is likely to demonstrate their choice of focus on certain issues, their sensitivity to particular concerns, and their readiness to ask certain questions.[88] Consequently, if the community of investment arbitrators is dense and homogenous, with developing countries or women being significantly underrepresented, 'one would expect a more narrowly informed body of doctrine.'[89]

Are developing countries well represented among the ranks of those who determine the scope and meaning of investment treaty rules? Sergio Puig's social network analysis of ICSID appointments offers a startling picture. It reveals that a core group of 25 arbitrators exercise inordinate influence over the development of the investment arbitration jurisprudence.[90] The investment arbitration network is 'a highly unequal one':[91] the entry barriers are very high, women and developing countries are woefully under-represented, and key players (those enjoying a high rate of appointment to arbitral panels) are primarily drawn from a small and strikingly homogenous pool of candidates.[92] The core group of arbitrators is dominated by white male individuals of seven nations (New Zealand, Australia, Canada, Switzerland, France, the UK, and the US).[93] While the reasons for this asymmetry have been discussed elsewhere[94] and fall outside the scope of this study, it is abundantly clear that the rules on arbitrator appointment perpetuate a highly inaccessible system that prevents

[87] Roberts, 'Clash or Paradigms', 54. For example, 'the commercial background of many investment treaty lawyers often manifested itself in investment treaty protections being treated as akin to contractual obligations between equal disputing parties' (ibid 77).

[88] ibid 56. See also David Kennedy, 'The Politics of the Invisible College: International Governance and the Politics of Expertise' (2001) 5 *European Human Rights Law Review* 463, 478: 'If we focus only on international lawyers … much will depend on the person's speciality—human rights lawyers, public international lawyers, international economic lawyers, comparative lawyers all see different things, worry about different things, bring a different stock of solutions, reach out to different non-legal disciplines for assistance.' See also Waible and Wu, noting that 'We would expect "conservative" arbitrators to tend to favor the protection of property rights without much reservation, whereas "progressive" arbitrators would tend to give greater weight to other societal values such as protection of the environment or public service delivery.' (Waibel and Wu, 'Are Arbitrators Political?' (2012), available at www.wipol.uni-bonn.de.).

[89] Sergio Puig, 'Social Capital in the Arbitration Market' (2014) 25 *EJIL* 387, 401; see also Michael Waibel 'ICSID Arbitrators: The Ultimate Social Network?' *EJIL:Talk!* 25 September 2014, available at www.ejiltalk.org/icsid-arbitrators-the-ultimate-social-network.

[90] ibid.

[91] Michael Waibel, 'Arbitrator Selection: Towards Greater State Control' in Andreas Kulick (ed), *Reassertion of Control over the Investment Treaty Regime* (Cambridge, Cambridge University Press, 2016) 344–47.

[92] ibid 348.

[93] Puig, 'Social Capital', 405. See also Susan D Franck, 'Development and Outcomes of Investment Treaty Arbitration' (2009) 50 *Harvard International Law Journal* 43, 78.

[94] Party autonomy, and the ensuing right by investor-claimants to have appoint their choice of arbitrator is said to be one of the chief reasons for the existing (skewed) pattern of appointments.

developing countries from making their input into shaping investment arbitration jurisprudence.

The mechanism of arbitrator appointment has prompted considerable concerns over its legitimacy and accountability and led to calls for radical reforms.[95] Seeking to address some of these concerns, the new mega-regional agreements such as the EU-US Transatlantic Trade and Investment Partnership (TTIP) and the EU-Canada Comprehensive Economic and Trade Agreement (CETA) envisage the establishment of a permanent investment court system.[96] For instance, CETA provides an alternative to party-appointed arbitrators and vests adjudicatory powers in the dispute settlement body comprising the tribunal of first instance and the appellate tribunal. The tribunal will be composed of 15 permanent members elected by the CETA Joint Committee, with five of these members to be selected from nationals of an EU Member State, five from nationals of Canada and five from nationals of third countries.[97]

Although the proposals to replace investor-state arbitration with a permanent adjudicatory body represent a significant shift from what long seemed to be immutable arbitration norms, the extent to which these reforms can meaningfully address concerns over the regime's lack of participation and inclusiveness is questionable. First, as Sornarajah pointed out in his scathing critique of the proposals, the appointment of five judges from third countries is not helpful. These judges may end up in a minority, and their stance could be overridden by a decision reached by the majority consisting of the developed country representatives. Furthermore, the proposals for the permanent judicial body do not elaborate on which geographical areas the third country judges may come from or how they would be selected.[98] Second, the proposals for an investment court system are at present effectively confined to the EU and its transatlantic partners, leaving a large number of developing states to endure the impenetrable and skewed arbitration structures inherited from the first generation of investment treaties. The fate of the European Commission's proposal to include an investment court system in TTIP remains uncertain.[99] Further still, the

[95] See eg Waibel, *Arbitrator Appointment*, 344–48; also Thomas Buergenthal, 'The Proliferation of Disputes, Dispute Settlement Procedures and Respect for the Rule of Law' (2006) 22 *Arbitration International* 495; James D Fry and Juan Ignacio Stampalija, 'Forged Independence and Impartiality: Conflicts of Interest of International Arbitrators in Investment Disputes' (2014) 30 *Arbitration International* 189.

[96] See further Stefanie Schacherer, 'TPP, CETA and TTIP: Between Innovation and Consolidation—Resolving Investor-State Disputes under Mega-regionals' (2016) 7 *Journal of International Dispute Settlement* 628, 630.

[97] Art 8.27(2) CETA; see also Schcherer, 'TPP, CETA and TTIP', 632.

[98] M Sornarajah, 'An International Investment Court: Panacea or Purgatory?' *Columbia FDI Perspectives*, No 180, 15 August 2016, available at ccsi.columbia.edu/files/2013/10/No-180-Sornarajah-FINAL.pdf.

[99] See the text of the proposal at trade.ec.europa.eu/doclib/docs/2015/september/tradoc_153807.pdf.

draft of another potentially standard-setting mega-regional agreement, the Trans-Pacific Partnership, showed clear preference for a fully-fledged investor-state arbitration mechanism.[100] Until a comprehensive overhaul of the entire network of investment treaties is undertaken, the recent reforms are likely to create a troublingly fragmented two-tier system, with the EU and its developed economy partners embracing alternatives to investor-state arbitration because the existing mechanism no longer suits them, and developing countries remaining bound by the rules that enable a close and non-representative group of decision-makers to exercise disproportionate control over the making of international investment jurisprudence.

IV. LACK OF STAKEHOLDER INPUT IN THE MAKING OF INVESTMENT TREATIES IN DEVELOPED COUNTRIES

A. Lessons from the Multilateral Agreement on Investment: Perils of Exclusionary Treaty-making

It has long been acknowledged that '[e]ven in operative democracies, processes giving rise to investment policy, like many other policy domains, are inaccessible, lacking in transparency and democratic inputs.'[101] A prime example is the (failed) Multilateral Agreement on Investment (MAI). MAI negotiations were initiated at the Annual Meeting of the OECD Council at Ministerial level in May 1995. The aim was to create a broad multilateral framework for international investment safeguarding high standards for the liberalisation of investment regimes and investment protection and providing for effective dispute settlement procedures. It was intended that the agreement would be open to non-OECD countries; however, from the outset, the negotiating process was marred by lack of a comprehensive and representative body of developing countries.[102] Likewise, civil society was not included in the negotiation process, with keen interest by NGOs stirred by an online publication of the leaked Consolidated Negotiating Text of the MAI in August 1997. The lack of publicity about the negotiations in the media led to a perception that the public and stakeholders were being debarred from the process.[103] The negotiations ultimately failed, largely due to the content of the agreement: it was

[100] The text of the agreement can be found at ustr.gov/trade-agreements/free-trade-agreements/trans-pacific-partnership/tpp-full-text. See further Schacherer, 'TPP, CETA and TTIP', 643.

[101] David Schneiderman, 'Power and Production in Global Legal Pluralism: An International Political Economy Approach' in Amanda Perry-Kessaris (ed), *Socio-legal Approaches to International Economic Law: Text, Context, Subtext* (Abingdon, Routledge, 2013) 116.

[102] Peter Muchlinski, 'The Rise and Fall of the Multilateral Agreement on Investment: Where Now?' (2000) 34 *International* Lawyer 1033, 1039.

[103] ibid 1039–40.

conceived as a pure investment protection instrument and premised on the idea that government regulation of businesses ought to be curtailed. This rendered the MAI unpalatable to a number of OECD member states, with the French Prime Minister branding it as 'an unacceptable threat to national sovereignty.'[104]

Although it was the OECD member states that opposed the MAI, NGOs played a significant part in precipitating its downfall. They fomented the political opposition through raising awareness of its one-sided nature, drawing attention to critical issues such as the unaccountability of corporate actors and of the international organisations that stood behind the negotiations.[105] As critics of the MAI observed in analysing the reasons for its failure, a more representative and inclusive negotiation process is a crucial precondition for any multilateral investment treaty instrument, and that 'the active involvement of developing countries and countries in transition is essential.'[106] Lessons from the failure of the MAI did not translate into concrete shifts in state approaches to investment treaties. Even in developed states, these treaties are still drafted and negotiated in the absence of a meaningful political debate, with limited or at times non-existent public input in the formulation of investment treaty priorities. It remains lamentably common for the executive agencies to negotiate such treaties 'in a sphere beyond the reach of the public.'[107]

B. New Trends in the Making of Mega-regional Investment Agreements: Towards a More Inclusive Process?

i. Innovations in Drafting and Negotiation of EU Investment Agreements

Recent developments in the EU and the US point to a burgeoning trend towards greater openness and participation in the process of drafting and negotiating international investment agreements. In January 2014, the European Commission announced the launch of an online public consultation on investment protection and investor-to-state dispute settlement (ISDS) in the TTIP.[108] The consultation was introduced in response to what the then

[104] See 'France Quits Investment Accord Talks on Multilateral Agreement, Jospin Says Structure "Not Open to Reform" and Sovereignty Threatened' *Financial Times* (15 October 1998).

[105] Muchlinski, 'The Rise and Fall', 1049.

[106] ibid 1050.

[107] Markus Gehring and Dimitrij Euler, 'Public interest in investment arbitration' in Dimitrij Euler, Markus Gehring and Maxi Scherer, *Transparency in International Investment Arbitration: A Guide to the UNCITRAL Rules on Transparency in Treaty-Based Investor-State Arbitration* (Cambridge, Cambridge University Press, 2015) 8.

[108] 'Commission to consult European public on provisions in EU-US trade deal on investment and investor-state dispute settlement', Brussels, 21 January 2014.

EU trade commissioner referred to as 'unprecedented public interest' in the negotiation of TTIP and CETA.[109] The consultation was made available in all official EU languages and, in departure from the usual assumption that the interests of the public are best mediated through the states, established a direct corridor of communication to allow interests that are not well-represented through member state governments to be heard in the negotiation process.[110] It was seen as a mechanism designed to facilitate direct public input into the process of making international investment agreements. Greater engagement of the general public and civil society with international treaty-making was in turn expected to facilitate a better-informed and publicly-backed EU investment policy, and create an investment treaty regime more directly connected to democratic processes.[111]

A burgeoning shift away from diplomacy to a more inclusive process of making international investment treaties has also manifested itself in an increased parliamentary scrutiny of the treaty-making process. For instance, in the context of the EU-US treaties, the process of drafting and negotiating international agreements was until recently 'dominated by governmental cooperation in opaque frameworks, which hampers democratic participation and oversight.'[112] The changes introduced by the Lisbon Treaty enabled the European Parliament, in its capacity as a co-legislator on the EU's trade agreements, to assume the responsibility of ensuring that the talks on EU investment agreements are transparent and that the final outcome 'respects European values, stimulates sustainable growth and contributes to the well-being of all citizens.'[113] The Parliament's involvement in the making of TTIP was therefore hailed as a step towards a more transparent and inclusive process of trade negotiations. By providing a platform for relevant political factions to voice their opposition to the investor-state arbitration mechanism and its inclusion in the EU investment agreements, the European Parliament has been facilitating dialogue about the contours of the future international investment treaties. It has done so by enabling the voices which had hitherto been dismissed for being too ideological to be heard as a

[109] ibid.

[110] Stephan W Schill, 'Editorial: Five Times Transparency in International Investment Law' (2014) 15 *Journal of World Investment and Trade* 363, 366.

[111] ibid 368.

[112] Davor Jančić, 'Transatlantic Regulatory Interdependence, Law and Governance: The Evolving Roles of the EU and US Legislatures' (2015) 17 *Cambridge Yearbook of European Legal Studies* 334, 336; see also Deidre Curtin, 'Official Secrets and the Negotiation of International Agreements: Is the EU Executive Unbound?' (2013) 50 *Common Market Law Review* 423.

[113] European Parliament, Committee on International Trade, 'Draft Report containing the European Parliament's recommendations to the Commission on the negotiations for the Transatlantic Trade and Investment Partnership (TTIP)' 2014/2228(INI) 5 February 2015, available at www.europarl.europa.eu/sides/getDoc.do?pubRef=-//EP//NONSGML+COMPARL+PE-549.135+01+DOC+PDF+V0//EN.

legitimate expression of concern and political contestation. Arguably, the European Parliament's involvement in treaty-making process is a crucial element of its mandate to promote the values of liberalism and democracy, thus also contributing to the democratisation of regional and global governance.[114]

The opening of the public consultation and increased parliamentary involvement has moved investment treaty protection into the realm of hotly-contested political issues and created the opportunities for a more open and inclusive treaty-making process. This re-politicisation of international investment law—or at least of the process of investment treaty making—has most certainly influenced the EU's evolving position on investment treaty protection. As evidenced by the Commission's statement following the analysis of the public consultation submissions, the EU had to acknowledge the existence of considerable scepticism against investment arbitration.[115] The Commission responded by stressing its commitment to the reforms aimed at designing 'more balanced investment chapters' in EU agreements.[116] One example of such reform is the incorporation of 'a set of modern provisions which rebalance the rights of the state and the investor in favour of the state, and its right to regulate in the public interest' in EU-Canada CETA.[117] Other proposed changes include measures to increase transparency of arbitral proceedings,[118] creating a code of conduct for arbitrators, access to an appeal system and, a medium term goal, working towards the establishment of a permanent multilateral investment court.[119]

ii. Re-politicisation of Investment Treaty-making in the United States

An overarching significance of the public consultation and increased parliamentary scrutiny over EU investment treaties is that these developments may be 'the precursor of more general changes in how international treaties, in particular those with immediate impact on domestic law and policy-making, are made in the future.'[120] Indeed, the

114 Jančić, 'Transatlantic Regulatory Interdependence', 336.

115 The European Commission, 'Online public consultation on investment protection and investor-to-state dispute settlement (ISDS) in the Transatlantic Trade and Investment Partnership Agreement', 13 January 2015 SWD(2015) 3 final, available at trade.ec.europa.eu/doclib/docs/2015/january/tradoc_153044.pdf.

116 See the statement by the Commissioner Cecilia Malmström, available at ec.europa.eu/commission/2014-2019/malmstrom/blog/investments-ttip-and-beyond-towards-international-investment-court_en.

117 ibid.

118 See eg 'European Commission pushes for full transparency for ISDS in current investment treaties', available at europa.eu/rapid/press-release_IP-15-3881_en.htm.

119 See C Malmström, 'Investments in TTIP and beyond—towards an International Investment Court', available at ec.europa.eu/commission/2014-2019/malmstrom/blog/investments-ttip-and-beyond-towards-international-investment-court_en.

120 Schill, 'Editorial: Five Times Transparency in International Investment Law' (2014) 15 *Journal of World Investment & Trade* 363, 369.

EU's approach inspired calls for a similar process to be introduced in the US.[121] For instance, in a letter addressed to the then Ambassador Froman, US-based labour, environmental, health, consumer, business, family farm, faith-based and other interest groups applauded the launch of the public consultation process for the European civil society and requested that the same opportunity be provided to stakeholders and NGOs in the US.[122]

In the US, public debates over investment treaties and investment arbitration have been a feature of the domestic political process since at least 1992 when one candidate in presidential elections campaigns agitated against the US membership in NAFTA.[123] The controversy reached its first tipping point after the first stream of NAFTA investment disputes made it clear that Chapter 11 rules on investment protection could be deployed to challenge environmental regulations and other public policies. To name a few, in 1999, a Canadian investor in *Methanex v United States* challenged California's ban of a certain gasoline additive.[124] Earlier in 1998, a Canadian investor in *Loewen v United States* initiated arbitral proceedings claiming damages for actions of a Mississippi court.[125] NGOs and civil society groups, academics, and other factions forming part of the 'anti-globalisation' movement raised concerns that NAFTA investment protection rules would hinder state capacity to regulate and legislate in the public interest.[126]

Civil society concerns might well have been ignored by those involved in the drafting and negotiation of US investment treaties, had it not been for increased publicity the controversy received. According to one online trade news resource, it was journalist Bill Moyers' documentary on NAFTA which helped to mobilise congressional leadership initial opposition to granting trade promotion authority to President GW Bush.[127] Trade promotion authority or 'TPA', also known as fast-track legislation, was first introduced in the Trade Act of 1974. Its overarching aim was to strike a balance between Presidential and Congressional authority in

[121] In the US, government agencies can and do obtain input from interested persons prior to initiation. Regulatory decision-making is far less inclusive and comprehensive, and the opportunities for direct input into international treaty making seem to be limited to representative democracy. See RT Bull, 'Public Participation and the Transatlantic Trade and Investment Partnership' (2014–2015) 83 *George Washington Law Review* 1262, 1283.

[122] The letter available at www.etuc.org/sites/www.etuc.org/files/press-release/files/letter_to_amb._froman_requesting_public_consultation_on_investment_2014.pdf.

[123] See James E Mendenhall, 'The Evolving U.S. Position on International Investment Protection and Its Impact on the U.S. Position in the Trans-Pacific Partnership Negotiations' in N Jansen Calamita and Mavluda Sattorova, *The Regionalization of International Investment Treaty Arrangements* (British Institute of International and Comparative Law, London, 2015) 255.

[124] *Methanex Corporation v United States*, Final Award on Jurisdiction and Merits, 3 August 2005 (2005) 44 ILM 1345.

[125] *Loewen v United States*, Award, 26 June 2003 (2003) 42 ILM 811.

[126] David Schneiderman, *Resisting Economic Globalization: Critical Theory and International Investment Law* (Basingstoke, Palgrave Macmillan, 2013) 80.

[127] ibid.

matters relating to US foreign trade policy. While the US Constitution confers Congress with a final say on trade-related issues, the 'fast-track' approval has shifted some powers to the President, enabling the government to negotiate trade agreements and bring them back to the Congress for an up-or-down vote only. The heightening of controversy over NAFTA investment protection rules coincided with the expiry of fast-track authority in 2002. For fast-track trade authority to be successfully renewed the Bush administration had to garner support within Congress, including by addressing the increasingly vociferous concerns of environmental and other groups over the implications of investment protection for public policy regulations.[128] In order to prevent members of the Congress from using the controversial NAFTA investment provisions as a ground to oppose the government's ambitious trade agenda, a binding interpretation of the NAFTA Chapter 11 clarifying the scope of certain substantive investment obligations contained in Article 1105 was pushed through, laying ground for what subsequently became a new generation of US investment treaties.[129] The NAFTA parties also took steps to demystify the process and enhance transparency of investor-state arbitration.[130]

Some criticised the amendments for not going far enough. As Public Citizen highlighted in its excoriating analysis of the interpretation, the clarification by the NAFTA governments sought to narrow the application of Article 1105 to treatment that is required by 'customary' international law, yet failed to define what is meant by 'customary', thus '[p]roviding enormous opportunity for a continuation of the expansive interpretation by the tribunals.'[131] Other critics argue that the amendments merely 'reinforce[] a policy of promoting US constitutional norms abroad while trumping local rules that regulate markets.'[132] Indeed, one of the key objectives of the 2002 Bipartisan Trade Promotion Authority Act was to ensure that

> foreign investors in the United States are not accorded greater substantive rights with respect to investment protections than United States investors in the United States, and to secure for foreign investors rights comparable to those that would be available under United States legal principles and practices.[133]

[128] ibid.

[129] Notes of Interpretation of Certain Chapter 11 Provisions (NAFTA Free Trade Commission, 31 July 2001).

[130] ibid. See further Alessandra Asteriti and Christian J Tams, 'Transparency and Representation of the Public Interest in Investment Treaty Arbitration' in Stephan W Schill (ed), *International Investment Law and Comparative Public Law* (Oxford, Oxford University Press, 2010) 793–94.

[131] NAFTA Chapter 11 Investor-to-State Cases: Bankrupting Democracy, available at www.citizen.org/publications/publicationredirect.cfm?ID=7076.

[132] Schneiderman, *Resisting Economic Globalization*, 20.

[133] Bipartisan Trade Promotion Act 2002, Title XXI of Pub L 107-210. See further Parvan Parvanov and Mark Kantor, 'Comparing U.S. Law and Recent U.S. Investment Agreements: Much More Similar Than You Might Expect' in Karl Sauvant (ed), *Yearbook on International Investment Law & Policy 2010–2011* (Oxford, Oxford University Press, 2012) 743.

The key achievement of the NAFTA amendments was not to ensure a more democratic and equitable application of investment protection rules but rather to shield the US from unbridled exposure to investor claims whilst ensuring that US investors abroad continue to enjoy strong protections. Notwithstanding these failings, the ensuing change of US international investment agreements has considerably influenced treaty drafting patterns globally.

iii. Towards a More Pluralist Conception of State in the Investment Treaty-making Process?

The political history of the binding interpretation to Article 1105 also shows that the formation and change of international investment agreements is becoming increasingly shaped by domestic politics—a factor that has been somewhat neglected in existing investment treaty scholarship. The importance of viewing state behaviour not just as a set of strategic calculations by a unitary actor but rather as a product of complex interactions between political players at the domestic level has been acknowledged in the more recent theories of compliance with international law. Notable among them is Joel Trachtman's domestic coalitions-based theory, which seeks to explain and predict state behaviour by uncovering 'the black box of the state in order to see the internal workings of the domestic political process' and focusing on the individuals and groups that influence governments through political institutions and social practices.[134] Trachtman exposes the cracks in the explanations based on the unitary model of the state—including their ignorance of the domestic political dynamics which underpin the state's decision to comply, modify or withdraw from international legal regimes.[135] He argues that 'there is no unified, ex ante national interest. The national interest is the result of a domestic political process, taking into account opportunities and risks in the international market.'[136]

As the recent developments in investment treaty practice demonstrate, the unitary model of the state may indeed have been a reasonable heuristic device where investment treaty rules were predominantly matters of foreign policy determined independently of domestic constituents' interests and preferences. It can still be used as an effective analytical tool in explaining the treaty practice of states where domestic political input is stifled or non-existent. However, as the investment treaty reforms in

[134] Joel P Trachtman, 'International Law and Domestic Political Coalitions: The Grand Theory of Compliance with International Law' (2010) 11 *Chicago Journal of International Law* 128–29.

[135] ibid 130.

[136] ibid 130–31.

the US and the EU have revealed so far, international investment law has been increasingly moving from the realm of 'beyond the border' to 'inside the border' issues.[137] With domestic political actors and constituencies becoming increasingly vocal in the debate over international investment agreements, the shape of the latter is likely to be correspondingly influenced by national politics within host states. In particular, much will depend on how a particular host state accommodates an inclusive and participatory interaction between various stakeholders and whether national political and constitutional arrangements enable such stakeholders to make an effective input in a debate about future investment agreements.

iv. One Step Forward, Two Steps Back?: The Role of Domestic Constitutional Arrangements in Enabling and Constraining Public Engagement in Investment Treaty-making

When examined through a less state-centric lens, the apparent willingness of the EU to allow the input by the general public in the debate concerning investment protection in mega-regional agreements should be seen in conjunction with the European Commission's refusal, the same year it launched public consultation, to register the *Stop TTIP* initiative. The European Citizens' Initiative (ECI) has been introduced by the Treaty of Lisbon as a platform for citizens to present a legislative proposal to the Commission, providing they collect over a million signatures from a minimum of seven member states.[138] The *Stop TTIP* initiative was formally submitted on 15 July 2014 and requested the Commission to halt the process of negotiating TTIP and CETA due to these agreements giving rise to 'several critical issues such as investor-state dispute settlement and rules on regulatory cooperation that pose a threat to democracy and the rule of law.'[139] Despite the initiative having met the expressly-stated admissibility requirements, the Commission refused to register it on what many have regarded as formalistic grounds.[140] Among other reasons, the Commission resorted to distinguishing between the conclusion of treaties and preparatory work. While conceding that, as a matter of

[137] ibid 131.

[138] Art 11(4) Treaty on European Union. For an overview of the ECI see Alex Warleigh, 'On the Path to Legitimacy? The EU Citizens Initiative Right from a Critical Deliberativist Perspective' in Carlo Ruzza and Vincent Della Sala (eds), *Governance and Civil Society in the European Union* (Manchester University Press, 2007) 55; Michael Dougan, 'What Are We to Make of the Citizens' Initiative?' (2011) *CML Rev* 1807; Bruno Kaufmann, 'Transnational "Babystep": The European Citizens' Initiative' in Maija Setala and Theo Schiller (eds), *Citizens' Initiatives in Europe Procedures and Consequences of Agenda-Setting by Citizens* (Basingstoke, Palgrave Macmillan, 2012) 228.

[139] ec.europa.eu/citizens-initiative/public/initiatives/non-registered/details/2041.

[140] ec.europa.eu/citizens-initiative/public/documents/2552.

principle, the signing and conclusion of an international agreement may be requested by a citizens' initiative, the Commission reasoned that the preparatory decisions authorising the opening of treaty negotiations or repealing such authorisation did not fall within the remit of a citizens' initiative.[141] Furthermore, the *Stop TTIP* initiative invited the Commission to stop something from occurring, in this case by repealing the mandate for the TTIP negotiations and refraining from the conclusion of CETA. In the Commission's view, a citizen's initiative would be admissible if it requested modifying law, not refraining from creating law.[142]

The refusal by the European Commission to register the *Stop TTIP* initiative was heavily criticised as being politically motivated and out of line with the Commission's previous practice.[143] One practical implication of the Commission's refusal is that, by precluding a citizens' initiative in respect of preparatory acts, citizens have been excluded from using the ECI process to try to influence the agenda of any external treaty that is being negotiated by the EU.[144] The Commission's distinction between proposals to modify law and to refrain from certain actions has also been found questionable. The approach it has taken dramatically reduces the range of situations in which citizens' initiative as a democratic instrument could be used. Concerns have been expressed that the Commission's interpretation of the ECI legislation has thereby restricted the scope for effective citizen engagement in the formation of EU international treaties.[145] The refusal to register the *Stop TTIP* initiative—along with the Commission's apparent preference for public consultation as a means of engagement with experts[146]—prompted questions as to whether the existing instruments of democracy continue to be deployed merely to build a wider basis of support and legitimise investment treaties and not as a means of facilitating effective citizens' participation in the making of investment treaties.[147]

Similar criticisms can be levelled in relation to the European Parliament's role in democratising investment treaty-making process. A closer and more critical look at the Parliament's commitment to progressive reform of international investment law can discern it as tokenistic and obscuring the underlying lack of truly inclusive treaty-making process. For instance, in the early days of preparatory work for CETA, the Parliament strongly

[141] ibid.

[142] ibid.

[143] See eg James Organ, 'Decommissioning Direct Democracy? A critical analysis of Commission decision making on the legal admissibility of European Citizens Initiative proposals' (2014) 10(3) *EuConst* 422.

[144] ibid.

[145] ibid.

[146] James Organ, 'EU Citizen Participation and the ECI: The TTIP Legacy' (2017), available at papers.ssrn.com/sol3/papers.cfm?abstract_id=2919810.

[147] ibid.

advocated to replace investor-state dispute settlement by state-to-state dispute settlement and the use of local judicial remedies.[148] However, later it welcomed the Commission's proposal for a new Investment Court System and some factions within the European Parliament have supported the inclusion of the investment court solution in CETA as well as TTIP.

The focus of the European Parliament's recommendations to the Commission throughout the recent negotiations lends some credence to the argument that rather than being committed to the idea of progressive transformation of international investment law in general, the Parliament is merely seeking to modify the law so as to preserve old asymmetries of power in global economic relations. For instance, the main thrust of the Parliament's proposals so far was to recommend that the Commission takes necessary steps to ensure that investment protection provisions are limited to post-establishment provisions and focus on national treatment, most-favoured nation, fair and equitable treatment and protection against direct and indirect expropriation, including the right to prompt, adequate and effective compensation; that standards of protection and definitions of investor and investment should be drawn up in a precise legal manner protecting the right to regulate in the public interest.[149] However, the Parliament did not question the extent to which investment protection provisions should be aligned with protections provided to investors under EU law (the latter offers greater policy space for host states). It did not throw its weight behind the debate over the desirability of maintaining two separate regimes for intra-EU investors and investors from third states. Neither did it question critically the extent to which substantive protections enshrined in EU investment treaties would be compatible with the ideals of democracy, participation and good governance.

The European Parliament could have played, but failed to, the role of an important global champion for a more sustainable, inclusive and fair investment protection regime. The opposition to investor-state dispute settlement by the European Parliament gained momentum and was fuelled by concerns over a prospect of developed member states of the EU being targeted by investor-state arbitration claims. This can be seen not so much as a laudable effort to address the shortcomings of the existing global investment treaty regime but rather as a parochial refusal to accept the norms which have long been binding (and biting) upon the rest of international community. European states invented and applied investor-state arbitration in over 1,500 investment agreements,[150] and yet

[148] European Parliament resolution of 8 June 2011 on EU-Canada trade relations, 8 June 2011, Strasbourg.

[149] EU-Canada Comprehensive Economic and Trade Agreement, Briefing, January 2016. EPRS, PE 573.929.

[150] Patricia Garcia-Duran and Leif Johan Eliasson, 'The Public Debate over Transatlantic Trade and Investment Partnership and Its Underlying Assumptions' (2017) 51 *Journal of World Trade* 23, 31.

the institution of investor-state protection turned into a hotly-contested political issue only after the launch of TTIP and CETA negotiations, which increased the risk of developed member states of the EU becoming a target of investor claims.

The symbolic rather than real input of the Parliament into investment treaty reform in the EU can be explained by unique constitutional arrangements underpinning the allocation of power between the EU institutions which arguably prevent the Parliament from exercising significant influence over international investment agreements. In terms of domestic, or in this case supranational constitutional configurations, it was the Lisbon Treaty that propelled the European Parliament to a prominent place in the process of negotiation and conclusion of investment treaties. By virtue of Article 218(6) and 10 TFEU the European Parliament has been vested with the power of consent to international trade agreements and has the right to be kept informed throughout the negotiation process. What is crucial for our understanding of the effectiveness of parliamentary engagement is the fact that 'power of assent (or dissent) to a final text on a take-it-or-leave-it basis, although important, is no real substitute for involvement in the shaping of legislation.'[151] As far as the process of setting an investment treaty negotiation agenda is concerned, Article 218(10) TFEU vests the European Parliament with a formal right to be 'informed' 'immediately and fully' at all stages of the conclusion of an international agreement.[152] However, it does grant the Parliament the power to approve the negotiating directives.[153] Neither does the Parliament have formal power of oversight of the negotiating process.[154] The European Parliament is therefore at an institutional disadvantage compared to the Commission and the Council. And this disadvantage has its impact not only within the EU but also globally, as the outcome of investment treaty negotiations are likely to shape the contours of the future international investment law.

The weakness of the European Parliament's response to the Commission's stance on investment treaty protection issues, however, cannot be attributed solely to the way the Lisbon Treaty allocated power between EU institutions. Even after having been granted consent powers, the Parliament has not always been consistent in fully utilising its authority to exercise democratic control and act as a conduit for citizens' concerns. The relevant example is its involvement with the Anti-Counterfeiting Trade

[151] Marise Cremona, 'Negotiating the Transatlantic Trade and Investment Partnership (TTIP): Context and scope of TTIP' (2015) 52 *Common Market Law Review* 351, 362.

[152] Art 218(10) TFEU.

[153] Szilárd Gáspár-Szilágyi, 'Transparency, Investment Protection and the European Parliament' (2017) *European Investment Law and Arbitration Review* 8–9.

[154] Art 207(3) TFEU. It must be acknowledged, however, that the European Parliament has on occasion compensated for this lack of oversight powers by informally using a threat to veto the outcome of a negotiation. See further Gáspár-Szilágyi, 'Transparency', 12.

Agreement (ACTA).[155] As Subramanian has shown in her recent critique, the European Parliament needed an external trigger before making the full use of its consent powers.[156] Prior to rejecting ACTA in 2012, the Parliament had effectively oscillated between voicing its displeasure over lack of transparency in the negotiation process and subsequently hailing it as a step in the right direction. The new Lisbon powers were not sufficient for the Parliament to take a more daring and consistent stance in confronting the Commission's efforts to push forward ACTA. It needed an external trigger, which presented itself in citizen protests and the submission of a petition in March 2012 with two and half million signatures urging the Parliament to reject the agreement. Only then did the European Parliament seize the opportunity to utilise its consent powers and to demonstrate 'its bond with the citizens' to counter the allegation of democratic deficit.[157] While such inertia on the part of the European Parliament may have ramifications for the future of international treaties globally and particularly those signed with developing states, ultimately it is also likely to shape the impact of treaties—including investment treaties—on host communities in developed EU member states.

V. CONCLUSION

Despite the significant changes which the investment treaty regime has undergone over the past decade, both investment treaty making and the formation of arbitral jurisprudence do not accommodate a meaningful participation by developing countries. Developing countries are still constrained in their ability to contribute to shaping the good governance standards which national institutions are expected to endorse and abide by in their treatment of foreign investors. While some of these constraints emanate from the lack of capacity, the fundamental problem is in the investment treaty regime's failure to address the historically-entrenched asymmetries at the heart of its treaty-making processes and arbitration mechanism.

Neither do the existing institutional and procedural arrangements enable an input from host communities into formulating investment protection priorities. Although the recent developments in investment treaty-making in the EU mark a significant shift towards a more participatory process, the manner in which the Commission conducted the public consultation, its refusal to register the *Stop TIIP* citizens' initiative, and the

[155] Sujitha Subramanian, 'The Changing Dynamics of the Global Intellectual Property Legal Order: Emergence of A 'Network Agenda'? (2015) 64 *ICLQ* 103.
[156] ibid 126.
[157] ibid.

European Parliament's ambivalence over (and its failure to mount effective opposition to) investor-state dispute settlement, all demonstrate that inequalities of power hold sway over the formation of investment treaty norms in the EU. While governments, as the only legitimate and accountable representatives of their populations, bear the ultimate responsibility for concluding binding international agreements, a genuinely inclusive and participatory treaty-making process necessitates that provision is made 'for representatives of civil society to be officially involved in the negotiations as advisers and not merely as observers.'[158] Furthermore, investment policies should account for the views and interests of local and regional stakeholders.[159] Greater strides towards a more participatory and inclusive treaty-making process will arguably not only counter the perceptions of remoteness of international investment agreements but also, crucially, could facilitate a 'bottom up' formulation of investment protection norms globally.

[158] Muchlinski, 'The Rise and Fall', 1050.
[159] ibid 1053.

7

Conclusion

WHAT IMPACT DOES investment treaty law have on host states? Does it enable good governance for both foreign investors and host communities as the proponents of the recent regime narratives argue? What does the growing invocation of good governance ideals in investment treaty law tell us about the shifting scope of investment treaty norms and their objectives?

The historical and doctrinal evaluation of the good governance narratives in investment arbitration practice point to both increasing mission creep and the attempts at what Tan described as 'crisis containment and rehabilitation of the normative and institutional credibility of the regime'.[1] Reliant on investors to purchase their services, arbitrators are interested in advancing interpretations that enhance the attractiveness and utility of investment treaties for the business community. By expanding the scope of state responsibility in investment treaty law through the creation of new causes of action that fall under the general rubric of 'failure to ensure and maintain good governance standards', arbitral tribunals have opened up new opportunities for investors to challenge governmental conduct in a significantly broader range of cases than customary international law or national laws previously allowed. At the same time, good governance has provided an attractive alternative to the increasingly contested economic development rationale traditionally used to justify the existence of both investment treaty law and its investor-state arbitration mechanism. Good governance is both a substantive standard to which host states (mostly developing countries) are expected to adhere in their treatment of foreign investors and a benefit which host states (again, mostly developing countries) are ultimately promised if they continue to participate in the investment treaty regime.

The harnessing of the good governance precepts by arbitral tribunals was supported by inadequate legal reasoning. Whilst potentially enhancing

[1] Celine Tan, 'Reviving the emperor's old clothes: the good governance agenda, development and international investment law' in Stephan W Schill, Christian J Tams and Rainer Hofmann (eds), *International Investment Law and Development: Bridging the Gap* (Cheltenham, Edward Elgar, 2015) 148.

the attractiveness of investment treaty law to foreign investors and supplying additional justification for investment treaty instruments, the introduction of the new standards into the corpus of positive international investment law highlights broader systemic issues in the design and functioning of the investment treaty regime. Whilst some of these issues are gradually attracting more attention in the course of ongoing investment treaty reforms, others still remain largely unaddressed. Our interrogation of investment treaty law and its good governance mission highlights the need to re-evaluate the existing rationales behind both investment treaties and the investor-state arbitration mechanism. Now that evidence increasingly points to the lack of positive correlation between investment treaties offering increased FDI and economic growth, who stands to gain from international investment agreements that grant foreign investors enhanced privileges? What is the overarching societal function of the contemporary investment treaty regime and to what extent is that function attainable given the existing design of investment treaty rules and associated investment arbitration procedures? Further studies are warranted to explore how those who ultimately bear the costs and benefits of investment rules—developing states and host communities—could be included in the process of redefining investment treaty objectives and shaping the content of investment treaty norms.

Does investment treaty law and its investor-state dispute settlement mechanism encourage host states to embrace good governance norms in their dealings with foreign investors? Does the imposition of monetary sanctions for a breach of good governance precepts deter the host government from committing such breaches in the future? The principal finding of our empirical investigation is that host states do not necessarily respond to their encounter with investment treaty law by becoming more risk-averse and compliant with good governance norms. There is also a pervasive lack of awareness about investment treaty law and its good governance prescriptions among government officials who deal with investors on a day-to-day basis. Whilst broader and systematic empirical analyses are still warranted, this study has nevertheless been useful in unveiling some of the hitherto less-visible patterns of host state behaviour. Our conversations with governmental officials have helped cast light onto the currently underexplored yet noteworthy aspects of the interplay between international norms and domestic change. For instance, the consistent message by international organisations about the significance of foreign investment protection appears to push host states in the direction of the solutions that prioritise 'good governance for foreign investors' rather than 'good governance for all.' There is a clearly discernible trend among developing states towards creating legal enclaves for foreign investors not only at the international but also national level. The proliferation of these enclaves does not inspire belief in international law as a force for change. Rather, over-valuing foreign investors entrenches the prevailing perceptions of international law as a forum for select privileged actors.

The case studies also highlight the significance of further empirically-driven and contextual studies of the effects of investment treaties on government behaviour. Among other things, the impact of investment treaty law should be investigated in conjunction with other transnational programmes and initiatives responsible for the diffusion of the so-called international norms and best practices on regulation of investment in developing states. Such an inquiry necessitates a broader, more comprehensive and longitudinal study, which in turn requires significant resources, networks to enable access to government officials, linguistic competence and even the ability to adapt conversation in line with cultural norms and expectations of interviewees. In combining a normative and doctrinal analysis with empirical insights and thereby seeking to make a contribution to the existing empirically-grounded discourse, this book has been greatly inspired by the richness of contextual data the conversations with government officials offered. Yet this author is also cognisant of the methodological constraints and practical hurdles that continue to stand in the way of empirical studies. Not only are the barriers to empirical studies involving government officials extremely high, but new entrants might also be discouraged by the eagerness with which some academics dismiss the usefulness of empirical approaches due to 'sampling issues'.

Throughout this book, the focus on those whom investment treaty law endeavours to govern has reaffirmed the growing importance of peering behind the unitary conception of state and identifying the actors who shape host state interaction with the investment treaty regime. According to Kingsbury, '[t]he fashion for abandoning focus on States is, at best, grossly premature.'[2] This book, however, does not advocate dispensing with the state as a principal unit of analysis, but rather makes a case for the incorporation of a broader range of actors into the existing analytic framework to enhance our understanding of how they set the state machinery in motion.

Take, for instance, international organisations and advisory agencies that have been active in compelling developing states to reform their regulatory frameworks for investment at the national level. While our empirical studies allude to the central role played by resource constraints in shaping the state capacity to internalise good governance norms, the interviews also suggest that external support may not always carry an enabling effect on recipient countries. It seems that the emerging transnational network of influence, primarily comprising international financial

[2] Benedict Kingsbury, 'The Concept of Compliance as a Function of Competing Conceptions of International Law' (1998) 19 *Michigan Journal of International Law* 345, 371.

and aid institutions, Western governments and those responsible for the production of investment treaty norms, may in fact suppress rather than enable improvements in domestic governance. With its emphasis on external (foreign) expertise, external (international) law and dispute settlement mechanisms, these transnational agents of diffusion are likely to have an emasculating effect on the national legal consciousness and thus hinder the emergence of new, innovative ways of interaction between developing states and the global investment protection regime. Governance reforms in developing states do require capacity-building support, but the latter needs to be designed so as to empower national actors rather than merely increase the sphere of influence of international agencies.[3]

The critique of the investment treaty regime's resistance to the ideas of democracy, participation and socio-political enablement of host communities also highlights the growing role of non-state actors in shaping the future contours of international investment law. Although the recent shifts towards greater openness in investment treaty-making could be criticised for merely creating an illusion of stakeholder participation to deflect the growing criticisms of the regime, domestic political actors and constituencies are becoming increasingly vocal in the debate over investment treaty law. The future of international investment agreements is therefore likely to be influenced by national constitutional arrangements governing the input by civil society and other non-state stakeholders in the treaty-making process. This, in turn, yet again calls for a re-orientation of existing discourse on investment treaties towards less state-centric and more pluralistic approaches. To quote Itamar Mann, the problem with most international legal scholarship today is that it displays more concern about the future of international law than about those it is supposed to govern.[4]

[3] Carol Harlow, 'Global Administrative Law: The Quest for Principles and Values' (2006) 17 *EJIL* 187.

[4] Itamar Mann (@itamann), Twitter, 20 June 2017, 12:04.

Bibliography

van Aaken, A, 'Primary and Secondary Remedies in International Investment Law and National State Liability: A Functional and Comparative View' in SW Schill, *International Investment Law and Comparative Public Law* (Oxford, Oxford University Press, 2010) 721–754.

——, 'Perils of Success? The Case of International Investment Protection' (2008) 9 *European Business Organization Law Review* 1.

Allee, T and Peinhardt, C, 'Evaluating Three Explanations for the Design of Bilateral Investment Treaties' (2014) *World Politics* 47.

Alvarez, JE, 'Remarks' (2012) 86 ASIL Proceedings 550.

——, 'Contemporary Foreign Investment Law: An "Empire of Law" or the "Law of Empire"'? (2008–2009) 60 *Alabama Law Review* 943.

Anghie, A, 'Civilization and Commerce: The Concept of Governance in Historical Perspective' (2000) 45 *Villanova Law Review* 887.

Asteriti, A and Tams, CJ, 'Transparency and Representation of the Public Interest in Investment Treaty Arbitration' in SW Schill (ed) *International Investment Law and Comparative Public Law* (Oxford, Oxford University Press, 2010) 788–816.

Avery, CL, 'Business and Human Rights in a Time of Change' in M Kaminga and S Zia-Zarifi (eds) *Liability of Multinational Corporations under International Law* (Kluwer Law International, 2000).

Baccini, L and Urpelainen, J, 'Before Ratification: Understanding the Timing of International Treaty Effects on Domestic Policies' (2014) 58 *International Studies Quarterly* 29.

Baetens, F and Bronckers, M, 'Reconsidering financial remedies in WTO dispute settlement' (2013) 16 *Journal of International Economic Law* 281.

Behn, D, Berg, TL and Langford, M, 'Poor States or Poor Governance? Explaining Outcomes in Investment Treaty Arbitration' (2017) *Northwestern Journal of International Law & Business*.

Bonnitcha, J, 'Foreign Investment, Development and Governance: What international investment law can learn from the empirical literature on investment' (2016) 7 *Journal of International Dispute Settlement* 31.

——, 'Investment Treaties and Transition from Authoritarian Rule' (2014) *15 Journal of World Investment and Trade* 965.

——, *Substantive Protection under Investment Treaties: A Legal and Economic Analysis* (Oxford, Oxford University Press, 2014).

——, 'Outline of a Normative Framework for Evaluating Interpretations of Investment Treaty Protections' in C Brown and K Miles (eds), *Evolution in Investment Treaty Law and Arbitration* (Cambridge, Cambridge University Press, 2011) 117–144.

Brewster, R, 'Pricing Compliance: When Formal Remedies Displace Reputations Sanctions' (2013) 54 *Harvard International Law Journal* 259.

Broches, A, 'Settlement of Investment Disputes' in A Broches (eds), *Selected Essays: World Bank, ICSID and Other Subjects of Public and Private International Law* (Dordrecht, Martinus Nijhoff Publishers, 1995) 161.

——, 'The Convention on the Settlement of Investment Disputes between States and Nationals of Other States' (1972) (II) *Recueil Des Cours* 136.

Brouder, T, 'Behavioral International Law' (2015) 163 *University of Pennsylvania Law Review* 1099.

Brown, C (ed), *Commentaries on Selected Model Investment Treaties* (Oxford, Oxford University Press, 2013).

Brownlie, I, *Principles of Public International Law*, 6th edn (Oxford, Oxford University Press, 2003).

——, 'Treatment of Aliens: Assumption of Risk and the International Standard' in W Flume and others (eds), *International Law and Economic Order: Essays in honour of F.A. Mann* (München, Verlag C.H. Beck, 1977) 3093–19.

Buergenthal, T, 'The Proliferation of Disputes, Dispute Settlement Procedures and Respect for the Rule of Law' (2006) 22 *Arbitration International* 495.

Calamita, NJ, 'Dispute Settlement Transparency in Europe's Evolving Investment Treaty Policy: Adopting the UNCITRAL Transparency Rules Approach' (2014) 15 *Journal of World Investment & Trade* 645.

Carkovic, M and Levine, R, 'Does foreign direct investment accelerate economic growth?' in T Moran, E Graham and M Blomstrom (eds), *Does Foreign Direct Investment Promote Development* (Institute for International Economics, 2005).

Caron, DD and Shirlow, E, 'Dissecting Backlash: The Unarticulated Causes of Backlash and Its Unintended Consequences' in G Ulfstein and A Føllesdal (eds), *The Judicialization of International Law—A Mixed Blessing?* (Oxford University Press, forthcoming).

Cengiz, F and Hoffmann, L, 'Rethinking Conditionality: Turkey's European Union Accession and the Kurdish Question' (2013) 51 *Journal of Common Market Studies* 416.

Chayes, A and Chayes, AH, *The New Sovereignty: Compliance with International Regulatory Agreements* (Cambridge MA, Harvard University Press, 1995).

Choudhury, B, 'Recapturing Public Power: Is Investment Arbitration's Engagement of the Public Interest Contributing to the Democratic Deficit? (2008) 41 *Vanderbilt Journal of Transnational Law* 775.

Coe, J Jr. and Rubins, N, 'Regulatory Expropriation and the *Tecmed* Case: Context and Contributions' in T Weiler (ed), *International Investment Law and Arbitration: Leading Cases from the ICSID, NAFTA, Bilateral Treaties and Customary International Law* (London, Cameron May, 2005) 597–668.

Cohen, D 'Regulating Regulators: The Legal Environment of the State' (1990) 40 *University of Toronto Law Journal* 245.

Côté, C, *A chilling effect? The impact of international investment agreements on national regulatory autonomy in the areas of health, safety and the environment*. PhD thesis, The London School of Economics and Political Science (LSE, 2014).

Cotterrell, R, 'Transnational networks of community and international economic law' in A Perry-Kessaris (ed), *Socio-legal Approaches to International Economic Law: Text, Context, Subtext* (Abingdon, Routledge, 2013) 133–149.

Crawford, J, 'International Law and the Rule of Law' (2003) 24 *Adelaide Law Review* 4.

Cremona, M, 'Negotiating the Transatlantic Trade and Investment Partnership (TTIP): Context and scope of TTIP' (2015) 52 *Common Market Law Review* 351.

Curtin, D, 'Official Secrets and the Negotiation of International Agreements: Is the EU Executive Unbound?' (2013) 50 *Common Market Law Review* 423.

Denza, E and Brooks, S, 'Investment Protection Treaties: United Kingdom Experience' (1987) 36 *ICLQ* 908.

Dezalay, Y and Garth, BG, *Dealing in Virtue: International Commercial Arbitration and the Construction of a Transnational Legal Order* (Chicago University Press, 1996).

Dolzer, R and Schreuer, C, *Principles of International Investment Law* (Oxford, Oxford University Press, 2008).

Dolzer, R, 'The Impact of International Investment Treaties on Domestic Administrative Law' (2005) 37 *New York University Journal of International Law and Policy* 972.

Dougan, M, 'What Are We to Make of the Citizens' Initiative?' (2011) *CML Rev* 1807.

Douglas, Z, 'Nothing if Not Critical for Investment Treaty Arbitration: *Occidental, Eureko*, and *Methanex*' (2006) 22 *Arbitration International* 27.

Echandi, R, 'What Do Developing Countries Expect from the International Investment Regime?' in. JE Alvarez and KP Sauvant (eds), *The Evolving International Investment Regime: Expectations, Realities, Options* (Oxford, Oxford University Press, 2011) 3–21.

Fairgrieve, D, *State Liability in Tort. A Comparative Law Study* (Oxford, Oxford University Press, 2003).

Falsafi, A, 'The International Minimum Standard of Treatment of Foreign Investors' Property: A Contingent Standard' (2006–2007) 30 *Suffolk Transnational Law Review* 318.

Franck, S, 'International Decision: *Occidental Exploration & Production Co v. Republic of Ecuador*' (2005) 99 *AJIL* 676.

——, 'The Legitimacy Crisis in Investment Treaty Arbitration: Privatising Public International Law Through Inconsistent Decisions' (2005) 73 *Fordham Law Review* 1521.

Franck, TM, *The Power of Legitimacy among Nations* (Oxford, Oxford University Press, 1990).

——, 'Legitimacy in the International System' (1988) 82 *American Journal of International Law* 705.

Fry, JD and Stampalija, JI, 'Forged Independence and Impartiality: Conflicts of Interest of International Arbitrators in Investment Disputes' (2014) 30 *Arbitration International* 189.

Gallus, N, 'The Influence of the Host State's Level of Development on International Investment Treaty Standards of Protection' (2005) 6 *Journal of World Investment Trade* 711.

García-Bolívar, OE, 'Economic Development at the Core of the International Investment Regime' in C Brown and K Miles (eds), *Evolution in Investment Treaty Law and Arbitration* (Cambridge, Cambridge University Press, 2011) 586–605.

Garcia-Duran, P and Eliasson, LJ, 'The Public Debate over Transatlantic Trade and Investment Partnership and Its Underlying Assumptions' (2017) 51 *Journal of World Trade* 23.

Gáspár-Szilágyi, S, 'Transparency, Investment Protection and the European Parliament' (2017) *European Investment Law and Arbitration Review* (forthcoming).

Gaukrodger. D and Gordon, K, 'Investor-state dispute settlement: A scoping paper for the investment policy community' (OECD Working Papers on International Investment, No 2012/3, OECD Investment Division).

Gehring, M and Euler, D, 'Public interest in investment arbitration' in D Euler, M Gehring and M Scherer, *Transparency in International Investment Arbitration: A Guide to the UNCITRAL Rules on Transparency in Treaty-Based Investor-State Arbitration* (Cambridge, Cambridge University Press 2015) 7–27.

Gilmore, AB, Collin, J and McKee, M, 'British American Tobacco's erosion of health legislation in Uzbekistan' (2006) 332 *British Medical Journal* 355.

Ginsburg, T, 'International Substitutes for Domestic Institutions: Bilateral Investment Treaties and Governance' (2005) 25 *International Review of Law and Economics* 107.

Gómez, KF and Titi, C, 'International Investment Law and ISDS: Mapping Contemporary Latin America' (2016) 17 *Journal of World Investment and Trade* 515.

Gotanda, JY, 'The Unpredictability Paradox: Punitive Damages and Interest in International Arbitration' (2010) 7 (1) *Transnational Dispute Management*.

——, 'Punitive Damages: A Comparative Analysis' (2004) 42 *Columbia Journal of Transnational Law* 391.

Guthrie, BK, 'Beyond Investment Protection: An Examination of the Potential Influence of Investment Treaties on Domestic Rule of Law' (2012–2013) 45 *New York University Journal of International Law and Politics* 1151.

Guzman, AT, 'Why LDCs Sign Treaties that Hurt Them: Explaining the Popularity of Bilateral Investment Treaties' (1997–1998) 38 *Virginia Journal of International Law* 639.

Hanna, J Jr, 'Is Transparency of Governmental Administration Customary International Law in Investor-Sovereign Arbitrations? Courts and Arbitrators May Differ' (2005) 21 *Arbitration International* 187.

van Harten, G, 'Investment Treaty Arbitration, Procedural Fairness, and the Rule of Law' in Stephan W Schill, *International Investment Law and Comparative Public Law* (Oxford, Oxford University Press, 2010) 629.

van Harten, G and Loughlin, M, 'Investment Treaty Arbitration as a Species of Global Administrative Law' (2006) 17 *EJIL* 121.

Hirsch, M, 'The Sociology of International Investment Law' in Z Douglas, J Pauwelyn and JE Viñuales (eds), *The Foundations of International Investment Law: Bringing Theory into Practice* (Oxford, Oxford University Press, 2014) 144–168.

Halle, M and Petersen, LE, 'Investment provisions in Free Trade Agreements and Investment Treaties: Opportunities and Threats for Developing Countries', Asia-Pacific Trade and Investment Initiative UNDP Regional Centre in Colombo, December 2005.

Hamida, WB, 'Investment Treaties and Democratic transition: Does Investment Law Authorise Not to Honor Contracts Concluded with Undemocratic Regimes?' in StW Schill, CJ Tams and R Hofmann (eds) *International Investment Law and Development: Bridging the Gap* (Cheltenham, Edward Elgar, 2015) 309–329.

Harlow, C, 'Global Administrative Law: The Quest for Principles and Values' (2006) 17 *EJIL* 187.

Hathaway, OA, 'Do Human Rights Treaties Make a Difference?' (2002) 111 *Yale Law Journal* 1935.

Hayek, F, *The Road to Serfdom* (London, Routledge, 1944).

Hewko, J, 'Foreign Direct Investment in Transitional Economies: Does the Rule of Law Matter?' (2002) 11 *European Constitutional Review* 71.

Higgins, R, 'The Taking of Property by the State: Recent Developments in International Law' (1982) 176 *Recueil des Cours* 259.

Hober, K, *Investment Arbitration in Eastern Europe: In Search of a Definition of Expropriation* (New York, JurisNet, 2007).

Hippolyte, A, 'Aspiring for a Constructive TWAIL approach towards the International Investment Regime' in SW Schill, CJ Tams and R Hofmann (eds), *International Investment Law and Development: Bridging the Gap* (Cheltenham, Edward Elgar, 2015) 180–219.

Jančić, D, 'Transatlantic Regulatory Interdependence, Law and Governance: The Evolving Roles of the EU and US Legislatures' (2015) 17 *Cambridge Yearbook of European Legal Studies* 334.

Johnson, L, 'The Transparency Rules and Transparency Convention: A good Start and Model for Broader Reform in Investor-State Arbitration' *Columbia FDI Perspectives*, No. 126, July 21, 2014.

Kalicki, J and Medeiros, S, 'Fair, Equitable and Ambiguous: What is Fair and Equitable Treatment in International Investment Law?' (2008) 22 *ICSID Review* 24.

Karl, J, 'International Investment Arbitration: A Threat to State Sovereignty' in W Shan, P Simons and D Singh (eds), *Redefining Sovereignty in International Economic Law* (Oxford, Hart Publishing, 2008) 225–245.

Kaufmann, B, 'Transnational 'Babystep': The European Citizens' Initiative' in M Setala and T Schiller (eds), *Citizens' Initiatives in Europe Procedures and Consequences of Agenda-Setting by Citizens* (Basingstoke, Palgrave Macmillan, 2012) 228–242.

Kaufmann, D, 'Governance Redux: The Empirical Challenge' (Washington DC, World Bank, 2004).

——, Kraay, A and Zoido-Lobaton, P, 'Governance Matters' (1999) *World Bank Policy Research Working Papers* No 2196.

Kentikelenis, AE, Stubbs, TH and King, LP, 'IMF conditionality and development policy space, 1985–2014' 560 (2016) 23 *Review of International Political Economy* 543.

Keohane, RO, *Power and Governance in a Partially Globalized World* (London, Routledge, 2002).

——, Moravcsik, A and Slaughter, AM, 'Legalized dispute resolution: interstate and transnational' (2000) 54 (3) *International Organization* 457.

Kill, T, 'Don't Cross the Streams: Past and Present Overstatement of Customary International Law in Connection with Conventional Fair and Equitable Treatment Obligations' (2008) 106 *Michigan Law Review* 853.

Kingsbury, B, 'Global Administrative Law in the Institutional Practice of Global Regulatory Governance' in H Cissé, DD Bradlow, and B Kingsbury, *International Financial Institutions and Global Legal Governance* (World Bank Publications, 2011) 3–33.

Kingsbury, B and Schill, SW, 'Investor-State Arbitration as Governance: Fair and Equitable Treatment, Proportionality, and the Emerging Global Administrative Law', Institute for International Law and Justice, NYU Law School, Working Paper 2009/6 (Global Administrative Law Series).

Koh, HH, 'How Is International Human Rights Law Enforced?' (1998) 74 *Indiana Law Journal* 1397.

——, 'Why Do Nations Obey International Law' (1977) 106 *Yale Law Journal* 2599.

Kotera, A, 'Regulatory Transparency' in P Muchlinski, F Ortino and C Schreuer (eds), *The Oxford Handbook of International Investment Law* (Oxford, oxford University Press, 2008) 617–636.

Krever, T, 'Quantifying Law: Legal Indicators Projects and the Reproduction of Neo-Liberal Common Sense (2013) 34 *Third World Quarterly* 131.

Kulick, A, *Global Public Interest in International Investment Law* (Cambridge, Cambridge University Press, 2012).

Kumm, M, 'An Empire of Capital? Transatlantic Investment Protection as the Institutionalization of Unjustified Privilege' *ESIL Reflections*, Volume 4, Issue 3, 25 May 2015.

Kurtz, J, 'Building Legitimacy through Interpretation in Investor-State Arbitration' in Z Douglas, J Pauwelyn and JE Viñuales (eds), *The Foundations of International Investment Law: Bringing Theory into Practice* (Oxford, Oxford University Press, 2014) 257–295.

Lim, K, 'Upholding Corrupt Investors' Claims Against Complicit or Compliant Host States—Where Angels Should *Not* Fear to Tread' in KP Sauvant, *Yearbook on International Investment Law & Policy 2011–2012* (Oxford, Oxford University Press, 2013) 601–680.

Litwin, D, 'On the Divide Between Investor-State Arbitration and the Global Fight Against Corruption' (2013) 10 (3) *Transnational Dispute Management*.

Llamzon, AP, *Corruption in International Investment Arbitration* (Oxford, Oxford University Press, 2014).

Ma, D, 'A BIT Unfair?: An Illustration of the Backlash Against International Arbitration in Latin America' (2012) *Journal of Dispute Resolution* 571.

Marboe, I, 'State Responsibility and Comparative State Liability for Administrative and Legislative Harm to Economic Interests' in SW Schill, *International Investment Law and Comparative Public Law* (Oxford, Oxford University Press, 2010) 377–412.

Mazumder, S, 'Can I stay a BIT longer? The effect of bilateral investment treaties on political survival' (2016) 11 *Review of International Organisations* 477.

McLachlan, C, Shore, L and Weiniger, M, *International Investment Arbitration: Substantive Principles* (Oxford, Oxford University Press, 2007).

McRae, D, 'Measuring the Effectiveness of the WTO Dispute Settlement System' (2008) 3 *Asian Journal of WTO and International Health Law and Policy* 1.

Mendenhall, JE, 'The Evolving U.S. Position on International Investment Protection and Its Impact on the U.S. Position in the Trans-Pacific Partnership Negotiations' in NJ Calamita and M Sattorova, *The Regionalization of International Investment Treaty Arrangements* (British Institute of International and Comparative Law, London 2015) 255–282.

Miles, CA, 'Corruption, Jurisdiction, and Admissibility in International Investment Claims' (2012) 3 *Journal of International Dispute Settlement* 329.

Miles, K, *The Origins of International Investment Law: Empire, Environment and the Safeguarding of Capital* (Cambridge, Cambridge University Press 2013).

Monebhurrun, N, 'Novelty in International Investment Law: The Brazilian Agreement on Cooperation and Facilitation of Investments as a Different

International Investment Agreement Model' (2017) 8 *Journal of International Dispute Settlement* 79.

Montt, S, *State Liability in Investment Treaty Arbitration: Global Constitutional and Administrative Law in the BIT Generation* (Oxford, Hart Publishing, 2009).

Muchlinski, P, Ortino, F and Christoph Schreuer, 'Preface'in P Muchlinski, F Ortino and C Schreuer (eds) *The Oxford Handbook of International Investment Law* (Oxford, Oxford University Press, 2008).

——, "Caveat Investor?' The Relevance of the Conduct of the Investor under the Fair and Fair Equitable Treatment Standard' (2006) 55 *ICLQ* 527.

——, 'The Rise and Fall of the Multilateral Agreement on Investment: Where Now?' (2000) 34 *International Lawyer* 1033.

Nelken, D, 'Comparative Sociology of Law' in R Banakar and Travers (eds) *An Introduction to Law and Social Theory* (Oxford, Hart Publishing, 2002).

Neumann, M, *The Rule of Law* (Burlingon VT, Ashgate, 2002).

Neumayer, E and Spess, L, 'Do Bilateral Investment Treaties Increase Foreign Direct Investment to Developing Countries?' (2005) 33 *World Development* 1567.

Newcombe, A and Paradell, L, *Law and Practice of Investment Treaties: Standards of Treatment* (Alphen aan den Rijn, Kluwer Law International, 2009).

Organ, J, 'Decommissioning Direct Democracy? A critical analysis of Commission decision making on the legal admissibility of European Citizens Initiative proposals', (2014) 10 *European Constitutional Law Review* 422.

——, 'EU Citizen Participation and the ECI: The TTIP Legacy' (2017), available at https://papers.ssrn.com/sol3/papers.cfm?abstract_id=2919810.

Ononaiwu, C, 'Regional Investment Treaty Arrangements in the Caribbean: Developments and Implications' in NJ Calamita and M Sattorova, *The Regionalization of International Investment Treaty Arrangements* (British Institute of International and Comparative Law, London, 2015) 199–224.

Paparinskis, M, 'Good Faith and Fair and Equitable Treatment in International Investment Law' in AD Mitchell, M Sornarajah, and T Voon, Good Faith and International Economic Law (Oxford, Oxford University Press, 2015) 144–172.

——, *The International Minimum Standard and Fair and Equitable Treatment* (Oxford, Oxford University Press, 2013).

Parra, AR, *The History of ICSID* (Oxford, Oxford University Press, 2012).

Paradell, L, 'The BIT Experience of the Fair and Equitable Treatment Standard' in F Ortino, L Liberti, A Sheppard and H Warner (eds), *Investment Treaty Law: Current Issues II* (London, British Institute of International and Comparative Law, 2007).

Pauwelyn, J, 'Different Means, Same End: The Contribution of Trade and Investment Treaties to Anti-Corruption Policy' in S Rose-Ackerman and P Carrington (eds), *Anti-Corruption Policy: Can International Actors Play a Constructive Role?* (Carolina Academic Press, 2013) 247–265.

——, 'The Calculation and Design of Trade Retaliation in Context: What is the Goal of Suspending WTO obligations?' in CP Bown and J Pauwelyn (eds), *The Law, Economics and Politics of Retaliation in WTO Dispute Settlement* (Cambridge, Cambridge University Press, 2010) 34–72.

Perry-Kessaris, A, 'What does it mean to take a socio-legal approach to international economic law?' in A Perry-Kessaris (ed), *Socio-legal Approaches to International Economic Law: Text, Context, Subtext* (Abingdon, Routledge, 2013) 3–18.

——, 'Prepare Your Indicators: Economics Imperialism on the Shores of Law and Development' (2011) 7 *International Journal of Law in Context* 401.

Perry, A, 'Effective Legal Systems and Foreign Direct Investment: In Search of the Evidence' (2000) 49 *ICLQ* 779.

Peterson, LE, 'Siemens, and its Argentine Subsidiary, Plead Guilty to Certain Breaches of Foreign Corrupt Practices Act', 1 Investment Arbitration Rep, No17, 17 December 2008.

Posner, EA and Sykes, AO, 'Efficient Breach of International Law: Optimal Remedies, "Legalized Noncompliance", and Related Issues' (2011–2012) 110 *Michigan Law Review* 243.

Puig, S, 'No Right Without a Remedy: Foundations of Investor-state Arbitration' in Z Douglas, J Pauwelyn and JE Viñuales (eds), *The Foundations of International Investment Law: Bringing Theory into Practice* (Oxford, Oxford University Press, 2014) 235–256.

——, 'Social Capital in the Arbitration Market' (2014) 25 *EJIL* 387.

Poulsen, LN, *Bounded Rationality and Economic Diplomacy: The Politics of Investment Treaties in Developing Countries* (Cambridge, Cambridge University Press, 2015).

Rajagopal, B, 'From Resistance to Renewal: The Third World, Social Movements, and the Expansion of International Institutions' (2000) 41 *Harvard International Law Journal* 529.

Rasulov, A, 'Central Asia and the Globalisation of the Contemporary Legal Consciousness' (2014) 25 *Law and Critique* 163.

Raustiala, K, 'Compliance and Effectiveness in International Regulatory Cooperation' (2000) 32 *Case Western Reserve Journal of International Law* 387.

Rawski, F, 'Wold Bank Community-driven Development Programming in Indonesia and East Timor: Implications for the Study of Global Administrative Law' (2005) 37 *International Law and Politics* 919.

Raz, J, 'The Rule of Law and Its Virtue' in J Raz, *The authority of law: Essays on law and morality* (Clarendon, Oxford, 1979) 211–229.

Reinisch, A, 'Legality of Expropriations' in A Reinisch, *Standards of Investment Protection* (Oxford, Oxford University Press, 2008).

Reisman, MW, and Arsanjani, MH, 'The Question of Unilateral Governmental Statements as Applicable Law in Investment Disputes' (2005) *ICSID Review* 328.

Reisman, MW and Sloane, RD, 'Indirect Expropriation and Its Valuation in the BIT Generation' (2004) 74 *British Yearbook of International Law* 115.

Roberts, A, 'Clash of Paradigms: Actors and Analogies Shaping the Investment Treaty System' (2013) 107 *AJIL* 45.

——, 'Power and Persuasion in Investment Treaty Interpretation: The Dual Role of States' (2010) 104 *AJIL* 179.

Root, E, 'The Basis of Protection to Citizens Residing Abroad' (1910) 4 *AJIL* 517.

Rose, C, *International Anti-Corruption Norms: Their Creation and Influence on Domestic Legal Systems* (Oxford, Oxford University Press, 2015).

Roth, AH, *The Minimum Standard of International Law Applied to Aliens* (Leiden, A W Sijthoff's Uitgeversmaatschappij, 1949).

Salacuse, JW, *The Law of Investment Treaties* (Oxford, Oxford University Press, 2010).

——, 'The Treatification of International Investment Law' (2007) 13 *Law and Business Review of the Americas* 155.

Sattorova, M, and Vytiaganets, O, 'Investment Treaty Law and Its Lessons for Developing States' (2017) available at https://papers.ssrn.com/sol3/papers.cfm?abstract_id=3002067.

Sattorova, M, Erkan, M and Omiunu, O, 'How Do Host States Respond to Investment Treaty Law?: Some Empirical Observations' (2017) *The European Yearbook of International Economic Law* (forthcoming).

——, 'International Investment Law in Central Asia: The Making, Implementation and Change of Investment Rules from a Regionalist Perspective' (2015) 16 *Journal of World Investment and Trade* 1089.

——, 'Denial of Justice Disguised: Investment Arbitration and the Protection of Foreign Investors from Judicial Misconduct' (2012) 61 *ICLQ* 223.

——, 'Return to the Local Remedies Rule in European BITs?: Power (Inequalities), Dispute Settlement, and Change in Investment Treaty Law' (2012) 39 (2) *Legal Issues of Economic Integration* 223.

Sauvant, K and Sachs, L, (eds), *The Effect of Treaties on Foreign Direct Investment: Bilateral Investment Treaties, Double Taxation Treaties and Investment Flows* (Oxford, Oxford University Press, 2009).

Schacherer, S, 'TPP, CETA and TTIP: Between Innovation and Consolidation—Resolving Investor–State Disputes under Mega-regionals' (2016) 7 *Journal of International Dispute Settlement* 628.

Schefer, KN, 'Poverty and Investment Law: Starting the Discussion' (2014) 15 *Journal of World Investment and Trade* 908.

Schefer, KN and Woldesenbet, MG 'The Revised Agreement on Government Procurement and Corruption' (2013) 47 *Journal of World Trade* 1129.

Schlemmer, EC, 'An Overview of South Africa's Bilateral Investment Treaties and Investment Policy' (2016) 31 *ICSID Review* 167.

Schill, SW, 'Editorial: Five Times Transparency in International Investment Law' (2014) 15 *Journal of World Investment and Trade* 363.

——, 'Illegal Investments in Investment Treaty Arbitration' (2012) 11 *Law and Practice of International Courts and Tribunals* 281.

——, 'System Building in Investment Treaty Arbitration and Lawmaking' (2001) 12 *German Law Journal* 1083.

——, 'Fair and Equitable Treatment, the Rule of Law, and Comparative Public Law' in SW Schill, *International Investment Law and Comparative Public Law* (Oxford, OUP 2010) 152–182.

——, 'Enabling Private Ordering: Function, Scope and Effect of Umbrella Clauses in International Investment Treaties' (2009) 18 *Minnesota Journal of International Law* 1.

——, *The Multilateralization of International Investment Law* (Cambridge, Cambridge University Press, 2009).

——, 'Revisiting a Landmark: Indirect Expropriation and Fair and Equitable Treatment in the ICSID case Tecmed' (2006) 3 (2) *Transnational Dispute Management*.

Schneiderman, D, *Resisting Economic Globalization: Critical Theory and International Investment Law* (Basingstoke, Palgrave Macmillan, 2013).

——, 'Power and Production in Global Legal Pluralism: An international political economy approach' in A Perry-Kessaris (ed), *Socio-legal Approaches to International Economic Law: Text, Context, Subtext* (Abingdon, Routledge, 2013) 98–117.

——, 'Investing in Democracy? Political Process and International Investment Law' (2010) 60 *University of Toronto Law Journal* 909.

——, *Constitutionalizing Economic Globalization: Investment Rules and Democracy's Promise* (Cambridge, Cambridge University Press, 2008).

——, 'Investment Rules and the New Constitutionalism' (2000) 25 *Law and Social Inquiry* 757.

Schreurer, C, Malintoppi, L, Reinisch, A and Sinclair, A, *The ICSID Convention: A Commentary*, 2nd edn, (Cambridge, Cambridge University Press, 2009).

Schreurer, C, 'Calvo's Grandchildren: The Return of Local Remedies in Investment Arbitration' (2005) 4 *Law and Practice International Courts and Tribunals* 1.

——, 'Non-pecuniary Remedies in ICSID Arbitration' (2004) 20 *Arbitration International* 325.

Schultz, T and Dupont, C, 'Investment Arbitration: Promoting the Rule of Law or Over-empowering Investors? A Quantitative Empirical Study' (2014) 25 *EJIL* 1147.

Schwarzenberger, G, *Foreign Investments and International Law* (London, Steven & Sons, 1969).

——, 'The Abs-Shawcross Draft Convention on Investments Abroad: A Critical Commentary' (1960) 9 *Journal Public Law* 147.

Schimmelfennig, F and Sedelmeier, U, 'Governance by conditionality: EU rule transfer to the candidate countries of Central and Eastern Europe' (2004) 11 *Journal of European Public Policy* 669.

Schwimmelfennig, F, Engert, S and Knobel, H, 'Costs, Commitment and Compliance: The Impact of EU Democratic Conditionality on Latvia, Slovakia and Turkey' (2003) 41 *Journal of Common Market Studies* 495.

Shaffer, G, 'Transnational Legal Process and State Change' (2012) 37 *Law and Social Inquiry* 229.

——, 'A New Legal Realism: Method in International Economic Law Scholarship' in CB Picker, ID Bunn, and D Arner (eds), *International Economic Law: The State and Future of the Discipline* (Oxford, Hart Publishing, 2008).

Shany, U, *Assessing the Effectiveness of International Courts* (Oxford, Oxford University Press, 2014).

Shawcross, H, 'The Problems of Foreign Investment in International Law' in (1961–1) 102 *Recueil des Cours* 335.

Shihata, IF, 'Corruption—A General Review with an Emphasis on the Role of the World Bank' (1997) 15 *Dickinson Journal of International Law* 451.

Simmons, BA, 'International Law and State Behavior: Commitment and Compliance in International Monetary Affairs' (2000) 94(4) *American Political Science Review* 819.

Snodgrass, E, 'Protecting Investors' Legitimate Expectations: Recognizing and Delimiting a General Principle' (2007) 21 *ICSID Review* 1.

Sohn, LB and Baxter, R, *Convention on the International Responsibility of States for Injuries to Aliens. Preliminary Draft with Explanatory Notes* (Cambridge, MA, Harvard Law School, 1959).

Sornarajah, M, 'An International Investment Court: Panacea or Purgatory?,' Columbia FDI Perspectives, No.180, 15 August 2016.

——, *The International Law on Foreign Investment* (Cambridge, Cambridge University Press, 2004).

Spalding, AB, 'The Irony of International Business Law: U.S. Progressivism and China's New Laissez Faire' (2011) 59 *UCLA Law Review* 354.

Stiglitz, JE, 'Regulating Multinational Corporations: Towards Principles of Cross-Border Legal Frameworks in a Globalized World Balancing Rights with Responsibilities' (2008) 23 *American University International Law Review* 451.

Stoker, G, 'Governance as theory: five propositions' (1993) 50 (155) *International Social Science Journal* 17.

Subramanian, S, 'The Changing Dynamics of the Global Intellectual Property Legal Order: Emergence of A 'Network Agenda'? (2015) 64 *ICLQ* 103.

Subedi, SP, *International Investment Law: Reconciling Policy and Principle*, 3rd edn (Oxford, Hart Publishing, 2016).

Sunstein, C, *Democracy's Constitution* (New York, Oxford University Press, 2001).

Stone Sweet, A, Chung, M and Saltzman, A, 'Arbitral Lawmaking and State Power: An Empirical Analysis of Investment Arbitration' (2017), available at https://papers.ssrn.com/sol3/papers.cfm?abstract_id=2919723.

Sykes, AO, 'Public Versus Private Enforcement of International Economic law: Standing and Remedy' (2005) 34 *Journal of Legal Studies* 631.

Tan, C, 'Reviving the emperor's old clothes: the good governance agenda, development and international investment law' in SW Schill, CJ Tams and R Hofmann (eds), *International Investment Law and Development: Bridging the Gap* (Cheltenham, Edward Elgar 2015).

——, 'Navigating New Landscapes: Socio-legal mapping of plurality and power in international economic law' in A Perry-Kessaris (ed), *Socio-legal Approaches to International Economic Law: Text, Context, Subtext* (Abingdon, Routledge, 2013) 19–35.

——, 'The New Disciplinary Framework: Conditionality, New Aid Architecture and Global Economic Governance' in J Faundez and C Tan (eds), *International Economic Law, Globalization and Developing Countries* (Cheltenham, Edward Elgar, 2010) 112–137.

Thomas, JC, 'Reflections on Article 1105 of NAFTA: History, State Practice and the Influence of Commentators' (2001) 17 *ICSID Review* 21.

Tienhaara, K, *The Expropriation of Environmental Governance: Protecting Foreign Investors at the Expense of Public Policy* (Cambridge, Cambridge University Press, 2009).

Trachtman, JP, 'International Law and Domestic Political Coalitions: The Grand Theory of Compliance with International Law' (2010) 11 *Chicago Journal of International Law* 128.

Trebilcock, MJ and Daniels, RJ, *Rule of Law Reform and Development: Charting the Fragile Path of Progress* (Cheltenham, Edward Elgar, 2008).

Trubek, DM and Santos, A, 'Introduction: The Third moment in Law and Development Theory and the Emergence of a New Critical Practice' in DM Trubek and A Santos (eds), *The New Law and Economic Development: A Critical Appraisal* (Cambridge, Cambridge University Press, 2006) 1–18.

Tucker, T, 'Investment Agreements v the Rule of Law?' (2013) available at http://investmentpolicyhub.unctad.org/Blog/Index/25.

Tudor, I, *The Fair and Equitable Treatment in the International Law of Foreign Investment* (Oxford, Oxford University Press, 2008).

Vandevelde, KJ, 'Model Bilateral Investment Treaties: The Way Forward' (2012) 18 *Southwestern Journal International Law* 313.

——, *Bilateral Investment Treaties: History, Policy, and Interpretation* (Oxford, Oxford University Press, 2010).

——, *U.S. International Investment Agreements* (Oxford, Oxford University Press, 2009).

Verwey, WD and Schrijver, NJ, 'The Taking of Property Under International Law: A New Legal Perspective?' (1984) 15 *Netherlands Yearbook of International Law* 3.

Vicuna, FO, 'Regulatory Authority and Legitimate Expectations: Balancing the Rights of the State and the Individual under International Law in a Global Society' (2003) *International Law FORUM du droit international* 188.

Vidigal, G, 'Re-assessing WTO Remedies: The Prospective and the Retrospective' (2013) 16 *Journal of International Economic Law* 505.

Vinuales, JE, 'Investor Diligence in Investment Arbitration: Sources and Arguments' (2017) 32 *ICSID Review* 346.

Waibel, M, 'Abitrator Selection: Towards Greater State Control' in A Kulick (ed), *Reassertion of Control over the Investment Treaty Regime* (Cambridge, Cambridge University Press, 2016) 333–355.

Walde, TW, 'The "Umbrella Clause" in Investment Arbitration. A Comment on Original Intentions and Recent Cases' (2005) 6 *Journal of World Investment and Trade* 183.

Waldron, J, 'Is the Rule of Law an Essentially Contested Concept (In Florida)?' (2002) 21 *Law and Philosophy* 137.

Warleigh-Lack, A, 'On the Path to Legitimacy? The EU Citizens Initiative Right from a Critical Deliberativist Perspective' in C Ruzza and VD Sala (eds), *Governance and civil society in the European Union* (Manchester University Press, 2007) 55–72.

Weiler, T and Walde, TW, 'Investment Arbitration under the Energy Charter Treaty in the Light of New NAFTA Precedents: Towards a Global Code of Conduct for Economic Regulation' (2004) 1 *Transnational Dispute Management* 1.

Weston, BH, 'The Charter of Economic Rights and Duties of States and the Deprivation of Foreign-Owned Wealth' (1981) 75 *AJIL* 437.

Weston, BH and Dawson, F, '"Prompt, adequate, and effective"?: A Universal Standard of Compensation' (1961-1962) 30 *Fordham Law Review* 727.

Williams, L, 'What Is TTIP? And Six Reasons Why the Answer Should Scare You', The Independent (6 October, 2015).

Wood, T, 'Political Risk or Political Right? Reconciling the International Legal Norms of Investment Protection and Political Participation' (2015) 30 (3) *ICSID Review* 665.

Woods, N, 'Order, Justice, the IMF, and the World Bank' in R Foot, J Gaddis and A Hurrell (eds), *Order and Justice in International Relations* (Oxford, Oxford University Press, 2003) 80–102.

World Bank, *World Development Report* (New York, Oxford University Press, 2005).

Yackee, JW, 'Investment Treaties and Investor Corruption: An Emerging Defence for Host States?' (2012) 52 *Virginia Journal of International Law* 723.

——, 'Do Bilateral Investment Treaties Promote Foreign Direct Investment? Some Hints from Alternative Evidence' (2010–2011) 51 *Virginia Journal of International Law* 397.

UNCTAD, Recent Developments in Investor-State Dispute Settlement (ISDS), No 1, April 2014.

——, *Best Practices in Investment for Development. How to prevent and manage investor-State disputes: Lessons from Peru*, Investment Advisory Series, Series B, number 10 (New York and Geneva, United Nations, 2011).

——, *Taking of Property* (United Nations, New York and Geneva, 2000).

Index

www.ingramcontent.com/pod-product-compliance
Lightning Source LLC
LaVergne TN
LVHW052314200926
848481LV00002B/558